Global ____

Dictionary of
Synonyms

Illustrated English Thesaurus

Martin H. Manser
Andrew Betsis

also ideal for learners of English preparing for exams:
IELTS, TOEFL, TOEIC, BULATS, PET, FCE, CAE, CPE

GlobalELT
ENGLISH LANGUAGE TEACHING BOOKS

Contents

Published by GLOBAL ELT LTD, 2015
www.globalelt.co.uk
email: orders@globalelt.co.uk

British Library Cataloguing-in-Publication Data
A catalogue record of this book is available from the British Library.

● *Global ELT Dictionary of Synonyms* - ISBN: 9781781642320
© **GLOBAL ELT LTD,** 2015

Preface

Learners of English may sometimes find it difficult to know which word to use in a particular context. Or they may have used a particular word several times already in what they are writing, and so they want to use a different expression; especially when you need to paraphrase.

Ordinary Thesauruses or dictionaries of Synonyms are not as helpful as they might first appear: to read a list of synonyms for a certain word is helpful only as far as it goes. This dictionary, however, goes beyond a mere listing of words with a similar meaning and helps distinguish them. The differences between similar words are shown by giving each one a definition and an example.

The definitions are intended to show the various shades of meaning of the group of synonyms. The examples show the context in which a word is used and which other words typically occur with each synonym.

restrain verb

not to allow something, someone, or yourself to become too violent or forceful or to express themselves openly, or to prevent someone, for example a prisoner, from behaving violendy by holding them, handcuffing them, etc.: *I couldn't restrain myself any longer and burst out laughing.*

control

not to allow something, someone, or yourself to act freely, especially to limit or restrain something or someone: *Government efforts to control immigration have so far failed.*

curb

to keep something under strict control and, usually, to reduce it: *He should try to curb his enthusiasm and act more rationally,*

hold back

to restrain something such as tears or laughter, or to stop something from progressing or developing as fast as it would like: *Business is being held back by government restrictions.*

inhibit

to prevent an event or process from developing: *Does the Internet encourage or inhibit learning?*

keep under control

to control: *If you can't keep your children under control, you'll have to take them out.*

limit

not to allow something to exceed a particular amount or extent, or not to allow someone complete freedom: *You'd be wise to limit the amount of time you spend on each question in the exam.*

restrict

to limit something, especially to allow less of something than something or someone needs or wants: *The amount that each candidate in the election can spend on publicity will be restricted to $20,000.*

Guidance on usage is given in two ways: showing context of use by style markers in round brackets, e.g., {informal), (formal) and by means of brief usage notes introduced by *.

clanger *(informal)*
a stupid or embarrassing mistake: *What a clanger; Linda said the capital of Belgium was Amsterdam!*

intransigent *(formal)*
completely unwilling to change your mind about something: *Senior party members remained intransigent in their opposition to any change in the constitution.*

engaged not free to speak to someone because you are speaking to someone or doing something else: *Mike is engaged at the moment. Shall I ask him to phone you when he's free?*

* In British English a telephone line is said to be engaged when someone is speaking on it; in US English, it is said to be busy.

Some entry words contain more than one list of synonyms, in which case the different lists are numbered 1, 2, etc.

Cross-references are given at the end of many entries to show additional words with a related meaning.

How to use this book

First, look up the word for which you want to find a synonym in the index at the back of the book. For example, if you want to find a word to use instead of *stubborn*, you could look that up in the index. In the index, the word **stubborn** is in bold, which means it is one of the main keywords in the dictionary. If you then look up **stubborn** in the main dictionary part of the book, you will find a list of alternative words. By looking at the definitions and examples, you can choose the one that most closely matches what you want to express.

stubborn *adjective*

showing an unwillingness to change your opinion or your course of action even when people try to persuade you to or when it seems reasonable to do so: *He can be very stubborn when he doesn't get his own way.*

difficult (*informal*)
unco-operative and unhelpful: *She's not really against the plan, she's just being difficult.*

dogged
showing an admirable determination to achieve something even if it takes a long time and many attempts: *Their dogged persistence eventually paid off.*

intransigent (*formal*)
completely unwilling to change your mind about something: *Senior party members remained intransigent in their opposition to any changes.*

obstinate
stubborn and usually unreasonable: *Her obstinate refusal to accept a compromise made it impossible for us to reach an agreement.*

persistent
not stopping what you are doing, or doing the same thing over and over again, in order to achieve something, often in a way that is annoying: *She was so persistent that in the end he had to agree to see her.*

unco-operative
unwilling to help other people do or get what they want: *The dispute could have been settled much sooner, if the unions hadn't been so unco-operative.*

200

common words & phrases
in **British English**

and their synonyms/counterparts
in **American English**

British English	American English
aerial (radio/tv)	antenna
aubergine	eggplant
autumn	fall
banger	sausage
bank holiday	national holiday
barrister	attorney, lawyer
solicitor	attorney, lawyer
basin	sink
bat (table tennis)	paddle (ping pong)
bath (run the bath)	fill the tub
bath gown	bath robe
bill (at restaurant)	check
bin (dust bin)	trash can
biscuit (bickie)	cookie
block of flats	apartment house/building
bloke	man / guy
Bobby	policeman / cop
bonnet	hood
booking	reservation
boot	trunk
box	tv / television
braces	suspenders
break time	recess
bungalow	house (one story) / ranch house
cafe	diner
car journey	road trip
car park	parking lot
caravan	trailer
cashier	teller
chap	man / guy
chemist	drug store / druggist
chest of drawers	dresser/bureau
chips	french fries

cinema	movie theater
city centre	downtown
clothes peg	clothespin
come round	come over
cooker	range or stove
copper	policeman / cop
couch	sofa
courgette	zucchini
crisps	potato chips
crossroads	intersection
cupboard	closet
curriculum vitae, CV	resume
curtains	drapes
diary (personal account)	journal
diversion	detour
drawing pins	pushpins / thumbtacks
dressing gown	robe
driving licence	driver's license
dummy (for babies)	pacifier
dustman	garbage man
eggy bread (fried)	french toast
engine	motor
estate agent	realtor
exhaust pipe	tail pipe / muffler
fairy cake	cup cake
film	movie
fire engine	fire truck
fizzy drink	pop, soda, coke
flat (one storey)	apartment
floor	storey
flyover	overpass
football	soccer
fortnight	two weeks
foyer	lobby

friend	buddy
fringe	bangs
full stop (punctuation)	period
gaol, prison, jail	prison, jail, penitentiary, pokey
garden	backyard / yard
gear-lever	gear shift
glue	gum
grill	broil
ground floor	first floor
grub	food
hand brake	parking brake, emergency brake
handbag	purse
head teacher	principal
headmaster, headmistress,	principal
hire (a car)	rent (a car)
holiday	vacation
hoover (noun)	*vacuum cleaner (noun)*
hoover (verb)	vacuum (noun and verb)
ice lolly	popsicle
gone off	spoiled
jab (injection)	shot
jacket potato	baked potato
jam	jelly
jelly	jello
john	toilet
jumper	sweater
kip	sleep
knackered (i'm knackered)	beat (i'm beat)
knickers	underwear / panties
lad	boy
lady bird	lady bug
lass	girl
lift	elevator
lollypop man/woman	crossing guard

loo	bathroom / restroom
lorry	truck
luggage	baggage, luggage
mac (slang for macintosh)	rain coat
maize	corn
man	man / guy
managing director	chief executive officer (CEO)
marking scheme	grading scheme
marks	grades
mate	friend / buddy
maths	math
mince	chopped beef
mobile phone	cell(ular) phone
motorway	freeway / highway
mum / mummy / mom	mom
nappy	diaper
nick	steal
nutter	crazy person
off you go	go ahead
open day / evening	open house
pal	friend / buddy
pants	underwear / panties
pavement	sidewalk
pedestrian crossing	cross walk
petrol	gas / gasoline
petrol station	gas station
phone box	telephone booth
pinafore dress	jumper
pinny	apron
plaster	band-aid
play time	recess
plimsolls	gym shoes
pocket money	allowance
policeman	policeman / cop

polo neck	turtle neck
postal code	zip code
postman	mailman
pram (perambulator)	baby carriage/(baby) buggy
primary school	elementary school
property	real estate
public school	private school
puddings	dessert
pullover	sweater
queue (n)	line
queue (v)	stand in a line
quid (slang for pound)	bucks (slang for dollars)
rasher	a slice of bacon
reception (hotel)	front desk
receptionist	desk clerk
reversing lights	back-up lights
ring up/phone	call/phone
rounders	baseball
row	argument
rubber	eraser
rubbish	garbage (or trash)
rucksack	backpack/backbag
runner beans	green beans
school dinner	hot lunch
scone	biscuit
scotch pancakes	flapjacks
secondary school	high school (junior high, senior high)
semi-detached house	duplex
serviette	napkin
settee	sofa
shop	store
single ticket	one-way ticket
skip (for debris, rubbish, etc)	dumpster
sleeping policeman	speed bump

staff room	teachers lounge
starter, entree	appetizer
state school	public school
stockholder	shareholder
surgery	doctor's office
surname (british preferred)	*last name (american preferred)*
suspenders	holds up stockings
sweets	candy
swimming costume	bathing suit
take-away	take out
tap	faucet
telly	tv / television
term	semester (or quarter)
terrace (row of houses joined)	town houses
tights	pantihose
timetable	schedule
tin	can
toilet	bathroom / restroom
torch	flashlight
trainers	sneakers
trodden on	stepped on
trousers	pants
tube, underground	subway
vest	undershirt
waistcoat	vest
wallet	wallet, billfold
wardrobe	closet
wedding ring	wedding band/ring
wellies	galoshes
wellington boots	galoshes
windscreen	windshield
zebra crossing	pedestrian crossing
zed (the letter z)	zee (z)
zip	zipper

INDEX

If you look up a word that is in BLACK in this index, you will be directed to the main keyword in BOLD (and colour) where other similar words are discussed.

For example, if you look up GIGGLE in the index, this will direct you to the keyword **laugh**, where GIGGLE is one of the synonyms listed in alphabetical order.

By looking up **laugh** in the main dictionary part of the book, you are given a wider range of alternatives. By looking at the definitions and examples you can choose the word that most closely matches what you want to express.

laugh *verb*

to make a sound in your throat because you are amused: I could hear the children laughing merrily in the garden.

cackle to laugh in a loud unattractive manner: *a group of women cackling.*

chortle to laugh quite loudly at something that amuses you: *'That's hilarious!' he chortled.*

chuckle to laugh quietly: *She sat, chuckling to herself as she read her magazine.*

giggle to give a high-pitched childlike laugh: *The girls started giggling and couldn 't stop.*

guffaw to give a loud deep laugh: *The men were guffawing with laughter at the comedian.*

roar to give a loud deep hearty laugh: *The audience was roaring with laughter.*
snigger to give a quiet mocking laugh: *The rest of the class sniggered at Sam's mistake.*

titter to give a high-pitched, embarrassed laugh: *Some of the children tittered nervously during the sex-education class.*

INDEX

anxiety
anxious - afraid
anxious - eager
anxious - impatient
ape - imitate
apex - top 1
appal - shock
apparent - clear
apparition - ghost
appeal to - beg
appealing - interesting
appealing - nice 1
appear - arrive
appetizing - delicious
applaud - praise
applicable - appropriate
apposite - appropriate
appreciate
appreciate - admire
appreciative - grateful
apprehend - capture
apprehension - anxiety
apprehensive - afraid
appropriate
approval
approve of - admire
approximate - rough 2
apt - appropriate
aptitude - gift 2
area - place
area - size
argue - disagree
argue - quarrel
argument
argument - subject
aroma - smell
arrange - organize 1
arrange - organize 2
arrest - capture
arrive
arrogant - proud
article - news
artificial
artless - naive
as clear as mud - obscure
ascend - climb
ascend - rise
ashamed
ashen - pale
ask
aspiration - hope
assassinate - kill
assault - attack 1
assault - attack 3

assemble - build 1
assemble - gather
assemble - make
assent - agree 1
assent to - accept 2
assertive - confident
assess - calculate
assessment - examina-
tion
assignment - duty
assimilate - learn
assist - help
assistant
associate - partner
associate with -
accompany
assume
assume - guess
assure - promise
astonish - surprise
astound - surprise
astute - clever
at fault - responsible
attach - join
attack
attack - invade
attempt - try
attend - accompany
attitude - opinion
attractive - beautiful
attractive - interesting
attribute - characteristic
augment - increase
austere - harsh
authentic - genuine
authenticate - prove
authoritarian - strict
authorization - approval
auxiliary - assistant
avaricious - greedy
avenue - road
average - ordinary
aversion - dislike
avert - prevent
avid - eager
avoid
avoid - prevent
await - expect
award - reward 1
aware
awe - fear
awfully - very
awkward - clumsy
awkward - difficult

back
back - support
backpack - travel
bad
baffle - puzzle
baffling - mysterious
balmy - warm
ban
band - group
banish
bunk on - expect
bankrupt - poor
banned - illegal
bar - ban
bare - empty
bare - naked
barking - mad
barmy - mad
bashful - shy
basic
basis
batter - beat 1
battle - fight
bawl - cry
bawl - shout
bay - shout
be against - oppose
be all ears - listen
be asleep - sleep
be at odds - conflict
be busy - work 2
be concerned - worry
be crazy about - love
be employed - work 2
be fond of - love
be in favour of - support
be infatuated with - love
be mistaken - err
be of one mind - agree 2
be on tenterhooks -worry
beam - smile
bear
bear - carry
bear out - prove
beat
beat up - attack 1
beating - defeat
beautiful
beefy - strong
beg
beg - ask
begin
behaviour

behind - late
beholden - grateful
belated - late
belief - opinion
believable - convincing
believe - assume
believe - consider
bellow - shout
bellyache - complain
beloved - favourite
beneficial - good 2
benefit - reward 1
benevolent - kind 1
bequest - gift 1
berate - attack 2
beseech - beg
best
best - favourite
betray
better - healthy
better off - rich
better yourself - improve
bewilder - puzzle
biased
bicker - quarrel
bide your time - wait
big
big business - business 2
bigoted - biased
bind - join
bit - part 1
bitch - woman
biting - cold
bitter - cold
bizarre - strange
black - dark 2
black-market - illegal
blame
blameless - innocent
blank - empty
blaring - loud
blast - attack 2
blatant - clear
blemish
blend - mix
blessing - approval
bliss - happiness
block - hinder
bloke - man
bloomer - mistake
blow your own trumpet
- boast
blub - cry
blubber - cry

blunder - err
blunder - mistake
blunt - frank
boast
boast - own
boastful - proud
body - build 2
bodyguard - guard
boiling - hot
bold
bold - brave
bolt - close 2
bolt - escape
bolt - run
bolt (down) - eat
bomb - fail
bona fide - genuine
bone-idle - lazy
bonkers - mad
bonus - gift 1
bonus - reward 1
bony - thin
boob - err
booming - loud
boost - increase
border
borderline - border
boring
boss - leader
bother - annoy
bother - disturb
bother - trouble 1
bother - trouble 2
bound - jump
boundary - border
bouquet - smell
bout - fight
boy - man
brag - boast
brain - mind
brainchild - idea
brainpower - mind
brainwave - idea
brainy - clever
brave
brawl - fight
brawny - strong
brazen - insolent
break
break - chance
break - holiday
break off - stop 2
break out - escape
break up - scatter

breather - break 2
brief
bright
bright - bold
bright - clever
brilliant - bright
brilliant - clever
brilliant - excellent
bring - carry
bring about - cause 2
bring into existence -
make
bring round - persuade
bring to justice - punish
bring to light - reveal
brisk - quick
briskly - fast
bristly - rough 1
broad - general
broadcast - advertise
broke - poor
bruise - hurt
brutal - cruel
buddy - friend
budget - cheap
buffoon - fool
bug - listen
build
build - make
bulk - size
bulky - big
btilky - heavy
bulletin - news
bully - threaten
bump into - hit
bump into - meet
bump off - kill
bumpy - rough 1
bunch - group
bungling - clumsy
buoyant - light
burden - duty
burglar - thief
burgle - steal
burning - hot
burrow - hole
bury - hide
business
bustling - busy 3
busy
busy - active
butt in - disturb
buy
by yourself - alone 1

bypass - road

cackle - laugh
cajole - tempt
calamity - disaster
calculate
calculated - shrewd
calculating - shrewd
call (out) - shout
call into question - question
call it a day - stop 2
call names - insult
call to mind - remember
calling - job
callous - cruel
calm
calm - patient
calm - peace
camouflage - hide
cancel - abolish
candid - frank
capable - able
capital - money
captain - leader
capture
care - anxiety
care for - love
career - job
careful
careless
caring - devoted
carry
carry - sell
carry out - achieve
cart - carry
cartoon - picture
carve - cut
case - inspect
cash - money
cast - throw
cast aspersions on -
    criticize
casual - accidental
casual - informal
cataclysm - disaster
catalogue - list
catapult - throw
catastrophe - disaster
catch - capture
catch a glimpse of - see
catch on - understand
catch sight of - see
category - kind 2

cause
caustic - sarcastic
cautious - careful 1
cavity - hole
cease - disappear
cease - stop 2
ceaseless - eternal
celebrated - famous
censure - blame
central - basic
certain - sure
certify - prove
challenge - question
champion - back
champion - defend
champion - support
chance - accidental
chance
chance upon - meet
change
change - affect 1
change - money
changeable - unpre-
dictable
chaos - disorder
chap - man
chaperone - accompany
character
characteristic
charade - pretence
charge - run
charitable - kind 1
charming - nice 2
chary - careful 1
chase - follow
chat - discussion
cheap
cheat
check
check out - inspect
checklist - list
cheeky - insolent
cheer up - please
cheerful - happy
cheerfulness - happiness
cherish - appreciate
chew - eat
chic - fashionable
chick - woman
chicken - cowardly
chief - leader
chilly - cold
chock-a-block - full
choose

choose - decide
chop - cut
chore - duty
chonle - laugh
chosen - favourite
chubby - fat
chuck (in) - abandon 2
chuckle - laugh
chum - friend
chunk - part 1
civil - polite
clamber - climb
clanger - mistake
clarify - explain
clash - conflict
class - group
classic - simple
classify - organize 2
classy - exclusive
clean
clear
clear - earn
clemency - mercy
clever
clever - able
climax - top 2
climb
climb - rise
clique - group
cloak - hide
close
close - finish
clown - fool
clued up - aware
clumsy
coach - teach
coarse - rough 1
coax - tempt
cocky - confident
cocky - proud
cogent - convincing
cognizant - aware
cold
cold - unfriendly
collaborator - partner
collapse - fail
colleague - assistant
colleague - partner
collect - gather
collide - hit
colloquial - informal
colossal - big
colourful - bright
comb - search 1

combine - mix
come - arrive
come across - find
come apart - separate 2
come by - buy
come clean - admit 1
come to grief - fail
come to rest - stop 1
come upon - meet
comfortable
comfy - comfortable
comical - funny
command - control
command - order
commandment - order
commence - begin
commend - praise
comment - say
commerce - business 1
commission - duty
commission - income
committed - devoted
common - general
common - ordinary
commotion - trouble 2
communicate - tell
commute - travel
compact - small
companion - friend
company - business 2
compassion - mercy
compassionate - kind 1
compelling - convincing
competent - able
complain
complaint - illness
complete
complete - achieve
complete - finish
complex - complicated
compliant - obedient
complicated
compliment - praise
complimentary - free 1
comply with - accept 2
composed - calm 1
composed - patient
comprehend - under-
stand
comprehensive - general
compromise - endanger
compulsory - necessary
compute - calculate
comrade - friend

con - cheat
con-artist - thief
conceal - hide
concede - admit 1
conceited - proud
concentrate - think
concept - idea
concern - affect 1
concern - anxiety
concern - business 2
concise - brief 2
conclude - decide
conclude - finish
concur - agree 2
condemn - blame
condense - shorten
condition - illness
condition - rule
condone - forgive
conduct - accompany
conduct - behaviour
conduct - control
confab - discussion
conference - discussion
confess - admit 1
confidence trickster -
thief
confident
confident - sure
confidential - secret
confirm - prove
conflict
conform to - observe
confront - oppose
confuse - puzzle
confusion - disorder
congratulate - praise
congregate - gather
conjecture - guess
con-man - thief
connect - join
conquer - beat 2
conquest - defeat
conscience-stricken -
ashamed
conscientious - reliable
conscious - aware
consent - agree 1
consequence - result
consider
consider - think
considerable - big
considerate - kind 1
consideration - respect

consign - send
conspicuous - clear
constant - continuous
constant - faithful
construct - build 1
construct - make
constructive - useful
consume - eat
consuming - intense
contemplate - think
contemplate - plan 2
contemporary - modern
contempt - mockery
content - happy
contentment - happiness
continual - continuous
continue - remain
continuous
contraband - illegal
contradict - conflict
contrast - difference
contribute - give
contribution - gift 1
contrition - regret
control
control - restrain
convention - custom
conventional - ordinary
conversation - discussion
conversion - change 1
convert - change 2
convert - persuade
convey - carry
convict - punish
conviction - opinion
convince - persuade
convinced - sure
convincing
cool - calm 1
cool - cold
cool - fashionable
coordinate - organize 1
copy
copy - imitate
core - basis
corporation - business 2
correct - accurate
correct - appropriate
cotrect - fix
correct - true
corroborate - prove
corrupt - bad 1
corrupt - dishonest
costly - valuable

cosy - comfortable
cough up - pay
counsel - advice
counsel - guide
counselling - advice
count - calculate
counterfeit - artificial
countless - many
courageous - brave
courteous - polite
cover - hide
cover - pretence
covert - secret
covetous - greedy
cow - threaten
cowardly
coy - shy
crack - break 1
crafty - shrewd
cram - fill
cramp - pain
crash into - hit
crater - hole
crave - beg
craven - cowardly
crawl
craze - fashion
crazy - mad
create - cause 2
credible - convincing
credulous - naive
creep - crawl
crest - top 1
crevice - hole
criminal - bad 1
criminal - illegal
critical - important
criticize
criticize - attack 2
criticize - blame
crooked - dishonest
crooked - illegal
cross - angry
crow - boast
crowded - busy 3
crowded - full
crown - top 1
crucial - important
crude - rude
cruel
crush - beat 2
cry
cry (out) - shout
cryptic - obscure

culmination - top 2
cunning - shrewd
curb - restrain
cure - improve
curious - strange
currency - money
current - modern
curtail - shorten
cushy - easy
custom
cut
cut - share
cut - shorten
cut out - stop 2

damage
damaging - bad 2
damp - wet
danger
dangerous
daring - brave
dark
dart - run
dash - hurry
dash - run
data - information
dawn on - understand
daydream - dream
dazzling - bright
dead
dead set on -determined
deafening - loud
deal in - sell
deal with - organize 1
dealings - business 1
dear - valuable
dearest - favourite
debatable - doubtful
debate - discussion
deceased - dead
deceit - trick
deceitful - dishonest
deceive - betray 1
deceive - cheat
decency - honour
decent
deception - trick
deceptive - dishonest
deceptive - false
decide
declare - say
decline - deteriorate
decline - refuse 1
decorous - decent

decrease
decree - order
decree - rule
dedicated - devoted
dean - consider
deep - intense
deface - damage
defeat
defeat - beat 2
defect - blemish
defective - bad 4
defend
defer - delay 1
deferential - polite
defiant - disobedient
defiant - insolent
deficiency - lack
define - explain
definite - sure
defonned - ugly
defraud - cheat
defunct - dead
defy - oppose
degenerate - deteriorate
degradation - disgrace
dejected - sad
delay
delectable - delicious
deliberate - think
delicate - weak
delicious
delight - entertain
delight - happiness
delight - please
delightful - nice 1
delightful - nice 2
deliver - release
deliver - save
demand - ask
demand - order
demanding - difficult
demeanour - behaviour
demented - mad
demolish - destroy
demonstrate - prove
demonstration - sign
demoralize - discourage
denounce - criticize
deny - refuse 1
deny - refuse 2
departed - dead
dependable - reliable
depict - draw
deplore - disapprove

deport - banish
deportment - behaviour
depressed - sad
deputize for - replace
deputy - assistant
derision - mockery
derisive - sarcastic
derogatory - rude
descend on - invade
describe - explain
desert - abandon 1
deserted - alone 2
deserted - empty
design - draw
designation - name
designer - fashionable
desire - hope
despise - hate
destitute - poor
destroy
destroy - damage
detach - separate 2
detached - separate 1
detain - delay 2
detect - find
deter - discourage
deteriorate
determine - decide
determined
detest - hate
detrimental - bad 2
development
devoted
devour - eat
devout - religious
diagram - picture
dialogue - discussion
dice - cut
dictate - order
die out - disappear
differ - conflict
differ - disagree
difference
different - separate 1
difficult
difficult - complicated
difficult - stubborn
difficulty - problem
diffident - shy
diligent - busy 1
dim - dark 1
dim - stupid
dimensions - size
diminish - decrease

dingy - dark 1
direct - control
direct - frank
direct - send
directive - order
directory - list
dirt-cheap - cheap
dirty
disadvantage - problem
disagree
disallow - ban
disappear
disappoint - discourage
disappointed - sad
disappointment - dismay
disapprove
disarray - disorder
disaster
discern - see
discharge - release
discipline - punish
disclose - betray 2
discomfort - pain
disconcert - puzzle
disconnect - separate 2
discontinue - abolish
discontinue - stop 2
discourage
discourteous - rude
discover - find
discredit - disgrace
discreet - secret
discrepancy - difference
discriminatory - biased
discussion
disdain - mockery
disease - illness
disgrace
disguise - pretence
disgusting
dishearten - discourage
dishonest
dishonest - illegal
dishonour - disgrace
disillusion - discourage
dislike
dislike - hate
dismal - sad
dismantle - separate 2
dismay
disobedient
disorder
disorder - illness
disorder - trouble 2

disorderliness - disorder
disparage - criticize
disparity - difference
dispassionate - fair
dispatch - send
dispel - scatter
disperse - scatter
display - reveal
displease - annoy
disposition - character
dispute - argument
dispute - disagree
dispute - question
disqualify - ban
disrepute - disgrace
disrespectful - insolent
disrupt - disturb
dissimilarity - difference
dissipate - scatter
dissuade - discourage
distant
distant - unfriendly
distaste - dislike
distinct - separate 1
distinction - difference
distinctive - special
distinguished - famous
distract - disturb
distress - dismay
distress - trouble 1
distrust - question
disturb
disturb - affect 2
disturb - trouble 1
disturbance - trouble 2
dither - hesitate
diversion - game
diversity - difference
divert - entertain
divide - separate 2
divorce - part 2
divulge - betray 2
do - achieve
do away with - abolish
do in - kill
do your best - try
do your bit - help
docile - obedient
dock - shorten
dodge - avoid
dodge - trick
dodgy - dangerous
dogged - stubborn
donate - give

donation - gift 1
doodle - draw
dosh - money
dote on - love
doting - devoted
double-check - check
double-cross - betray 1
doubt - question
doubtful
dough - money
down - drink
down to earth - sensible
downcast - sad
downpour - rain
doze - sleep
drag - pull
drained - tired
draw
draw - pull
draw up - stop 1
drawback - problem
drawing - picture
dread - fear
dreadful - bad 3
dream
dream - hope
dreary - boring
drenched - wet
drill - teach
drink
drive - push
drizzle - rain
droll - funny
drop - fall
drop off - decrease
drop off - sleep
drowsy - tired
drudgery - work 1
drunk
dubious - doubtful
duck out of - avoid
dude - man
dull - boring
dumb - stupid
dump - abandon 1
dunce - fool
dupe - cheat
duplicate - copy
dusky - dark 2
dusty - dirty
dutiful - obedient
duty
dwindle - decrease

eager
earn
earn your living - work 2
earnings - income
ear-piercing - loud
ease - crawl
easy
easygoing - informal
eat
eavesdrop - listen
ebb - deteriorate
eccentric
ecclesiastical - religious
economical - cheap
ecstasy - happiness
edge - border
edge - crawl
educate - teach
education - knowledge
effect - cause 2
effect - result
effort - work 1
effortless - easy
egg on - urge
egotistic - selfish
egotistical) - selfish
eject - banish
elaborate - complicated
elaborate - explain
elated - happy
elation - happiness
elderly - old
elect - choose
elect - decide
elegant - fashionable
elementary - basic
elementary - easy
elevated - high
elite - exclusive
elude - avoid
emaciated - thin
emancipate - release
embarrassed - ashamed
embezzle - steal
eminent - famous
emotion - feeling
emotional - moving
emotional - sentimental
employment - job
empty
empty - hungry
emulate - imitate
encounter - meet
encourage - back

encourage - support
encourage - urge
end - finish
endanger
endeavour - try
endless - continuous
endoise - back
endorsement - approval
endure - bear
endure - remain
enemy
energetic - active
energy - vigour
engaged - busy 1
engrossed - busy 1
enhatice - improve
enigmatic - mysterious
enjoy - appreciate
enjoy - own
enjoyable - nice 1
enlarge - increase
enlighten - explain
enormous - big
enquire - ask
enraged - angry
entail - involve
enter - arrive
enterprise - adventure
enterprise - business 2
entertain
entertaining - interesting
entertainment - game
enthral - entertain
enthusiastic - eager
entice - tempt
entire - complete 1
entreat - beg
envisage - plan 2
ephemeral - brief 1
episode - event
epithet - name
eradicate - abolish
erect - build 1
err
erroneous - false
error - mistake
erudition - knowledge
escapade - adventure
escape
escape - avoid
eschew - avoid
escort - accompany
escort - guard
esoteric - obscure

especial - special
essential - basic
essential - necessary
essentials - basis
establish - prove
establishment -
  business 2
esteem - respect
estimate - calculate
estimate - guess
estimated - rough 2
estimation - respect
eternal
euphoria - happiness
evade - avoid
evaporate - disappear
even-handed - fair
event
eventful - busy 2
everlasting - eternal
everyday - ordinary
everyday - simple
evict - banish
evidence - sign
evident - clear
evil - bad 1
evolution - development
exact - accurate
exacting - difficult
exam - examination
examination
examine - check
exasperate - annoy
exceedingly - very
excellent
exceptional - excellent
exceptional - special
excessively - very
excited
exciting - interesting
exclude - ban
exclusive
excuse - forgive
execute - kill
exemplary - excellent
exertion - work 1
exhausted - tired
exhibit - reveal
exhilarated - excited
exile - banish
exonerate - forgive
expand - increase
expect
expectation - hope

expel - banish
expensive - valuable
experience - event
expert - able
explain
exploit - adventure
exploration - adventure
expose - betray 2
expose - endanger
expose - reveal
express - speak
extend - increase
extended - long 1
extensive - big
extensive - long 2
extent - size
extinct - dead
extraordinary - special
extraordinary - unusual
extreme - intense
extremely - very
exuberant - happy
eye - inspect

fabricate - make
façade - pretence
facetious - funny
facts - information
fad - fashion
fade - disappear
fail
faint - quiet
faint - weak
faint-hearted - cowardly
fair
fairly - quite
faithful
faithful - devoted
faithful - true
fake - artificial
fall
fall - defeat
fall apart - separate 2
fall asleep - sleep
fall out (with) - quarrel
fall through - fail
false
false - artificial
false - dishonest
falsehood - lie
falter - hesitate
familiar - informal
famished - hungry
famous

fantastic - excellent
fantasy - dream
far - distant
faraway - distant
farcical - ridiculous
far-flung - distant
far-off - distant
fascinating - interesting
fashion
fashion - build 1
fashionable
fashionable - exclusive
fast fast - quick
fasten - close 2
fasten - join
fastidious - careful 2
fat
fathom - understand
fault - blemish
faultless - innocent
faux pas - mistake
favourable - good 2
favourite
favourite - popular
fax - copy
faze - affect 2
faze - puzzle
fear
fearful - afraid
fearless - brave
feature - characteristic
feeble - weak
feel - handle
feeling
feeling - opinion
fellow - man
female - woman
ferret out - find
fervent - sincere
feud - argument
few
fib - lie
fickle - unpredictable
fiddly - complicated
fierce - violent
fight
fight - argument
fight - quarrel
figure - build 2
fill
fill in - tell
fill in for - replace
filthy - dirty
filthy lucre - money

finalize - finish
find
fine - beautiful
fine - punish
finest - best
finger - handle
finish
firm - business 2
firm - hard
firm - strict
first-rate - excellent
fisticuffs - fight
fit - agree 3
fit - healthy
fitting - appropriate
fix
fix (up) - organize 1
fix on - decide
flabby - fat
flair - gift 2
flat - boring
flatter - praise
flavour - taste 1
flaw - blemish
flee - escape
fleeting - brief 1
flimsy - light
flimsy - weak
fling - throw
flop - fail
flunk - fail
fly - hurry
focused - determined
foe - enemy
foil - hinder
follow
follow - observe
follow - understand
fond - devoted
fondle - handle
fool
foolish - silly
foolproof - easy
foot the bill - pay
footpath - road
for nothing - free 2
forage - search 2
forbearing - patient
forbid - ban
forceful - strong
foreboding - anxiety
foremost - best
forestall - prevent
forgery - copy

forgive
forgiveness - mercy
fork out - pay
forlorn - alone 2
form - build 1
form - build 2
fomial - polite
formation - development
formidable - difficult
forthright - frank
fortuitous - accidental
fortuitous - fortunate
fortunate
fortune - wealth
forward - send
foster - support
foul - disgusting
foundation - basis
founder - fail
fracture - break 1
fragile - weak
fragment - part 1
fragrance - smell
frail - weak
frame - build 2
frank
frank - sincere
fraudulent - dishonest
freak out - trouble 1
free
free - release
freezing - cold
fresh - new
fret - worry
friend
friendly - nice 2
fright - fear
frighten
frightened - afraid
fritter away - waste
front -pretence
frontier - border
frosty - cold
frown on - disapprove
frozen - cold
fruitless - useless
full
full - busy 2
full - complete 1
function - duty
function - purpose
function - work 3
fundamental - basic
fundajnentals - basis

funds - money
funny
funny - unusual
furious - angry
furnish - give
furtive - secret
fuss - trouble 2
futile - useless

gaffe - mistake
gag - joke
gain - get
gallop - run
game
gang - group
gap - hole
gash - cut
gather
gauche - clumsy
gauge - calculate
gaunt - thin
gaze - look
general
general - rough 2
generate - cause 2
generous - kind 1
genial - nice 2
gentleman - man
genuine
genuine - sincere
gesture - sign
get
get - understand
get a move on - hurry
get away - escape
get back to - answer 1
get better - improve
get divorced - part 2
get on someone's nerves
  - annoy
get rid of - abolish
get the better of - beat 2
ghastly - disgusting
ghost
ghoul - ghost
gift
gifted - able
gifted - clever
gigantic - big
giggle - laugh
girl - woman
give
give away - betray 2
give the once-over -check

give up - abandon 2
give your word - promise
glad - grateful
glance - look
glare - look
glee - happiness
glide - crawl
glimpse - see
gloomy - dark 1
glowing - bright
gluttonous - greedy
gnarled - rough 1
go
go - travel
go - work 3
go against - conflict
go along -with - agree 1
go downhill - deteriorate
go for - choose
go on - remain
go pear-shaped - fail
go through - search 1
go through the roof -
  increase
go wrong - err
go your separate ways -
  part 2
goad - urge
go-ahead - approval
goal - hope
goal - purpose
gobble - eat
gone - dead
good
good - kind 1
good - nice 1
good-looking - beautiful
good-natured - nice 2
goodness - honour
gorge - fill
gorgeous - beautiful
govern - guide
gradual - slow
grand
grant - gift 1
grasp - understand
grasping - greedy
grasping - mean
grass on - betray 1
grateful
gratify - please
gratis - free 2
gratuity - gift 1
grave - serious

graze - hit
great - big
great - excellent
great - famous
greedy
green - inexperienced
grief - regret
grill - ask
grim - serious
grimy - dirty
grin - smile
gripe - complain
gripping - interesting
gross - disgusting
gross - earn
grotesque - ugly
ground-breaking - new
grounds - basis
grounds - cause 1
groundwork - basis group
grow - increase
growth - development
grubby - dirty
gruelling - difficult
grumble - complain
guarantee - promise
guard
guard - defend
guess
guess - assume
guffaw - laugh
guidance - advice
guide
guidelines - rule
guiltless - innocent
guilty - ashamed
guilty - responsible
gullible - naive
gulp - drink
gutless - cowardly
gutsy - brave
guy - man
guzzle - drink

habit - custom
hack off - annoy
hairy - dangerous
hale and hearty - healthy
hallucination - dream
halt - stop 1
ham-fisted - clumsy
hammer - beat 1
hamper - hinder
hand - give

handle
handsome - beautiful
handy - close 1
handy - useful
hang around - wait
hang on - wait
happening - event
happiness
happy
happy - fortunate
hard
hard - difficult
hard - harsh
hard up - poor
hark back - remember
harm - damage
harm - hurt
harmful - bad 2
harsh
harsh -cruel
hassle - problem
hasten - hurry
hastily - fast
hasty - careless
hasty - quick
hate
hatred - dislike
haughty - proud
haul - pull
have - own
have a crack - try
have a crush on - love
have a go - try
have a nap - sleep
have a row (with) -
  quarrel
have a stab - try
have butterflies (in your
stomach) - worry
have forty winks - sleep
have reservations about
  - question
have-a-go - brave
hawk - sell
hazard - danger
hazy - rough 2
head - control
head - leader
head - mind
headline - news
headstrong - disobedient
healthy
hear - listen
heart - basis

heart-felt - sincere
heartless - cruel
heart-rending - moving
heart-warming - moving
heated - angry
heave - pull
heavy
heavy-handed - clumsy
hectic - busy 2
hefty - heavy
height - top 2
hell-bent - determined
help
helper - assistant
helpful - kind 1
helpful - useful
heroic - brave
hesitate
hide
hideous - ugly
high
high - excited
high street - road
high-class - exclusive
highly - very
hike - walk
hilarious - funny
hinder
hint - suggest 2
hip - fashionable
hit
hit - beat 1
hitch - problem
hoard - gather
hobby - game
hold - own
hold - keep
hold back - restrain
hold on - wait
hold up - delay 2
hole
holiday
hollow - empty
holy - religious
homely - simple
homophobic - biased
honest - reliable
honest - sincere
honesty - honour
honour
honour - reward 2
honourable - decent
hop - jump
hope

hope for - expect
hopeless - inferior
horrify - shock
horror - fear
hostile - unfriendly
hostility - dislike
hot
hound - follow
howl - cry
huge - big
humane - kind 1
humanity - mercy
humbled - ashamed
humdrum - boring
humid - wet
humiliated - ashamed
humiliation - disgrace
humorous - funny
humour - please
hungry
hunt - search 2
hurt - throw
hurried - quick
hurriedly - fast
hurry
hurt
hurt - damage
hush - peace
hushed - quiet
hygienic - clean
hype up - advertise
hyper - excited
hyperactive - active

icy - cold
idea
idiosyncrasy - character-
istic
idiosyncratic - eccentric
idiot - fool
idiotic - stupid
idle - lazy
idolize - admire
ignoramus - fool
ignorant
ignorant - stupid
ill
illegal
illicit - illegal
ill-mannered - rude
illness
illustrate - draw
illustration - picture
illustrious - famous

image - character
image - picture
imagination - mind
imagine - assume
imbecile - fool
imitate
imitation - artificial
imitation - copy
immaculate - clean
immature - naive
immature - young
immense - big
immoral - bad 1
immortal - eternal
impair - hurt
impartial - fair
impatient
impede - hinder
impenetrable - obscure
imperative - necessary
imperfect - bad 4
imperfection - blemish
imperil - endanger
impersonate - imitate
impertinent - insolent
impinge on - affect 1
implore - beg
imply - involve
imply - suggest 2
impolite - rude
important
imposing - grand
impoverished - poor
impression - opinion
impressive - grand
improve
imprudent - silly
impudent - insolent
in - fashionable
in charge (of) - responsible
in demand - popular
in favour - popular
in length - long 2
in one piece - safe
in the dear - innocent
in the nude - naked
in the pink - healthy
in vain - useless
in your birthday suit -
naked
inaccuracy - mistake
inaccurate - careless
inaccurate - false

inactive - lazy
inadequate - inferior
inadvertent - accidental
inanimate - dead
inaudible - quiet
inaugurate - begin
incensed - angry
incessant - continuous
inch - crawl
incident - event
incite - persuade
include - involve
income
inconsiderate - selfish
incorporate - involve
incorrect - false
increase
indebted - grateful
indecent - rude
independent - separate 1
index - list
indicate - suggest 2
indication - sign
indignant - angry
indispensable - basic
indispensable - necessary
indisposed - ill
individual - separate 1
indolent - lazy
induce - persuade
industrious - active
industry - business 1
inebriated - drunk
ineffective - useless
inexorable - relentless
inexpensive - cheap
inexperienced
inexperienced - ignorant
inexpert - inexperienced
inexplicable - mysterious
infamous - famous
infamy - disgrace
infection - illness
inferior
infinite - eternal
inflexible - strict
influence - affect 1
influence - guide
influence - persuade
info - information
inform - tell
inform on - betray 1
informal
information

informed - aware
infrequent - few
ingenious - clever
ingenuous - naive
inhibit - restrain
inhibited - shy
inhospitable - unfriendly
initiate - begin
injure - damage
injure - hurt
innocent
innocent - ignorant
innocent - naive
innovative - new
innumerable - many
insane - mad
insatiable - greedy
inscrutable - mysterious
insecure - dangerous
insinuate - suggest 2
insistent - relentless
insolent
inspect
inspiration - idea
instigate - begin
instinct - feeling
instruct - teach
instruction - advice
instruction - order
insufficiency - lack
insufficient - few
insult
insulting - rude
intact - complete 1
intact - safe
integrity - honour
intellect - mind
intelligence - information
intelligence - mind
intelligent - clever
intend - plan 2
intense
intent - determined
intention - hope
intention - plan 1
intention - purpose
interest - entertain
interesting
interfere
interminable - long 1
interpret - explain
interrogate - ask
interrogation - examina-
tion

interrupt - disturb
intersperse - mix
intervene - interfere
intimate - suggest 2
intimidate - frighten
intimidate - threaten
intoxicated - drunk
intransigent - stubborn
intrepid - brave
intricate - complicated
intriguing - interesting
intrude - disturb
intuition - feeling
invade
invaluable - valuable
inveigle - tempt
inventory - list
invert - turn 2
invest - pay
investigate - check
invite - ask
involve
involved - complicated
irate - angry
ironic(al) - sarcastic
irreproachable - innocent
irresponsible - silly
irritate - annoy
isolated - alone 2
isolated - separate 1
issue - subject
itch - pain

jaded - tired
jam - fill
jam-packed - full
jeering - mockery
jeopardize - endanger
jiggle - shake
jilt - abandon 1
job
job - duty
jog - run
join
joke
jot down - write
journey - go
journey - travel
joy - happiness
joyful - happy
judge - consider
jumble - mix
jump
just - fair

justification - cause 1
juvenile - young

keen - eager
keep
keep - observe
keep - own
keep an eye on - watch
keep from - prevent
keep tabs on - watch
keep under control -
  restrain
keep under surveillance
  - watch
keep watch - watch
key - basic
key - important
kick off - begin
kick your heels - wait
kill
kind
kindness - mercy
knock - hit
knock back - drink
knock dawn - destroy
knotty - complicated
know-bow - knowledge
knowing - shrewd
knowledge
knowledge - information
knowledgeable - aware
kosher - fair

label - name
laborious - difficult
labour - work 1
labour - work 2
lacerate - cut
lack
lady - woman
laid-back - calm 1
land - arrive
lane - road
large - big
lass - woman
last - remain
last-minute - late
late
late - dead
laugh
laughable - ridiculous
laughing stock - fool
launch - throw law - rule
law-abiding - obedient

lax - careless
lay bare - reveal
lazy
lead - control
lead - guide
leader
leading - best
lean on - threaten
leap - jump
learn
learning - knowledge
leave - abandon 1
leave - holiday
leave behind - abandon 2
leave in the lurch -
  abandon 1
leave off - stop 2
lecture - speech
lecture - teach
leer - smile
leg it - escape
legacy - gift 1
legal tender - money
legendaty - famous
legitimate - genuine
legless - drunk
leisurely - slow
lend a hand - help
lengthy - long 1
lengthy - long 2
leniency - mercy
lessen - decrease
let go - release
let in - admit 2
let know - tell
let off - forgive
let slip - betray 2
lethargic - lazy
level-headed - sensible
liable - responsible
liberate - release
lie
lifeguard - guard
lifeless - dead
light
light - pale
likable - nice 2
like a shot - fast
likelihood - chance
lily-livered - cowardly
limit - restrain
limitless - eternal
limits - border
linger - wait

lingering - long 1
link - join
list
listen
literal - true
little - small
little - young
liveliness - vigour
lively - active
load - fill
loaded - full
loaded - rich
loads of - many
loathe - hate
loathing - dislike
lob - throw
locate - find
location - place
lock up - punish
lofty - high
lonely - alone 2
long
long weekend - holiday
long-suffering - patient
look
look after - organize 1
look around - search 1
look back - remember
look down your nose at -
  disapprove
look for - search 2
look forward to - expect
look on - watch
look over - inspect
look up - improve
look up to - admire
lookout - guard
loom (up) - rise
loot - steal
lose sleep - worry
lots of - many
loud
loud - bold
love
lovely - beautiful
lovely - nice 1
loving - devoted
low-cost - cheap
lower - decrease
loyal - devoted
loyal - faithful
lucky - fortunate
ludicrous - ridiculous
lug - carry

lukewarm - warm
lumbering - clumsy
luminous - bright
lump - part 1
lumpy - rough 1
lure - tempt
luscious - delicious
luxury - wealth

mad
mad - angry
magnificent - grand
magnitude - size
mail - send
maim - hurt
main - important
maintain - own
majestic - grand
major - bad 3
major - important
make
make - earn
make a fuss - complain
make a note of - write
make an effort - try
make arrangements -
  organize 1
make off with - steal
make out - see
make over - improve
make pay - punish
make up your mind -
  decide
make your way - go
makeover - change 1
make-up - character
malady - illness
male - man
malicious - bad 1
malnourished - hungry
man
manage - control
manager - leader
man-made - artificial
manners - behaviour
manoeuvre - trick
manufacture - make
many
march - walk
march into - invade
margin - border
mark - blemish
mark - sign
market - advertise

marvellous - excellent
massacre - kill
massive - big
master - learn
match - agree 3
mate - friend
mate - partner
material - information
materialistic - greedy
matter - subject
mature - reliable
mawkish - sentimental
meagre - few
mean
mean - involve
mean - plan 2
means - wealth
measured - slow
meddle - interfere
mediocre - inferior
meet
meet the cost of - pay
melancholy - sad
melt away - disappear
memorable - special
memorize - learn
menace - danger
menace - threaten
mend - fix
mendacious - dishonest
mentality - mind
mentally ill - mad
mention - say
menu - list
mercy
merge - mix
merry - happy
mess - disorder
message - news
messy - dirty
method - plan 1
meticulous - careful 2
middle-aged - old
mighty - strong
mild - warm
mimic - imitate
mind
mindful - aware
mindless - stupid
mingle - mix
mini - small
miniature - small
minute - small
miscalculate - err

mischievous - bad 1
mischievous -disobedient
miserable - sad
miserly - greedy
miserly - mean
misfortune - disaster
misguided - silly
misleading - false
misspend - waste
mistake
mistaken - false
mistrust - question
misunderstand - err
mix
moan - complain
mock - artificial
mockery
mocking - sarcastic
moderately - quite
modern
modem - fashionable
modest - shy
modification - change 1
modify - affect 1
modify - change 2
moist - wet
momentary - brief 1
momentous - important
momentum - speed
money
monitor - watch
monotonous - boring
moral - good 1
morality - honour
moron - fool
motivation - cause 1
motive - cause 1
motorway - road
mount - climb
mount (up) - increase
mournful - sad
move - affect 2
move - go
moving
muck in - help
mucky - dirty
muddy - dirty
muffled - quiet
mug - attack 1
mugger - thief
mull over - think
multiply - increase
munch - eat
murder - kill

murky - dark 1
mysterious
mystify - puzzle
mystifying - mysterious

naive
naked
name
narrative - story
narrow - thin
nasty - bad 1
nasty - bad 3
nasty - cruel
natural - informal
nature - character
naughty - bad 1
naughty - disobedient
nauseating - disgusting
near - close 1
nearby - close 1
necessary
necessary - basic
necessitate - involve
need - lack
needy - poor
neighbouring - close 1
nervous - afraid
nervous - impatient
net - earn
new
new - inexperienced
new - modern
new-fangled - modern
news
news - information
nibble - eat
nice
nick - capture
nick - steal
nickname - name
niggardly - mean
nigh - close 1
night watchman - guard
nightmare - dream
nip in the bud - prevent
nobility - honour
noble - good 1
nod off - sleep
no-frills - cheap
noisy - loud
no-nonsense - simple
nonsensical - ridiculous
nonstop - continuous
norm - custom

normal - ordinary
nostalgic - sentimental
not decent - naked
not guilty - innocent
notable - famous
notable - special
note down - write
noted - famous
noteworthy - special
notice - see
notify - tell
notion - idea
notorious - famous
novel - new
novel - story
nude - naked
nudge - push
numerous - many
nuts - mad

obedient
obese - fat
obey - observe
object - disapprove
object - oppose
object - purpose
objective - fair
objective - purpose
obligatory - necessary
oblige - help
oblige - please
obliged - grateful
obscure
observe
observe - say
observe - watch
obstinate - stubborn
obstruct - hinder
obtain - buy
obtain - get
obvious - clear
occasion - cause 1
occasion - chance
occasion - event
occupation - job
occupied - busy 1
occupied - full
occupy - invade
occurrence - event
odd - eccentric
odd - strange
odour - smell
of unsound mind - mad
off your own bat - alone1

offend - insult
offend - shock
offensive - attack 3
offensive - disgusting
offensive - rude
offhand - careless
off-putting - disgusting
ogle - look
old
old-fashioned - old
omission - mistake
on special offer - cheap
on the go - active
on the house - free 1
on your doorstep - close1
on your man - alone 1
on your tod - alone 1
onslaught - attack 3
open - frank
opening - chance
operate - work 3
opinion
opinion - advice
opponent - enemy
opportune - fortunate
opportunity - chance
oppose
opposite number -
  partner
opposition - enemy
opt - choose
optimum - best
oral - examination
order
order - organize 2
ordinary
organize
organize - control
origin - cause 1
original - genuine
original - new
originate - begin
out of danger - safe
out of sorts - ill
out of the ordinary -
  unusual
out of your mind - mad
outcome - result
outdo - beat 2
outfit - business 2
outlandish - strange
outlying - distant
out-of-date - old
outrage - shock

outright - complete 2
outspoken - frank
outstanding - excellent
over the limit - drunk
overall - general
overcame - beat 2
overdue - late
overhaul - fix
overhear - listen
overlook - forgive
overrun - invade
oversee - control
oversee - inspect
overthrow - defeat
overweight - fat
overweight - heavy
overwrought - excited
own
own up - admit 1

pace - speed
pack - fill
pack - group
packed - full
pain
pain - hurt
painstaking - careful 2
painting - picture
pal - friend
palatial - grand
pale
pallid - pale
panic - fear
panic - frighten
paper - examination
parable - story
paralytic - drunk
pardon - forgive
park - stop 1
parrot - imitate
parsimonious - mean
part
part company (with) -
   part 2
partial - biased
particular - careful 2
particular - separate 1
partisan - biased
partner
partner - accompany
pass - disappear
pass - give
pass - go
pass up - refuse 1

passion - feeling
passionate - eager
passionate - intense
past its sell-by date - old
past your/its prime - old
pastel - pale
pastime - game
pasty (-faced) - pale
patch - fix
patch up - fix
patent - clear
patient
pause - hesitate
pavement - road
paw - handle pay
pay - income
pay - reward 2
pay attention - listen
pay back - pay
pay tribute - praise
peace
peaceful - calm 2
peak - top 1
peak - top 2
peaky - pale
peculiar - eccentric
peculiar - strange
peculiarity -characteristic
peddle - sell
peep - look
pejorative - rude
pen - write
penalize - punish
penance - regret
penitence - regret
penniless - poor
penny-pinching - mean
pensive - serious
perceive - see
perceptive - shrewd
perfect - accurate
performance - behaviour
peril - danger
perilous - dangerous
perimeter - border
perjury - lie
pennission - approval
perpetual - eternal
perplex - puzzle
persist - remain
persistent - relentless
persistent - stubborn
persona - character
personality - character

persuade
persuasive - convincing
perturb - trouble 1
pester - disturb
pet - favourite
petite - small
petrified - afraid
petrify - frighten
phantom - ghost
philosophical - patient
phobia - fear
photocopy - copy
photograph - picture
physique - build 2
pick - choose
pick up - buy
pick up - handle
pick up - improve
pickpocket - thief
picture
picturesque - beautiful
piece - part 1
pilfer - steal
pinch - steal
pinnacle - top 2
pioneering - new
pious - religious
pit - hole
pithy - brief 2
pitiless - relentless
pity - mercy
place
placid - calm 1
plain - clear
plain - simple
plain - ugly
plan
plan - hope
plan - idea
plan - picture
plausible - convincing
play - game
plead - beg
pleasant - nice 1
please
pledge - promise
plenty - many
plight - problem
plod - walk
plot - plan 1
plot - plan 2
plot - story
ploy - trick
plucky - brave

plug - advertise
plump - fat
plump for - choose
plunge - fall
pocket - small
podgy - fat
poignant - moving
point - purpose
point - subject
point of view - opinion
point out - say
pointless - useless
poised - confident
poke - push
poke your nose in -
  interfere
polite
polluted - dirty
poltergeist - ghost
pompous - proud
ponder - think
ponderous - slow
pong - smell
poor
poor - bad 4
poorly - ill
popular
porky (pie) - lie
portable - light
portion - share
portrait - picture
portray - draw
posh - exclusive
position - job
position - place
positive - confident
positive - sure
possess - own
possibility - chance
post - job
post - send
postpone - delay 1
poverty - lack
poverty-stricken - poor
powerful - strong
powerful - violent
practical - sensible
practical - useful
practice - custom
praise
praise to the skies -praise
precarious - dangerous
precious - valuable
precious few - few

precise - accurate
preclude - prevent
predicament - problem
preferred - favourite
prejudiced - biased
premium - reward 1
preoccupied - serious
present - gift 1
present - give
presentation - speech
present-day - modern
preserve - keep
preserve - save
press - push
pressurize - threaten
presume - assume
presumptuous - insolent
pretence
pretty - beautiful
prevail (up) on - per-
suade
prevent
prevent - hinder
priceless - valuable
primary - basic
primary - important
principal - leader
pristine - clean
private - secret
privileged - fortunate
prize - appreciate
prize - reward 1
prize money - reward 1
probability - chance
problem
proceed - go
procrastinate - delay 1
procure - buy
procure - get
prod - push
produce - cause 2
produce - make
profession - job
profit - reward 1
profitable - useful
profits - income
profound - intense
progress - development
progress - go
prohibit - ban
prohibited - illegal
project - plan 1
prolonged - long 1
promise

promote - advertise
promote - back
promote - support
prompt - quick
promptly - fast
pronounce - speak
pronto - fast
propel - push
propel - throw
proper - appropriate
proper - decent
propitious - good 2
proportions - size
proposal - plan 1
propose - plan 2
propose - suggest 1
prospect - chance
prosperity - wealth
prosperous - rich
protect - defend
protest - complain
protracted - long 1
proud
prove
provide - give
providential - fortunate
provoke - cause 2
prudent - careful 1
prudent - sensible
prune - shorten
pry - interfere
publicize - advertise
puckish - hungry
pull
pull off - achieve
pull up - stop 1
pummel - beat 1
pun - joke
punch - beat 1
punctilious - careful 2
punish
puny - weak
purchase - buy
pure - clean
purpose
pursue - follow
push
push - advertise
push to - close 2
put - interfere
put an end to - abolish
put at risk - endanger
put down - insult
put forward - suggest 1

put in an appearance - arrive
put in order - organize 2
put in writing - write
put off - delay 1
put off - discourage
put to sleep - kill
put together - build 1
put together - make
put up - build 1
put up with - bear
put your oar in - interfere
puzzle
puzzling - mysterious

quaff - drink
quake - shake
quality - characteristic
quarrel
quarrel - argument
quash - abolish
queasy - ill
queer - strange
query - question
quest - adventure
question
question - ask
question - subject
questionable - doubtful
quick
quickly - fast
quiet
quip - joke
quirk - characteristic
quirky - eccentric
quit - stop 2
quite
quite - very
quiver - shake
quiz - ask
quiz - examination
quota - share

R and R - holiday
race - run
racist - biased
radiant - beautiful
raid - attack 3
rain
rainfall - rain
rainy - wet
raise your voice - shout
rally round - help
ram - hit

random - accidental
range - size
rapid - quick
rapidity - speed
rapidly - fast
raring to go - eager
raring to go - healthy
rash - silly
rate - consider
rate - speed
rather - quite
ration - share
rational - sensible
ravenous - hungry
reach - achieve
reach - arrive
reaction - result
real - genuine
realistic - sensible
realize - achieve
realize - understand
really - very
reason - cause 1
reasonable - cheap
reasonable - fair
reasonable - sensible
reasonably - quite
rebellious - disobedient
recall - remember
receive - accept 1
receive - admit 2
receive - get
recent - modern
reckless - silly
reckon - calculate
reckon - consider
reckon - guess
recognize - admit 1
recognize - praise
recognize - remember
recollect - remember
recommend - guide
recommend - suggest 1
recommendation - advice
recompense - reward 2
recondite - obscure
recount - tell
recover - save
recreation - game
rectify - fix
redeem - save
redress - revenge
reduce - decrease
reek - smell

reel - turn 1
refer to - say
reflect - think
refrain (from) -abandon 2
refuse
regal - grand
regale - entertain
regard - respect
regard as - consider
register - list
regret
regular - ordinary
regulation - rule
reject - refuse 1
rejoinder - answer 2
relate - tell
relaxed - calm 1
relaxed - informal
relaxing - comfortable
release
relentless
relevant - appropriate
reliable
religious
remain
remark - say
remarkable - unusual
remember
remind - remember
reminisce - remember
remit - send
remorse - regret
remorseless - relentless
remote - distant
remunerate - reward 2
rendezvous - meet
renounce - abandon 2
renovate - fix
renowned - famous
repair - fix
repay - pay
repentance - regret
repercussions - result
replace
replace with - replace
replenish - fill
replica - copy
reply - answer 2
report - news
report - tell
reprisal - revenge
reproduction - copy
repugnant - disgusting
repulsive - disgusting

repulsive - ugly
request - ask
request - order
require - involve
required - necessary
requisite - necessary
reschedule - delay 1
rescue - save
reserved - shy
resigned - patient
resilient - strong
resist - oppose
resolute - determined
resolve - decide
resonant - loud
respect
respect - admire
respect - observe
respectable - decent
respectful - polite
respite - break 2
respond - answer 1
response - answer 2
responsibility - duty
responsible
responsible - reliable
responsible - sensible
rest - break 2
rest - sleep
restful - comfortable
restless - impatient
restore - fix
restrain
restrict - restrain
result
retail - sell
retain - keep
retain - own
retaliation - revenge
reticent - shy
retiring - shy
retort - answer 2
retribution - revenge
reveal
reveal - betray 2
revenge
reverence - respect
reverent - religious
reverie - dream
reversal - change 1
reverse - change 2
reverse - turn 2
review - inspect
revise - learn

revolting - disgusting
revolution - change 1
revolutionize - change 2
revolve - turn 1
reward
reward - gift 1
rewarding - good 2
ribbing - mockery
rich
riches - wealth
ride - travel
ridicule - mockery
ridiculous
right - accurate
right - appropriate
right - fair
rigid - hard
rigorous - strict
rim - border
ring road - road
ringleader - leader
riot - trouble 2
rip off - cheat
rip off - steal
riposte - answer 2
rise
rise - increase
risk - danger
risk - endanger
risky - dangerous
ritual - custom
rival - enemy
road
roam - travel
roar - laugh
roar - shout
robber - thief
robust - strong
roll - list
rolling in it - rich
rolling in money - rich
root - cause 1
rotate - turn 1
rotund - fat
rough
rough - violent
round off - finish
round up - gather
rout - defeat
routine - custom
routine - ordinary
row - argument
rubbish - inferior
rude

rudimentary - basic
rugged - rough 1
ruin - damage
ruin - destroy
rule
rule - decide
rule out - prevent
ruminate - think
rummage - search 1
run
run - control
run - work 3
run away - escape
run down - criticize
run into - meet
ruse - trick
rush - hurry
rush - run
rushed off your feet -
   busy 1

sabbatical - holiday
sacred - religious
sad
sadistic - cruel
sadness - dismay
safe
safeguard - defend
saga - story
salary - income
salvage - save
sample - taste 2
sanction - approval
sarcastic
sardonic - sarcastic
satisfied - happy
saunter - walk
savage - violent
save
save - keep
savour - appreciate
savour - taste 1
savour - taste 2
say
say goodbye (to) - part 2
say no (to) - refuse 1
scalding - hot
scale - climb
scale - size
scan - look
scandal - disgrace
scandalize - shock
scarce - few
scarcity - lack

scare - fear
scare - frighten
scared - afraid
scatter
scene - place
scent - smell
scheme - plan 1
scheme - plan 2
scholarship - knowledge
scoff - eat
scold - attack 2
scope - size
scorching - hot
scornful - sarcastic
scour - search 1
scramble - climb
scrap - fight
scrawny - thin
scream - shout
screen - hide
scribble - draw
scribble - write
scrumptious - delicious
scrutinize - check
scuffle - fight
seal - close 2
search
second - back
second-in-command -
  assistant
second-rate - inferior
secret
secrete - hide
section - part 1
secure - close 2
secure - confident
secure - get
see
see - understand
see about - organize 1
see eye to eye (with) -
  agree 2
see to - organize 1
seedy - ill
seek - search 2
seek - try
seemly - appropriate
seize - capture
select - choose
select - exclusive
self-absorbed - selfish
self-assured - confident
self-centred - selfish
self-conscious - shy

self-effacing - shy
self-important - proud
selfish
self-possessed - confi-
dent
self-seeking - selfish
sell
sell off- sell
send
send up - imitate
senile - old
sense - feeling
senseless - silly
sensible
sentence - punish
sentiment - feeling
sentimental
sentinel - guard
sentry - guard
separate - scatter
separate
separate - part 2
sequel - result
serene - calm 1
serenity - peace
serious
serious - bad 3
sermon - speech
set - group
set back - delay 2
set free - release
set off - begin
setback - disaster
setback - problem
setting - place
settle (up) - pay
settle on - choose
sever - break 1
sever - separate 2
several - many
severe - bad 3
severe - harsh
sexist - biased
shadow - follow
shady - dark 1
shake
shame - disgrace
shape - build 2
share
sharp - fashionable
sharp - shrewd
shatter - break 1
shed light on - explain
sheepish - ashamed

shelve - delay 1
shield - defend
shift - turn 2
shiftless - lazy
shilly-shally - hesitate
shin up - climb
shiver - shake
shock
shock - dismay
shoddy - bad 4
shoplift - steal
shoplifter - thief
short - brief 1
short - brief 2
short - small
short story - story
shortage - lack
shorten
shout
shove - push
shove your oar in -
  interfere
show - pretence
show - prove
show - reveal
show off - boast
show up - arrive
shower - rain
showery - wet
shrewd
shrewd - clever
shriek - shout
shrill - loud
shrink - decrease
shudder - shake
shuffle - mix
shun - avoid
shut - close 2
shy
sick - ill
sickening - disgusting
sickness - illness
side-splitting - funny
sidestep - avoid
sift - search 2
sight - see
sign
sign - write
signal - sign
significant - important
silence - peace
silent - quiet
silly
simper - smile

simple
simple - easy
simulated - artificial
sincere
sing your own praises - boast
single out - choose
sink - fall
sip - drink
site - place
situation - place
size
sketch - draw
sketch - picture
sketchy - rough 2
skewed - biased
skilful - able
skinny - thin
skip - jump
skirmish - fight
slacken (off) - disappear
slag off - criticize
slag off - insult
slam - close 2
slam - criticize
slanted - biased
slapdash - careless
slash - cut
slaughter - kill
sleep
sleepy - tired
slender - thin
slice - cut
slice - part 1
slight - insult
slight - light
slight - small
slightly - quite
slim - thin
sling - throw
slip up - err
slipshod - careless
slit - cut
sloppy - careless
slow
slug - drink
sluggish - lazy
sluggish - slow
sly - shrewd
smack - taste 1
small
smart - clever
smash - break 1
smash - destroy

smash into - hit
smashed - drunk
smell
smile
smiling - happy
smirk - smile
snag - problem
snap - break 1
snide - sarcastic
snigger - laugh
snip - cut
snivel - cry
snobbish - proud
snoop - interfere
snooze - sleep
snub - insult
snug - comfortable
soaked - wet
soaking wet - wet
soar - rise
soaring - high
sob - cry
sober - serious
sodden - wet
soft - quiet
soft-hearted -sentimental
soggy - wet
soiled - dirty
solemn - serious
solid - continuous
solid - hard
sombre - serious
somewhat - quite
soppy - sentimental
soreness - pain
sorrow - regret
sort - kind 2
sort - organize 2
sort out - organize 2
sought-after - popular
sound - sensible
source - cause 1
spacious - big
spacious - comfortable
sparse - few
speak
speak up for - defend
special
special - favourite
spectre - ghost
speculate - guess
speech
speed
speed - hurry

speedy - quick
spick and span - clean
spin - turn 1
spineless - cowardly
spiral - turn 1
spirit - ghost
spiritual - religious
splendid - grand
splinter - break 1
split - break 1
split - hole
split up (with) - part 2
spoil - damage
spoil - destroy
spook - ghost
sport - game
spot - blemish
spot - place
spot - see
spotless - clean
spot-on - accurate
spread - scatter
spring - jump
sprint - run
spur on - urge
spurn - refuse 1
squabble - argument
squabble - disagree
squabble - quarrel
squad - group
squalid - dirty
squajider - waste
squeaky-clean - innocent
squeeze - push
stagger - surprise
stale - boring
stalk - follow
stamina - vigour
stance - opinion
stand - bear
stand in for - replace
stand up to - oppose
standard - ordinary
stare - look
stark - harsh
stark naked - naked
starkers - naked
start - begin
starting point - basis
startle - frighten
startle - surprise
startling - bold
starving - hungry
stash away - hide

state - say
state - speak
stately - grand
state-of-the-art - modern
statistics - information
statute - rule
staunch - faithful
stay - remain
steadfast - faithful
steal
stealthy - secret
steep - high
stench - smell
sterile - clean
stern - serious
stern - strict
stick up for - defend
stick your oar in -
  interfere
stiff - hard
still - calm 2
stillness - peace
stingy - mean
stink - smell
stirring - moving
stitch - pain
stock - fill
stock - sell
stockpile - gather
stoical - patient
stomach - bear
stop
stop - prevent
store - keep
storm - attack 1
storm - rain
story
story - news
stout - fat
straightforward - easy
straightforward - frank
straightforward-sincere
strange
stratagem - trick
strategy - plan 1
street - road
strength - vigour
stress - anxiety
strict
strict - accurate
stride - walk
strident - loud
strike - attack 3
strike - beat 1

strike - hit
striking - bold
stringent - strict
strive - try
stroll - walk
strong
strong - bold
strong - hard
strong - healthy
strong - intense
struggle - try
strut - walk
stubborn
study - learn
stuff - fill
stumble - hesitate
stumble across - find
stun - surprise
stunning - beautiful
stupid
sturdy - strong
style - fashion
style - kind 2
stylish - fashionable
stymie - hinder
subconscious - mind
subject
subject matter - subject
submissive - obedient
submit - suggest 1
subservient - obedient
subside - decrease
substandard - bad 4
substantial - heavy
substitute for - replace
subterfuge - trick
succeed - achieve
succeed - replace
succinct - brief 2
succulent - delicious
suffering - pain
suggest
suggestion - advice
suggestion - idea
suitable - appropriate
sultry - hot
summit - top 1
summit - top 2
sunny - warm
supersede - replace
supervise - control
supplant - replace
supply - give
support

support - back
support - defend
support - help
suppose - assume
suppress - restrain
supreme - best
supremo - leader
sure
sure of yourself -
  confident
surmise - guess
surprise
surprise - dismay
surprising - unusual
surreal - strange
surreptitious - secret
surroundings - place
survive - remain
sustained - long 1
svelte - thin
swallow - drink
swallow - eat
swarm up - climb
swarming - busy 3
swarthy - dark 2
sway - persuade
sway - shake
swear - promise
sweeping - general
sweet-talk - tempt
swell (up) - rise
sweltering - hot
swerve - turn 2
swift - quick
swiftly - fast
swig - drink
swindle - cheat
swindler - thief
swivel - turn 1
swot - learn
symbol - sign
sympathy - mercy
symptom - sign
synthetic - artificial

tag - name
tag along with -
  accompany
tail - follow
take - accept 1
take - carry
take - steal
take a dim view of -
  disapprove

take a nap - sleep
take a trip - travel
take aback - surprise
take apart - separate 2
take captive - capture
take exception to -
  disapprove
take for granted -
  assume
take home - earn
take in - admit 2
take in - involve
take issue with - disagree
take issue with - oppose
take off - imitate
take on - accept 1
take stock - think
take stock of - inspect
take your hat off to -
  admire
take your leave (of) -
  part 2
takings - income
tale - story
talent - gift 2
talented - able
talk - discussion
talk - speak
talk - speech
talk into - persuade
talk out of - discourage
tall - high
tall story - lie
tally - agree 3
tang - taste 1
tap - beat 1
tap - listen
tardy - late
task - duty
taste
tasty - delicious
taunt - insult
taunting - mockery
tea break - break 2
teach
team - group
tear - hole
tear - run
tear-jerking - moving
tedious - boring
teeming - busy 3
teenage - young
tell
tell - speak

temper - character
temperament - character
temperate - warm
tempo - speed
tempt
tender - sentimental
tepid - warm
term - name
terminate - abolish
terminate - finish
terrible - bad 3
terribly - very
terrific - excellent
terrified - afraid
terrify - frighten
terror - fear
test - check
test - examination
thankful - grateful
theme - subject
thesis - subject
thick - stupid
thief
thin
thin on the ground - few
think
think - assume
think - consider
think of - remember
think the world of -
  admire
think twice - hesitate
thorough - careful 2
thorough - complete 2
thorough - reliable
thoroughly - very
thought - idea
thoughtful - serious
thoughtless - selfish
thrash - beat 1
thrashing - defeat
threat - danger
threaten
threaten - endanger
thrilled - excited
throw
throw away - waste
thunderstorm - rain
thwart - hinder
tickle - entertain
tiddly - drunk
tidings - news
tight-fisted - mean
time off - holiday

time-consuming - long 1
timid - cowardly
timid - shy
tiny - small
tip - gift 1
tip - reward 2
tipsy - drunk
tired
tiresome - boring
tiring - busy 2
tiring - difficult
title - name
titter - laugh
to blame - responsible
toil - work 1
toil - work 2
token - sign
tolerant - patient
tolerate - bear
top
top - best
top dog - leader
topic - subject
topless - naked
topple - fall
toss - throw
total - complete 2
touch - affect 2
touch - handle
touching - moving
touching - sentimental
tough - hard
tough - harsh
tow - pull
tower - rise
towering - high
trace - draw
track - follow
track - road
track down - find
trade - business 1
trade - job
tradition - custom
tragedy - disaster
train - teach
traipse - walk
trait - characteristic
tranquil - calm 2
tranquillity - peace
transform - change 2
transformation -change 1
transitory - brief 1
transport - carry
trap - capture

travel
travel - go
treacherous - dangerous
treasure - appreciate
treasure - wealth
treasured - valuable
tremble - shake
trend - fashion
trendy - fashionable
trick
trick - cheat
trigger - cause 2
trim - cut
trim - shorten
trip - fall
trip - holiday
tropical - hot
trot - run
trouble
trouble - disturb
trouble - problem
troublesome - difficult
trouncing - defeat
true
true - accurate
true - faithful
true - genuine
truly - very
trustworthy - reliable
truthful - sincere
try
try - taste 2
trying - difficult
tubby - fat
tug - pull
tumble - fall
turn
turn a blind eye to -
  forgive
turn down - refuse 2
turn up - arrive
turn upside down - turn 2
tutor - teach
twinge - pain
twirl - turn 1
twist - turn 1
twit - fool
twitchy - impatient
type - kind 2
typical - ordinary

ugly
ultimate - best
unaccompanied - alone 1

unaccustomed -
  inexperienced
unaffected - informal
unaffected - sincere
unaided - alone 1
unattractive - ugly
unaware - ignorant
unbiased - fair
unbroken - complete 1
uncertain - doubtful
unclear - obscure
uncommon - unusual
uncomplicated - easy
uncompromising - strict
unconnected - separate 1
unconscious - ignorant
unconventional -
  eccentric
unco-operative -stubborn
uncoordinated - clumsy
uncover - find
uncover - reveal
undemanding - easy
under the weather - ill
undercover - secret
underfed - hungry
underground - secret
understand
understanding - patient
undertake - promise
undertaking - adventure
underweight - light
undressed - naked
undying - eternal
unease - anxiety
unending - eternal
uneven - rough 1
uneventful - boring
unexpected -
  unpredictable
unexplained - mysterious
unfamiliar -
  inexperienced
unfeigned - sincere
unflappable - calm 1
unflinching - determined
unforeseeable -
  unpredictable
unfriendly
unfurnished - empty
ungainly - clumsy
unhappy - sad
unhealthy - bad 2
unhealthy - ill

unhurried - slow
uninhabited - empty
unintelligent - stupid
unintentional - accidental
uninterupted -
  continuous
unite - join
unlawful - illegal
unleash - release
unlikely - doubtful
unlit - dark 1
unmitigated- complete 2
unoccupied - empty
unorthodox - unusual
unpaid - free 1
unplanned - accidental
unpleasantness-trouble 2
unpredictable
unpretentious - simple
unpunctual - late
unqualified - complete 2
unrelated - separate 1
unrelenting - relentless
unreliable -
  unpredictable
unrest - trouble 2
unruly - disobedient
unsatisfactory - inferior
unscathed - safe
unsettle - shock
unsightly - ugly
unsociable - unfriendly
unsophisticated - naive
unsophisticated - simple
unstable - unpredictable
unsurpassed - best
unswerving - faithful
untidiness - disorder
untrained -inexperienced
untrue - false
untrustworthy -dishonest
untruth - lie
untruthful - dishonest
unusual
unveil - reveal
unwelcoming - unfriendly
unwell - ill
unwise - silly
unwitting - accidental
unworldly - naive
up-front - frank
uphill - difficult
uphold - back
up-market - exclusive

upright - decent
upset - affect 2
upset - dismay
upset - sad
upset - shock
upset - trouble 1
upsetting - moving
upshot - result
uptight - impatient
up-to-date - modern
urge
useful
useless
useless - inferior
usher - accompany
usual - ordinary
utter - complete 2
utter - speak

vacant - empty
vacate - abandon 1
vacation - holiday
vacillate - hesitate
vague - rough 2
vain - proud
vain - useless
valiant - brave
valuable
value - appreciate
vandalize - damage
vanish - disappear
vanquish - beat 2
variable unpredictable
variation - difference
variety - difference
variety - kind 2
vast - big
vault - jump
veer- turn 2
velocity - speed
vendetta - revenge
veneer - pretence
venerate - admire
veneration - respect
vengeance - revenge
venture - adventure
veracious - true
verifiable - true
verify - check
verify - prove
very
vet - inspect
veto - ban
vex - annoy

vibrant - bold
vibrant - busy 3
vibrate - shake
vicious - cruel
vicious - violent
view - opinion
vigilant - careful 1
vigorous - active
vigorous - healthy
vigour
vilify - attack 1
violent
virtuous - good 1
vision - dream
vital - basic
vital - important
vital - necessary
vitality - vigour
vivid - bold
vocation - job
vogue - fashion
voice - speak
voracious - hungry
volv - promise

wacky - eccentric
wages - income
wail - cry
wait
walk
walk - go
wan - pale
wander - walk
wane - deteriorate
want - lack
warder - guard
warm
wary - careful 1
waste
watch
watchful - careful 1
waver - hesitate
ways - behaviour
wayward - disobedient
weak
weaken - deteriorate
wealth
wealthy - rich
weary - tired
weep - cry
weigh up - think
weightless - light
weighty - heavy
weird - eccentric

weird - strange
welcome - accept 1
welcome - admit 2
welcome - appreciate
well - healthy
well off - rich
well-behaved - polite
well-bred - polite
well-brought-up - decent
well-known - famous
well-mannered - polite
well-to-do - rich
wet
whereabouts - place
whiff - smell
whimper - cry
whine - complain
whinge - complain
whirl - turn 1
whisper - speak
white - pale
white lie - lie
whole - complete 1
wholehearted - sincere
whopper - lie
wicked - bad 1
widespread - popular
wield - handle
wilful - disobedient
will - urge
wily - shrewd
wimpish - cowardly
win over - persuade
wind - turn 2
wisdom - knowledge
wise - sensible
wisecrack - joke
wistful - sad
withdrawn - shy
withhold - keep
withhold - refuse 2
without charge - free 2
witness - see
witticism - joke
witty - funny
wolf - eat
woman
wonderful - excellent
word - news
work
work - job
work out - calculate
worked up - excited
worm - crawl

worn out - tired
worry
worry - anxiety
worry - trouble 1
worsen - deteriorate
worship - love
worthwhile - useful
worthy - decent
wound - hurt
wrap up - finish
wreck - damage
wreck - destroy
wriggle - crawl
write
write down - write
wrong - false

yank - pull
yarn - story
yell - shout
yellow - cowardly
young
youthful - young
yummy - delicious

zealous - eager
zest - vigour
zonked - tired

abandon *verb*

1 to go away from a person, place, or thing, usually hurriedly or without warning: *She was abandoned by her parents when she was a baby.*

desert to leave or to stop supporting someone or something that you have a duty to stay with or help: *All his friends deserted him when he was in trouble.*

dump (*informal*) to end a romantic relationship with someone suddenly in a way that hurts their feelings: *He dumped his girlfriend when he met someone else.*

jilt to end a romantic relationship suddenly with someone, especially someone who expects you to marry them: *Her fiancé jilted her the day before the wedding.*

leave to stop living with your husband or wife: *She left her husband after twelve years of marriage.*

leave in the lurch (*informal*) to leave someone to cope with a difficult situation: *The speaker cancelled at the last minute and left me in the lurch.*

vacate to leave a place that you have been staying in: *They vacated the premises on Friday.*

2 stop doing something: *She abandoned her attempts to help and left them to sort the mess out for themselves.*

chuck (in) (*informal*) to stop doing a job or task, especially because you are tired of it: *He chucked the job in, because he was fed up with all the paperwork.*

give up to stop doing something, especially something that you have been doing for a long time or that has become a habit: *When I tried to give up smoking, I put on a lot of weight.*

leave behind to stop being involved in an activity permanently, especially because you are older and wiser or have new interests: *I had to leave my acting career behind and concentrate on being a diplomat's wife.*

refrain (from) not to do something that you want, or are intending, to do: *I was sorely tempted to tell the boss exactly what was wrong with his management style, but decided it was wiser to refrain.*

renounce to stop holding a belief or opinion, or give up a particular type of behaviour, especially by making a formal declaration that you now consider it to be wrong: *The regime agreed to renounce all forms of violence.*

able *adjective*
having above average skill or intelligence: *an able student.*

capable very good at dealing with situations or people: *I will leave you in the hands of my capable assistant.*

clever showing a lot of intelligence or skill: *She deceived her opponent with a clever trick.*

competent having the skill necessary to do a particular job or activity well: *He's not a computer expert, but he's perfectly competent to carry out ordinary tasks on a computer.*

expert having a thorough knowledge of a particular subject or great skill in a particular type of work: *It took me two days to do a job that an expert dressmaker would have finished in two hours.*

gifted born with a high degree of skill or intelligence: *She thinks that she's naturally gifted and that she doesn't need to study or practise.*

skilful having or showin a lot of skill: *A more skilful driver would have avoided the obstacle.*

talented naturally very good at something, especially in the arts or sport: *His art teacher realized that he was an exceptionally talented painter.*

See also **clever**.

abolish *verb*
to take official action to stop a practice or ensure that a law or regulation is no longer in effect: *Slavery was abolished a long time ago.*

cancel to decide that something that has been arranged will not after all take place: *The party has been cancelled.*

discontinue to stop something after it has been going on for some time: *The doctor discontinued my treatment.*

do away with to stop a practice or remove something completely: *The government did away with free school milk.*

eradicate to stop or remove something harmful permanently and make sure that it cannot start again: *The school aims to eradicate bullying.*

get rid of to remove something that causes problems: *Isn't it time that we finally got rid of all restrictions on free trade?*

put an end to to prevent something from continuing: *The accident put an end to her dancing career.*

quash to state officially that a decision or punishment is wrong or unjust: *His drink-driving conviction was quashed.*

terminate to end an agreement: *Your contract has been terminated.*

accept *verb*

1 to be willing to take, or say yes to, something that is offered to you: *She accepted his proposal of marriage.*

receive to be given something: *I* *received a beautiful bouquet of flowers.*

take to receive or make use of something when it is offered to you: *If they offer me the job, I shall definitely take it.*

take on to agree to be responsible for doing something: *They have taken on too much work.*

welcome to receive something or someone gladly: *I welcome this opportunity to give my side of the story.*

2 to be willing to allow yourself to be governed by something such as a decision, a rule, or someone else's right to do something: *Tick this box to show that you accept the company's terms and conditions.*

abide by to obey a rule: *You must abide by the rules of the game.*

agree to to say that you are willing to do what is required by a suggestion or proposal: *They agreed to the terms of the house sale.*

assent to (*formal*) to agree to do what someone asks you to do: *I assented to their request to give a slide show.*

comply with to do what is required by a rule or expressed in a wish: *Your car must be fitted with seatbelts to comply with the laws on vehicle safety.*

See also **admit 1, 2.**

accidental *adjective*
happening without anyone planning or wishing it should happen: *Can you prove that the damage was accidental and not inflicted on purpose?*

casual unexpected and of little importance: *a casual encounter with a stranger.*

chance happening unexpectedly: *a chance remark.*

fortuitous not planned but having a happy outcome: *a fortuitous meeting with a new business contact.*

inadvertent done by mistake: *his inadvertent revelation of the winner's name.*

random not selected according to a plan or system: *a random sample of viewers.*

unintentional not deliberate: *If I offended you, it was unintentional.*

unplanned happening without being planned: *an unplanned pregnancy.*

unwitting doing something without realizing that you are doing it: *He became an unwitting accomplice in her plan.*

accompany *verb*
to go with a person to a place or an event: *Will you accompany me to the concert?*

associate with to spend a lot of time with someone: *I mostly associate with work colleagues.*

attend to go with and look after someone as a servant: *The princess was attended by her lady-in-waiting.*

chaperone to go somewhere, especially to a social event, with a young person in order to make sure that they do not get into trouble: *She chaperoned her daughter when she was invited to her first ball.*

conduct to lead someone to or around a place that they do not know: *The guide conducted us to the monastery.*

escort to go somewhere with someone either as a guard or as their partner at a social occasion: *The security guard escorted her out of the building.*

partner to act as a partner to someone, especially in a game or dance: *Will you partner me in the bowling competition?*

tag along with (*informal*) to go somewhere with someone, especially when you have not been invited to go with them: *My little sister always wants to tag along with me and my friends.*

usher to show someone where they have to go or sit, usually in a very polite way: *The head waiter ushered us to a small table in a quiet corner of the restaurant.*

accurate *adjective*
conforming to fact, reality, or the actual state of affairs: *An accurate description.*

correct without error: *the correct* *answer.*

exact correct in every detail: *an exact copy.*

perfect having no faults: *His grammar is perfect.*

precise exactly as specified: *at that precise time.*

right correct, or correct in what you say or think: *You were right about her; she isn't a very nice person.*

spot-on (*informal*) absolutely correct or true to life: *Yesterday's weather forecast was spot-on.*

strict not allowing for any deviation or vagueness: *in the strict sense of the word.*

true not a lie and not invented: *true story.*

See also **true.**

achieve *verb*

gain something through effort or ability: *He achieved worldwide fame as a rock guitarist.*

accomplish be successful in finishing a task or reaching a goal, especially one that you have set yourself: *She accomplished her goal of winning an Olympic gold medal.*

carry out to put an idea or a plan into action: *We carried out my father's wish to have his ashes scattered at sea.*

complete to finish a task: *Julia completed the crossword puzzle.*

do (*informal*) to perform a task or an action successfully: *We did it! We did it! We won the UEFA Cup!*

pull off (*informal*) to be unexpectedly successful in doing something: *Nobody thought Lawrie had a chance of winning but somehow he pulled it off!*

reach to manage to get to a level, standard, or goal that you have been working towards: *She reached her target weight loss of ten pounds.*

realize to fulfil an ambition, hope or dream: *I finally realized my ambition to visit China.*

succeed manage to do what you wanted or planned to do: *Janet succeeded in being elected a Member of Parliament.*

See also **get.**

active *adjective* able and eager to move about and do things: *an active 70-year-old who plays golf four times a week.*

busy dealing with work or involved in an activity so that you cannot stop to do anything else: *I was too busy to take a day off.*

energetic having or requiring a lot of energy: *an energetic dance routine.*

hyperactive having a medical condition that makes you unable to sit still, be quiet or concentrate on something: *Looking after a hyperactive child can be very tiring.*

industrious (*formal*) working hard and steadily: *an industrious student.*

lively cheerful and full of energy: *lively youngsters running about the place.*

on the go (*informal*) extremely busy: *She is always on the go, looking after her six kids.*

vigorous having or requiring great strength and energy: *a vigorous workout.*

See also **vigour.**

admire *verb*

to feel that someone or something is worthy of respect and praise: *I really admire you for standing up to the bullies.*

appreciate to enjoy something, such as an art form, and understand what makes it good: *He doesn't appreciate opera.*

approve of to think that an action or a person's behaviour is morally good or is sensible and correct: *I don't approve of teenagers smoking.*

idolize have an unrealistically high opinion of someone, usually a famous person: *Many young girls idolize pop stars.*

look up to to have respect for someone, usually an older person, who is a model of how you would like to be: *She looked* up to her older sister and wanted to be like her.

respect have a high opinion of someone or their actions: *I respect him for sticking to his principles.*

take your hat off to (*informal*) to think that someone has done something that deserves praise or admiration: *Well, I take my hat off to him. I wouldn't have dared to try anything so risky myself.*

think the world of (*informal*) to be very fond of someone: *He thinks the world of his wife and kids.*

value to consider a person or a quality important: *I really value your friendship.*

venerate (*formal*) to regard someone with deep almost religious feelings of respect, because of their age or their achievements: *She is venerated as a leader of the Women's Movement.*

See also **appreciate**; **respect**.

admit *verb*

1 say that something is true, especially that it is true that you have done something wrong or made a mistake: *I admit that I was rather drunk when I said that.*

accept to regard what someone says as true: *The police accepted his version of events.*

acknowledge to say, sometimes reluctantly, that you realize that something is true: *He finally acknowledged that my advice had been helpful.*

agree to say that something that someone else has said is right, often before adding a comment about something that you think is not so good: *They agreed that the meeting had been useful, but wished that more time had been spent discussing the budget for the following year.*

allow (*formal*) to say that someone or something may be right, but in a rather cautious or reluctant way: *She allowed that*

she might have been somewhat hasty.

come clean (*informal*) to admit to some wrongdoing that you have been keeping secret: *In the end he decided to come clean about cheating on his wife.*

concede to say that a point or an argument made by someone who is arguing against you is right: *I concede your point that it may be difficult to complete the work in the time available.*

confess to tell someone, especially

the police or a priest, that you have done something wrong: *She confessed to killing her husband.*

own up to admit that you are responsible for some wrongdoing: *Unless the person who stole the money owns up, the whole class will be punished.*

recognize to say that you realize that something is true or possible: *I recognize that her intentions were good.*

2 to allow someone to enter a building or place, especially because they have something such as a ticket that gives them the right to enter: *You won't be admitted if you haven't got a valid ticket.*

accept allow someone to join a group or organization: *The golf club is not accepting new members at the moment.*

let in to allow someone to enter a building or other place: *He came home drunk, and his wife would not let him in.*

receive to greet and welcome a guest or visitor as they enter a place: *The host and hostess were standing at the door to receive their guests.*

take in to give someone shelter and a

place to stay: *After their parents died, relatives took the children in.*

welcome to greet a guest or newcomer warmly: *We had a party to welcome the new neighbours.*

adventure *noun*
a journey or activity that is exciting and unusual for you and perhaps slightly risky: *I live in a very quiet little village, so a trip to London is always a bit of an adventure.*

enterprise an attempt to do something important or exciting, which shows you have initiative or courage but also involves a risk of failure: *The enterprise was so badly planned that many people thought it was doomed from the start.*

escapade an act that is exciting, but often comical or foolish: *They recalled some daring escapades from their schooldays.*

exploit an act of bravery: *the heroic exploits of the mountain-rescue service.*

exploration the activity of making journeys to unknown places in order to learn about them: *rockets for space exploration.*

quest a journey to search for something important or valuable: *They set out on a quest to find the hidden treasure.*

undertaking an action or a task that

involves a lot of effort and often an element of risk: *Going into the mountains without a guide was a risky undertaking.*

venture an attempt to achieve success or make a profit, usually in the world of business or finance: *I have invested in a new business venture.*

advertise *verb*
to give information about something, or display it, in order to make people want to buy it or go to it: *The concert was advertised in all the newspapers.*

announce make a piece of information known to a lot of people: *The winner of the art competition will be announced tomorrow at morning assembly.*

broadcast to make information publicly known, for example on television or radio: *The Prime Minister's speech will be broadcast in full.*

hype up (*informal*) to make exaggerated claims about how good or exciting someone or something is: *This new band has been so hyped up that people are expecting it to be as good as U2.*

market to advertise a product in a way that is designed to appeal to a specific section of the public: *This new drink is being marketed as a young person's drink.*

plug (*informal*) to give an interview

on television or radio or in the press, in order to promote your latest recording, film, book, etc.: *Not another actor plugging his autobiography!*

promote to present a product or an idea to the public in such a way as to encourage interest in it: *a campaign to promote breast-feeding.*

publicize to make the public aware of a certain product or event by advertising it on television or radio or on posters: *The actors paraded through the street in costume to publicize the show.*

push (*informal*) to give a product a lot of publicity to try to convince the public to buy it: *They are really pushing this new magazine, with loads of TV adverts and posters.*

advice *noun*
an opinion on something that is meant to be helpful to someone: *Can I ask your advice on how to remove ink stains?*

counsel (*formal*) advice about a serious matter from a wise or knowledgeable person: *In despair, he sought counsel from the parish priest.*

counselling professional advice given by a trained counsellor to people who have a specific type of problem: *They went for counselling when their marital problems got really serious.*

guidance help and advice that might be offered to a person who is undecided about something, such as which career to pursue: *The careers teacher will give you guidance on which subjects to study if you want to become a lawyer.*

instruction a direction to do something that people are expected to follow: *I followed the instructions on how to install the new software in my computer.*

opinion someone's personal view on a subject, which the person hearing it may or may not agree with: *I would value your opinion on which car I should buy.*

recommendation a statement saying that a particular thing or course of action is definitely good and that you think a person should try it: *On my sister's recommendation, we visited Barcelona.*

suggestion a statement putting forward an idea that you think may be good or helpful: *Do you have any suggestions as to what I could give Mum for her birthday?*

See also **guide; opinion; suggest 1.**

affect *verb*

1 to have an effect on someone or something: *The flooding doesn't seem to have affected the bus service in this area.*

alter make changes to something, such as a garment: *My trousers were too long, so I had them altered.*

change to make someone or something different in some way: *His mother's death when he was a child changed his whole life.*

concern to be relevant to someone: *The state of my finances does not concern you.*

impinge on (*formal*) to be an external factor that has an influence on something, especially by restricting it in some way: *Any form of censorship necessarily impinges on the ordinary citizen's freedom of speech.*

influence to use power or persuasion to change someone's thoughts, feelings, or actions: *He tried to influence the way other members voted.*

modify to change something, usual-ly in quite a small way, in order to create an improvement or advantage: *The design may have to be modified to suit the new customer's requirements.*

2 to cause an emotional reaction in someone, especially sadness: *I was deeply affected by the famine reports.*

disturb to make someone feel worried and upset: *His obsessive behaviour disturbs me.*

faze (*informal*) to make someone feel uneasy and lose their composure: *She was totally fazed by his rudeness.*

move to make someone feel strong emotion, especially sadness: *Her speech moved me to tears.*

touch to make someone feel an emotion such as love, gratitude, or sympathy: *I was touched by my colleagues' concern.*

upset to cause someone to feel distressed or offended: *It upsets me to see cruelty to children.*

See also **moving.**

afraid *adjective*

feeling fear in a particular situation, or worried about something because you think it may harm you: *Louise is afraid of spiders.*

anxious worried and tense: *I start to feel anxious if she's more than 10 minutes late.*

apprehensive worried because you feel that something that you are going to do will be bad experience for you: *She felt apprehensive about driving again so soon after the accident.*

fearful (*formal*) nervous about doing something that other people might dislike or disapprove of: *Fearful of offending her guests, she restricted her conversation to the weather and similarly safe topics.*

frightened in a state of fear: *Don't*

be frightened if you hear a loud noise. It's only me drilling a hole in the floor.

nervous being worried and having physical symptoms such as trembling hands and an uneasy feeling in your stomach because of something you are about to do: *I always get terribly nervous just before I have to go on stage.*

petrified so afraid that you are almost unable to move: *The thunderstorm left the child petrified.*

scared afraid of someone or something: *scared of the dark.*

terrified extremely frightened: *The terrified child was hiding behind the sofa.*

See also **cowardly; fear.**

agree *verb*

1 to say that you will do something that someone has asked you to do: *She agreed to reconsider her decision.*

acquiesce (*formal*) to say that you

will do what someone else wants, although you have reservations: *She acquiesced in the group's decision, even though she had her doubts.*

assent (*formal*) to say that you are willing to accept a request, proposal or suggestion: *The Prime Minister assented to their request for an interview.*

consent to give someone permission to do something: *He reluctantly consented to have his photograph taken.*

go along with (*informal*) to be willing to accept something such as opinion or suggestion or what someone says: I went along with the suggestion, because I couldn't think of anything better to do.

2 to have the same opinion about something as someone else: *I agree with Katie. It's too cold to go swimming.*

be of one mind (*formal*) said about

two or more people: to have the same opinion on a subject: *The prime minister and I are of one mind on this issue.*

concur (*formal*) to accept that someone else's statement or decision is correct: *I concur with Mr Justice Smythe in holding the case against the defendant to be unproven.*

see eye to eye (with) (*informal*) to have the same or similar views on a subject: *Politics is one subject on which I don't exactly see eye to eye with my father.*

3 to be the same as, or compatible with, one another: *Their accounts of the incident agree on some points and differ on others.*

accord (*formal*) to be consistent with what someone else has said or found out: *This accords with the findings of the original investigation.*

fit to be the same as, or exactly adapted to, something: *His face fits the description given by the police.*

match to be the same as something, very like it, or a good accompaniment to it: *The curtains don't match the carpet.*

tally to be consistent with one another; to accord with something: *The two witnesses' statements about the incident do not tally.*

See also **accept 2**; **admit 1**.

alone without anyone else being with you

1 *adverb* *He prefers to travel alone.*

by yourself without anyone else being with you or helping you: *I decorated the room all by myself.*

off your own bat (*informal*) without anyone else telling you what to do: *He gave me a ring to say sorry off his own bat.*

on your own without anyone else being with you or helping you: *She has been living on her own since her husband died.*

on your tod (*informal*) with no one else present: *They all shoved off and left me on my tod.*

unaccompanied without an escort: *Claire went to the wedding unaccompanied.*

unaided without the help or support  of someone or something, such as a walking stick: *Can the old lady walk unaided?*

2 *adjective* not with anyone else: *I was alone in the office.*

Not used before a noun.

deserted abandoned by a partner, parent, or friend: *a deserted wife.*

forlorn sad and lonely because you have been deserted: *a forlorn figure all alone on the beach.*

isolated feeling lonely because you have no friends nearby: *I felt isolated when I moved from the city to the country.*

lonely unhappy because you are alone: *It can be very lonely at first when you go away to university.*

angry *adjective* having a strong negative feeling about something and a wish to do something, possibly something violent, to change things or take revenge: *I was so angry about the way the shop assistant treated me, I complained to the manager.*

annoyed feeling mildly angry and impatient: *She was annoyed by his persistence.*

cross (*informal*) moderately angry: *My mum was cross with me for breaking a vase.*

enraged feeling intensely angry and likely to do something violent: *He was so enraged by their refusal to let him in that he threatened to break down the door.*

furious feeling or showing extreme anger: *Furious at being ignored, she stormed out.*

heated in which angry words are spoken: *a heated argument*

incensed feeling extremely angry because you feel that a moral wrong has been done: *Incensed by his brother's treachery, the king ordered his immediate execution.*

indignant feeling or showing anger and resentment because of something that seems unfair or unjust: *She got very indignant when I suggested that it was her fault that we had to cancel the party.*

irate (*formal*) very angry and upset: *appeasing an irate customer.*

mad (*informal*) feeling anger: *He went mad just because I was ten minutes late!*

See also **annoy**.

annoy *verb*

to make someone feel mildly angry: *It annoys me when you leave the lid off the toothpaste.*

aggravate (*informal*) to annoy and provoke someone deliberately: *He's only playing that stupid drum because he knows it aggravates me!*

bother to hinder or prevent someone from doing something by persistently trying to get their attention: *Stop bothering your dad when he's trying to rest!*

displease (*formal*) to make someone mildly unhappy and annoyed by what you do: *He didn't voice his misgivings for fear of displeasing the President.*

exasperate to make someone feel more and more annoyed and frustrated, usually because you will not or cannot do what they want you to do: *I was exasperated by his failure to understand my point of view.*

get on someone's nerves (*informal*) to make someone irritable or cause them to lose patience, usually by doing something annoying again and again or over a long period of time: *It really gets on my nerves when you repeat everything I say.*

hack off (*informal*) to make someone feel frustrated and impatient: *I'm getting seriously hacked off with that racket from upstairs.*

irritate to cause someone to feel a mild degree of anger and impatience: *His whiney voice really irritates me.*

vex to make someone feel angry and upset: *It vexed him to see the old lady struggling to make ends meet.*

See also **angry**.

answer

1 *verb* to say something in reaction to question that you have been asked: *She refused to answer any questions about her marriage break-up.*

acknowledge to show that you have received something such as a letter, or noticed something such as a greeting, by doing something in return: *I am writing to acknowledge receipt of your message sent yesterday.*

get back to (*informal*) to contact someone again to give your response to a subject previously discussed: *I'll get back to you later about the stag night.*

reply to say in response to a question or remark: *'No, thank you. I've had enough,' he replied.*

respond to react to what someone has said or done: *She responded to his threat by calling his bluff.*

2 *noun* something said in reaction to a question that has been asked: *The answer to your question is 'No'.*

rejoinder (*formal*) a clever reply, usually spoken and made during an argument or discussion in response to another person's reply to a question: *Simpson's brilliant rejoinder brought their witty repartee to a close.*

reply a spoken or written response to what someone has said or written: *I am waiting for a reply to my job application.*

response a reaction to an event or to what someone says: *Her only response to his comment was a coy smile.*

retort a spoken reply that is made in a sharp tone and attacks the person who asked the original question: *'I'll start minding my own business, when you stop letting your business go to rack and ruin' was Stephen's witty retort.*

riposte a quick witty spoken response

made in retaliation: *Joan's quick-witted riposte silenced her detractors.*

anxiety *noun*

a feeling of worry about possible harm that may happen to you or to someone or something else: *The thought of driving in the snow filled her with anxiety.*

anguish intense mental suffering: *Having to report her own son to the police caused her great anguish.*

apprehension a feeling of nervous-

ness and fear that something bad may be about to happen: *Sue was filled with apprehension about*
her first parachute jump.

care something that causes you to worry because you feel an emotional involvement or responsibility: *She seemed weighed down with cares.*

concern a state of worry combined with caring about someone's wellbeing: *I appreciate your concern for my safety.*

foreboding a strong feeling that something bad is going to happen in the future, often quite soon: *The house was unusually quiet, and I had a terrible sense of foreboding as I walked up the path to the front door.*

stress a state of being under mental or emotional pressure: *She is under stress because of the exams.*

unease a feeling that something is wrong or that there may be danger or difficulty, which makes you uncomfortable and nervous: *His obvious unease was because he had a guilty conscience.*

worry a troubled state of mind arising from a difficult situation or from something bad that you fear might happen: *Her husband's gambling has caused her a great deal of worry.*

See also **fear**.

appreciate *verb* to enjoy something because you understand what makes it good: *You don't appreciate good music.*

cherish to hold dear something such

as a gift, memento or memory that is important to you on a personal level: *I cherish every little gift she ever gave me.*

enjoy to get great pleasure from an activity or an object: *He has always enjoyed fine wine.*

prize to place a high value on something, such as a possession or a quality: *He prizes that battered old guitar above any other item in his collection.*

savour to take the time and enjoy something pleasurable, especially a taste or smell, fully: *I like to eat slowly and savour my food.*

treasure to consider something, such as a memory, precious: *I treasure the time we spent together.*

value to hold something, such as someone's opinion or a quality, in high esteem: *My grandmother is one person whose opinion I value.*

welcome to accept gratefully something such as an opportunity or a break: *I welcome the opportunity to present my side of the story.*

appropriate *adjective*
of the right kind or nature to suit a particular event or situation: *an outfit appropriate for a wedding.*

applicable that concerns or has to do with a particular person or a particular case: *These sections are only applicable if you are applying for a passport for the first time.*

apposite (*formal*) that is relevant, made at the right time, and comments interestingly on the subject: *a most apposite remark.*

apt that suits the circumstances or describes something very well: *an apt description.*

correct in accordance with the rules or conventions, especially those that deal with social behaviour: *He's never been taught the correct way to behave at a formal dinner.*

fitting particularly suitable or well deserved: *a fitting tribute to a courageous woman.*

proper being the only one that is considered right for a particular purpose: *That's not the proper place for that CD.*

relevant to do with the matter that is being discussed or dealt with and not with something else: *If what you have to say is relevant to the discussion, say it; if it isn't, don't.*

right that is needed in or is best for a particular situation: *There's no doubt that she's the right person for the job.*

seemly (*old-fashioned*) correct in a particular situation, according to convention: *His remarriage so soon after his wife's death was not considered seemly.*

suitable right for a particular purpose or occasion: *She was not considered suitable for the job.*

approval *noun*
the act of stating that you think something is good or that you will allow something to take place: *The matter has been settled, subject to approval by the board of directors.*

agreement the act of saying or showing that you give permission for a course of action: *He is making this journey with his doctor's agreement.*

authorization official permission to do something, for example to enter a private area: *Do you have authorization to go beyond this barrier?*

blessing warm approval of a proposed course of action, such as a marriage: *We don't need your permission to get married but we would like your blessing.*

endorsement support for someone's course of action or opinion: *Your silence on the matter will be seen as endorsement of their view.*

go-ahead (*informal*) permission to proceed with a plan: *We finally got the go-ahead to take on extra staff.*

permission the act of allowing someone to do something they want to do: *I have my son's permission to show you his letter.*

sanction official permission to follow a particular course of action: *This information was made public with the Government's sanction.*

argument *noun*
a situation in which two or more people disagree about something and try to change each other's views, often getting angry in the process: *She stormed out after an argument with her boyfriend.*

altercation (*formal*) an angry exchange of words: *There was a vehement altercation between an irate customer and the restaurant manager.*

dispute a difference of opinion between individuals or groups about a matter that is considered serious, often resulting in hostility: *an industrial dispute between management and the union.*

feud a long-running disagreement or hostile relationship, especially between two families: *a bitter five-year feud with our next-door neighbours.*

fight (*informal*) an angry disagreement, especially between partners, friends, or members of a family: *We had another fight about money last night.*

quarrel an angry disagreement between friends: *The two girls had a quarrel but made up soon after.*

row a noisy disagreement, usually between partners or family members: *My brother and his wife had a huge row at the dinner table.*

squabble an argument over something trivial: *a squabble over whose turn it is to take the rubbish out.*

See also **disagree**; **quarrel.**

arrive *verb*

reach a place, especially after a journey: *After a long trek through the mountains, we arrived safely in the village.*

appear to come into view or to be present in a place: *When I fell over, a nice young man appeared as if from nowhere and helped me to my feet.*

come to move towards the place where you are: *What time are the children coming home?*

enter to come into a place: *The Prime Minister entered the building, surrounded by police officers.*

land to come to the end of a journey by air: *We land at Miami Airport at 10.00 am.*

put in an appearance to attend a social event for a short time only, although you may not be keen to attend at all: *Simon put in an appearance at the wedding reception just before the bride and groom left.*

reach to arrive at a place, especially at the end of a journey: *The climbers reached the top of the mountain without mishap.*

show up (*informal*) to arrive at a place as arranged or expected: *I was expecting ten guests but only eight showed up.*

turn up (*informal*) to appear somewhere, often unexpectedly: *My aunt's ex-husband turned up unexpectedly at her funeral.*

artificial *adjective*

not natural, but made by human beings; often to look like something natural: *artificial flowers.*

counterfeit made to look like something genuine, especially money, but false and intended to defraud: *He was arrested trying to use a counterfeit £20 note.*

fake not genuine, especially because manufactured using non-natural ingredients to produce the effect of something natural: *fake fur.*

false manufactured to look like and take the place of something such as a part of the body or of a structure: *false teeth.*

imitation manufactured to look like something natural, but usually regarded as inferior to the natural version: *imitation leather.*

man-made not produced naturally but manufactured, usually from non-natural materials, and sometimes having advantages over the natural version: *man-made fibres.*

mock made in imitation of something and generally regarded as inferior to the genuine article: *mock-Tudor beams.*

simulated done in such a way as to imitate a natural action or recreate conditions in the real world: *Police cadets have to deal with simulated riot conditions as part of their training.*

synthetic produced by combining chemical substances and used as a substitute for something natural: *synthetic rubber.*

ashamed *adjective*

having a strong feeling of guilt and embarrassment about something wrong that you have done: *I was deeply ashamed of the way I had treated her.*

abashed feeling embarrassed, self-conscious, or rather humiliated, usually because someone has called attention to a mistake you made or a wrong you did: *She was not in the least abashed, though it was perfectly plain that she was the cause of all this unnecessary trouble.*

conscience-stricken feeling very guilty about some wrongdoing: *Beth was conscience-stricken about having offended her hostess.*

embarrassed feeling shy or uncomfortable in a particular situation, e.g., when talking about sex: *I was so embarrassed when I forgot my lines in the play.*

guilty knowing that you did something wrong and feeling rather bad about it: *I felt guilty about not including Jackie in our plans.*

humbled feeling that someone else's

actions show great goodness or generosity and that you might not be as good or generous in the same situation: *He felt humbled by the generosity of these people who had so little but were willing to share what they had.*

humiliated having been made, often deliberately, that you are very bad or very unimportant person: *I felt humiliated when the whole class laughed at my answer.*

sheepish looking embarrassed or self-conscious, for example because you have been caught doing something wrong: *She looked rather sheepish as I caught her taking the last biscuit.*

See also **disgrace.**

ask *verb*

to direct a question or request at someone: *'What time is it?' he asked.*

beg to ask someone earnestly to give you something or to do something for you: *The dying woman begged her friend to make sure her children were looked after.*

demand to ask for information insistently or forcefully: *'Where's your purse?' the burglar demanded.*

enquire to try to find out information about something: *I'm enquiring about the availability of flights to Barcelona.*

The spelling *enquire* is commoner in British English, but in US English the word is usually spelt *inquire.*

grill (*informal*) to question someone

very thoroughly, sometimes in a hostile way, to find out how much they know, what they think, etc.: *They grilled me on my reasons for wanting to work for the company.*

interrogate to ask someone a series of probing questions, especially in some official capacity: *The murder suspect was interrogated by the police.*

invite to ask someone to join you at a social event: *We have been invited to a party on Saturday.*

question to ask someone a series of questions, especially during an interview or an investigation: *Police questioned the man for several hours, but eventually released him.*

quiz to ask someone a lot of questions: *Her grandmother quizzed her about her new boyfriend.*

request to ask if you can have something: *I have requested a window seat.*

assistant *noun*
a person whose job or task is to help someone: *The director would be totally disorganized without his personal assistant.*

accomplice a person who helps someone to commit a crime: *The thief stole my purse while his accomplice distracted me.*

aide a person whose job is to assist an important person: *The President arrived, surrounded by his aides.*

auxiliary an untrained person who assists trained colleagues, especially in a hospital or in the armed forces: *a nursing auxiliary.*

colleague a person who works for the same organization or in the same department as you: *She has gone out for dinner with her colleagues from the office.*

deputy a person who substitutes for a superior when he or she is absent: *While the head teacher is away having an operation, her deputy will take over her duties.*

helper any person who helps another: *I am looking for a helper to tidy up after the party.*

right-hand man or *woman* a person who assists someone in authority and on whom they rely heavily: *The prime minister often called his press assistant his right-hand man.*

second-in-command the person who has second most authority in an organization: *The manager has had invaluable support from his second-in-command.*

assume *verb*
to accept that something is true without checking that it is true: *I assumed the woman he was with was his wife.*

believe to think quite strongly that something is true, even though you cannot be certain about it or prove that it is true: *I believe the new neighbours are American.*

guess (*informal*) to suppose something is the case without knowing or thinking very much about it: *I guess we must have been a bit drunk at the time.*

imagine to think that something is the case, based on a certain amount of information plus imagination: *I imagine that must have been a frightening experience.*

presume to act as if something is the case, without knowing for certain that it is, unless or until it is proven not to be: *Legally you are presumed innocent until proven guilty.*

suppose to think that something is likely to be the case, but realizing that you could quite easily be wrong: *I suppose the heavy rain must have caused the car to skid.*

take for granted to believe something to be the case without questioning it: *The singer took it for granted that everyone would pander to her wishes.*

think to have an idea or opinion about something, often a rather vague one and always without being sure about it: *I took my umbrella because I thought it was going to rain.*

See also **guess.**

attack

1 *verb* to use force to try to harm or capture someone or something: *He was attacked by a mountain lion.*

ambush to attack someone after hiding and waiting for them to come by: *The travellers were ambushed by bandits.*

assault to attack someone violently:

The old lady was assaulted by a strange man in her own home.

beat up (*informal*) to hit or kick someone repeatedly: *He got beaten up by a gang of thugs.*

mug to attack someone physically and rob them: *She was mugged on her way home from the bank.*

storm make a swift and sudden attack on a building or other place with a large force, in order to capture it or the people inside it: *The army stormed the citadel.*

vilify (*formal*) to say bad things about a person's character in a vicious way: *He was vilified by the media for his association with prominent figures in the world of organized crime.*

2 *verb* use words to show your negative feelings or opinions about someone or something: *The right-wing press attacked the government's policy on immigration.*

berate (*formal*) to scold someone angrily: *I was berated for being obstructive.*

blast (*informal*) to criticize someone severely: *He was blasted in the tabloids for his racist remarks.*

criticize to say that someone has behaved badly or that something is bad or faulty: *She was heavily criticized for putting her career before her family.*

scold use angry words to show your

disapproval of someone or their behaviour: *My mother scolded me for coming home so late.*

3 *noun* an attempt, using force, to harm or capture someone or something: *The city is under attack from the air.*

assault a sudden violent attack on a person or on enemy territory: *a serious assault on a homeless man.*

offensive an attack or series of attacks on a military target: *The latest offensive has resulted in heavy casualties among the allies.*

onslaught a violent and forceful physical or verbal attack: *Few of his colleagues thought he would survive the onslaught from the media.*

raid a sudden small-scale attack by

military forces into enemy territory, or an unexpected attack on a building or other place by police or criminals: *a bank raid.*

strike a military attack on a place, usually from the air: *an air strike on the capital.*

See also **invade.**

avoid *verb*

not to hit an object, not to meet a person, or not to become involved in a situation: *She crossed the road to avoid her ex-boyfriend.*

dodge to move aside quickly in order to avoid being hit: *The boy dodged out of the way of the oncoming car.*

duck out of (*informal*) to avoid doing something you have arranged to do: *He ducked out of taking the kids swimming.*

elude avoid being caught or discovered

by someone: *The singer eluded the paparazzi by slipping out by the back door.*

escape to succeed in avoiding an unpleasant situation or outcome: *The boys escaped punishment by giving each other alibis.*

eschew (*formal*) not to do something or become involved in something that you think is undesirable: *an artistic genius who eschews commercialism.*

evade to deliberately avoid doing something that you should do: *He was arrested for evading income tax.*

shun to deliberately avoid someone because you do not like them or are displeased with them: *She was shunned by her family when she married a gangster.*

sidestep to skilfully avoid dealing with a subject you don't want to deal with: *The prime minister sidestepped all questions about the war.*

See also **prevent**.

aware *adjective*
having knowledge or consciousness of sthing: *Are you aware that Sam has a black belt in karate?*

acquainted well informed about a subject: *fully acquainted with the rules of backgammon.*

alert watching and concentrating, so as to notice anything unusual, especially danger, immediately: *alert to the dangers of windsurfing.*

clued up (*informal*) having detailed knowledge about a subject: *He is well clued up on hip-hop.*

cognizant (*formal*) having full knowledge and understanding of a subject: *Are you cognizant of the terms of the contract?*

conscious noticing or feeling something that is happening: *conscious of being stared at.*

informed having a lot of information about a particular subject: *politically informed.*

knowledgeable knowing a lot about a particular subject: *We need someone who is knowledgeable about civil rights.*

mindful bearing in mind the importance of something: *ever mindful of the need for caution.*

B

back *verb*
to give help and encouragement to someone, or to show approval and support for something: *If you decided to oppose the management on this issue, we'd back you all the way.*

advocate to argue in favour of a course of action or a cause: *an MP who advocates capital punishment.*

champion to support and defend a person or a cause: *He championed the Cubist movement.*

encourage to give someone emotional support and boost their confidence: *He could always depend on his wife to encourage him when he felt low.*

endorse to show strong approval of someone's course of action or opinion: *I heartily endorse your views on complementary medicine.*

promote to speak or take action in order to encourage other people to adopt a particular course of action or to support a cause: *The local authority promotes recycling by providing households with separate containers for different types of refuse.*

second to speak in support of a motion made by a previous speaker in a meeting or debate: *Kathy proposed that we accept the company's offer, and Paul seconded the motion.*

support to take action to help someone or something that you approve of: *We support various charities, not only by giving money, but also by taking part in fund-raising events.*

uphold to defend a belief or a decision, often against opposition: *She always upheld the cause of women's rights.*

See also **support**.

bad *adjective*

1 doing things that are wicked or harmful: *The bad fairy cast a spell on the princess.*

corrupt committing acts that are morally wrong, usually for money: *a corrupt police officer who accepts bribes.*

criminal committing acts that are against the law: *He is known to have criminal tendencies.*

evil capable of committing extremely wicked acts, such as murder: *an evil dictator.*

immoral committing acts that are generally considered morally wrong: *Many people consider prostitution immoral.*

malicious intending to cause people harm: *malicious gossip.*

mischievous deliberately causing trouble, but not of a serious nature: *The mischievous child rang the doorbell and ran away.*

nasty unpleasant and cruel: *By betraying his best friend, Craig has shown that he has a nasty streak.*

naughty badly behaved, but not in a serious way: *Tom was sent to bed early because he had been a naughty boy.*

wicked deliberately causing harm to people: *Stealing your sister's boyfriend was a wicked thing to do.*

2 having a harmful effect: *Smoking is bad for your health.*

adverse causing difficulties or problems, or unfavourable to what you want to do: *The adverse effects of using the drug were not pointed out in the report.*

damaging causing usually non-physical damage, e.g., to someone's health or reputation: *This story could be seriously damaging to your chances of promotion.*

detrimental having a harmful effect: *Living in a damp flat would be detrimental to the children's health.*

harmful causing danger to people or damage to objects: *substances that are harmful to the environment.*

unhealthy harmful to your health: *unhealthy living conditions.*

3 causing a lot of trouble, pain, or worry: *She went to bed with a bad headache.*

dreadful (*informal*) very unpleasant or severe: *I had dreadful toothache.*

major large in scale and causing great difficulties: *major problems.*

nasty unpleasant and troublesome, but not necessarily serious: *a nasty cold.*

serious causing, or likely to cause, a great deal of harm or trouble: *a serious illness.*

severe worse than serious, very threatening to people's well-being: *The man sustained severe burns in the explosion.*

terrible (*informal*) very unpleasant or severe: *He had a terrible hangover the morning after the party.*

4 of low quality or lacking in skill: *Bill is a really bad singer.*

defective having a fault or defect: *I returned the hairdryer to the shop because it was defective.*

imperfect containing mistakes or flaws: *He seemed to understand my imperfect French.*

poor of a low standard or low quality: *The leading man gave a poor performance on opening night.*

shoddy done or made without skill:

shoddy workmanship.

substandard not reaching the required or expected standard: *an excellent CD with no substandard tracks.*

See also **inferior.**

ban *verb*

to forbid someone, officially, to do something: *She has been banned from driving for a year.*

bar to forbid someone to enter a place, such as a pub or club: *Wayne has been barred from the rugby club for starting a fight.*

disallow to reject something, such as a score in a game, as being invalid because it breaks a rule: *The last goal was disallowed because it was offside.*

disqualify to stop a competitor from taking part in a race or competition because they have broken a rule: *Jones was disqualified after two false starts.*

exclude to prevent someone from

entering a place, especially a school, often as a punishment: *Matthew was excluded from school for a week for persistent bad behaviour.*

forbid not to allow someone to do something or to go somewhere: *Children are forbidden to use the swimming pool unless accompanied by an adult.*

prohibit not to allow an activity: *Smoking is prohibited in the cinema.*

veto to prevent something, such as a piece of legislation, being passed: *The President vetoed the welfare-reform bill.*

banish *verb*

to send a person away, especially to another country, because of something bad that they have done: *The king banished the duke to Ireland following his involvement in a murder.*

deport to force someone to leave the country where they are living, especially to return to their country of origin: *She was deported because her working visa had expired.*

eject to remove someone by force

from a place, such as a night club or a party: *The man was ejected from the theatre for causing a disturbance.*

evict to force someone to leave their home, for example because they have broken a contract: *The family was evicted because they had not been paying their rent.*

exile force someone to leave their country and go and live in another country, often for political reasons: *Napoleon was exiled to St Helena for the rest of his life.*

expel to force someone to leave a place, especially to force a pupil to leave a school as punishment for very bad behaviour: *John was expelled for setting fire to the school.*

basic *adjective* simple but necessary
and important, especially as a starting point for expansion or development: *the basic qualifications for the job.*

central being the main and most important one among several: *the central theme of the film.*

elementary very simple and easy to understand, or dealing with the simplest aspects of something: *an evening class in elementary motor mechanics.*

essential very important because it plays a part in determining the nature or identity of something: *all the essential ingredients of a great party.*

fundamental very important, often because it serves as a basis for other things: *Food and shelter are fundamental human rights.*

indispensable so important or so highly valued that you could not manage without it or them: *an indispensable aid to navigation.*

key being the most important person or thing in a particular situation: *the key witness at a murder trial.*

necessary which is needed in order to enable something to happen: *They did not have the necessary funding to make an offer for the property.*

primary coming first in order of importance: *Alcohol abuse is the primary cause of his health problems.*

rudimentary very simple, especially because it has not been developed: *With my rudimentary knowledge of Polish, I had great difficulty understanding what she said.*

vital very important and hard to do without: *We think of you as a vital member of the department.*

basis *noun*
something, (a fact, reason, or situation) that underlies and supports something else such as a claim or argument: *It's an exciting story, but it has no basis in history.*

core the central or most important part of a problem or an issue: *We must tackle the core of the problem, not just the details.*

essentials the basic and most important parts of something, especially all the things that you need to know if you want to be able to understand a subject sufficiently to be able to proceed: *Some of the details of what she said were rather obscure, but I think I grasped the essentials.*

foundation a strong background element on which to base something important, such as a relationship or a belief: *You need a solid foundation of love and trust on which to build a marriage.*

fundamentals the basic and most important principles of something, such as a system or a subject: *The artist taught me the fundamentals of portrait painting.*

grounds a justifiable reason for a course of action, such as divorce or dismissal from a job: *Stealing is regarded as grounds for instant dismissal.*

groundwork preliminary work done in preparation for something more important: *At today's meeting we laid the groundwork for the pay negotiations.*

heart the essential or most important part of something, such as a problem: *Jealousy was at the heart of the matter.*

starting point something that serves as a beginning for something else, such as a discussion: *The company's pay offer was the starting point for negotiations.*

bear *verb*
be able to experience something without suffering or getting angry: *She couldn't bear to be parted from her children.*

abide to remain calm and not get angry when faced with someone or something that is extremely trying: *One thing he could never abide was rudeness.*
Only used in the negative.

endure to experience physical or emotional pain or hardship, especially with courage or without complaining: *Paula bravely endured the other children's taunts.*

put up with to cope patiently with a difficult person, situation, or type of behaviour: *I don't know how she puts up with her boyfriend's jealousy.*

stand to bear someone or something that you find very unpleasant or annoying: *I couldn't stand his arrogant attitude a minute longer.*

stomach (*formal*) tolerate something that you find very unpleasant or unacceptable: *Cruelty to animals was something George simply could not stomach.*

tolerate to accept someone or something even though you do not like them or do not approve of them: *I tolerate my sister's husband for her sake, but I don't like him.*

See also **carry.**

beat *verb*

1 to hit someone or something repeatedly with hard blows of your fists or hands or a weapon or tool, especially a stick: *The young man was beaten senseless by a gang of youths.*

batter hit someone or something hard and repeatedly, usually implying greater and more concentrated and destructive force than 'beat': *They picked up a bench and used it to batter down the door.*

hammer to strike against something with heavy blows, as if using a hammer: *She hammered on the door to be let in.*

hit to make hard and harmful contact with something or someone once: *The man hit the burglar over the head with a baseball bat.*

pummel to punch someone repeatedly: *The toddler threw a tantrum, pummelling his mother's legs in frustration.*

punch to hit someone with a clenched fist: *He drew back his fist and punched me right in the face.*

strike to hit someone or something sharply, either with the hand or with a weapon: *It's against the law for a teacher to strike a pupil.*

 tap to hit someone or something lightly, either with the open hand or with an object: *She tapped him lightly on the hand with a ruler.*

thrash to strike someone hard and repeatedly, especially as a punishment: *His father thrashed him with a belt buckle until he bled.*

2 to win a contest, battle, game, or race (which may be a friendly one or one where there is not much at stake) against someone or something: *England beat Australia at cricket.*

conquer to defeat an enemy in a war or battle and take control of them and their territory: *The Roman emperor conquered Sicily.*

crush to beat someone easily, or comprehensively so that they are no longer able to resist: *Stalin's purges effectively crushed all opposition to his regime.*

defeat to beat someone in a contest, fight, race, etc., usually where there is something serious at stake: *Octavius Caesar defeated the combined naval forces of Antony and Cleopatra at the Battle of Actium.*

get the better of to gain an advantage over someone: *Because she is more intelligent than him, she always gets the better of him in an argument.*

outdo to do better than someone else at some activity: *Val can always outdo the rest of us when it comes to witty repartee.*

overcome to defeat someone or something, usually after a long struggle: *In the end the army was overcome by a superior force.*

vanquish (*formal*) to defeat an army or a leader thoroughly in a war or battle: *Their foes were vanquished in a bloody battle.*

See also **attack 1, 2.**

beautiful *adjective* very pleasing to the senses, especially sight or hearing, or very satisfying when judged by aesthetic criteria (mostly used when making a serious assessment of something or someone): *a beautiful woman.*

attractive having an appearance or character that appeals to people: *She has a very attractive warm personality.*

fine beautiful because well made, done, or performed: *There is some fine singing on this disc.*

good-looking having a very pleasing appearance: *For his age, he is a very good-looking man.*

gorgeous extremely attractive in personal appearance, or rich and splendid in colour and decoration: *a gorgeous evening dress.*

handsome having attractive, regular, and usually masculine features: *She is in love with a handsome film star.*
lovely beautiful or attractive (but often used in a more casual way than 'beautiful'): *Katie has a lovely singing voice.*

picturesque (said about a place or scene) so pleasing in appearance as to make a beautiful picture: *a picturesque village in the foothills.*

pretty pleasing in appearance (but without the more striking qualities that make a person or thing 'beautiful'): *a pretty little girl.*

radiant looking beautiful and very happy: *The bride looked positively radiant.*

stunning extraordinarily beautiful or

impressive: *When we reached the top of the hill, we had a stunning view of the coastline.*

beg *verb* to ask for something earnestly and humbly: *The hostages begged their captors for mercy.*

appeal to to ask someone earnestly and urgently for something, such as help or co-operation: *The murdered girl's parents appealed to the public to come forward if they know anything that might help find the killer.*

beseech (*literary*) to ask someone earnestly and anxiously to do something for you: *We beseech Thee to hear us, good Lord.*

crave to ask someone earnestly to grant you something such as indulgence or understanding: *I crave your indulgence on this matter.*

entreat (*formal*) to ask someone earnestly and persuasively for something: *Treat this matter with the utmost urgency, I entreat you.*

implore (*formal*) to ask someone for something by appealing to their emotions: *I implore you to examine your conscience and make a donation to the disaster fund.*

plead to make an emotional appeal

to someone to do something: *In tears, she pleaded with her husband not to leave her.*

See also **ask.**

begin *verb* to happen, or to do something, for the first time or for the first time in the period in question: *After a while, it began to rain.*

commence (*formal*) to begin, usually

in accordance with a plan or previous arrangement: *Festivities will commence at 7.30 pm.*

inaugurate (*formal*) to begin something, such as a new system or service, officially, especially by means of a ceremony: *The President of France travelled to London on the first train to inaugurate the new cross-Channel rail link.*

initiate to begin something, such as a relationship or a discussion, by making the first move: *Sunita was too shy to initiate a conversation with a stranger.*

instigate (*formal*) to cause something, especially a troublesome event, to happen: *The shop steward instigated a walkout in protest against the working conditions.*

kick off to start, especially to start a football match by kicking the ball from the centre of the pitch: *The game kicks off at three o'clock.*

originate to happen, or cause something to happen, for the first time: *The game of golf originated in Scotland.*

set off to begin a course of action, especially a journey: *We set off for Rome first thing in the morning.*

start to begin to happen or begin doing something: *The baby woke up and started crying.*

behaviour *noun*
the way that a person behaves: *Children should be rewarded for good behaviour.*

conduct the way that a person behaves, often with reference to morality: *His conduct in the face of severe provocation was admirable at all times.*

demeanour (*formal*) the way that a person behaves and the impression that gives of their character: *His demeanour is very intimidating.*

deportment (*formal*) the way that a

person stands and moves: *She has the elegant deportment of a fashion model.*

manners ways of behaving towards other people, especially judged by how much courtesy and consideration a person shows: *His good manners won over his new girlfriend's parents.*

performance the way that a person behaves in a testing situation: *Najma was happy with her performance in the job interview.*

ways a person's characteristic habits or style of behaviour: *Alex has his own little ways, which some people find eccentric.*

best *adjective* better than any other: *the best holiday I have ever had.*

finest of the best possible quality: *made from the finest coffee beans.*

foremost best, most important, or

best-known in a particular field: *the foremost philosopher of his time.*

leading most important or among the most important in a particular field: *a leading neurosurgeon.*

optimum most effective or most advantageous: *For optimum benefit, you should exercise for half an hour three or four times a week.*

supreme the greatest in achievement or power: *the supreme champion at Cruft's Dog Show.*

top the most successful or most important in a particular area of activity: *the top golfer in the world.*

ultimate being the best possible example of something: *the ultimate feelgood movie.*

unsurpassed having never been bettered: *The quality of his workmanship is unsurpassed.*

betray *verb*

1 to do something, especially to give information, that enables an enemy to defeat or capture someone who trusts you: *His best friend betrayed him to the secret police.*

deceive to make someone believe that you are a friend or supporter in order to betray them: *They discovered too late that they had been deceived by a traitor in their midst.*

double-cross (*informal*) to betray an ally by working against them while pretending to be on their side: *If you double-cross a gangster, you're likely to come to a sticky end.*

grass on (*informal*) to inform on

someone: *Somebody grassed on me to the cops!*

inform on to give someone in authority, such as the police, information that incriminates someone: *One of the neighbours informed on him for working while claiming benefits.*

2 to show something that was

intended to be kept hidden, especially inadvertently: *The look on his face betrayed his distaste.*

disclose to reveal information that has previously been unknown or kept secret: *Details of the tour dates will be disclosed in due course.*

divulge (*formal*) to allow something to be known, usually by saying it to someone: *I am not permitted to divulge the present whereabouts of the prime minister and his wife.*

expose make someone's true character known publicly: *The Minister was exposed in the media as a liar and a cheat.*

give away to reveal information that was meant to be kept secret: *The actress gave her real age away when she said she had been at President Kennedy's inauguration.*

let slip to say something unintentionally that reveals information that was meant to be kept secret: *She let slip that she had lost her engagement ring.*

reveal to make visible or known, deliberately or inadvertently, something that has previously been unseen or unknown: *I am now able to reveal the name of the lucky winner.*

biased *adjective*
not impartial, showing favour or antipathy to a particular kind of person or thing: *biased in favour of pretty young women.*

bigoted having a strong irrational

dislike of certain people or groups of people: *a man so bigoted he would not even shake hands with a Black person.*

discriminatory unfairly treating one person or one group better than others: *a discriminatory practice.*

homophobic biased against homosexuals: *homophobic bullying in the workplace.*

partial favouring one contestant, team, or group over others: *A football referee must not appear to be partial to either side.*

partisan biased in favour of a particular person or group: *She is too partisan to judge the competition.*

prejudiced having a preconceived opinion of someone, something, or a group of people: *prejudiced against Irish people.*

racist holding or betraying the belief that one race is superior to all others: *The broadcaster was fired for making racist remarks on television.*

sexist holding or betraying the belief that one sex is superior to the other, usually that men are superior to women: *Ron's female colleagues found his sexist attitude offensive.*

skewed presented in a biased way that distorts the truth: *a skewed account of events.*

slanted showing bias in favour of a particular person, group, or view: *The article was slanted in favour of the rebels.*

big *adjective*

above the average in size or amount: *a big strong man.*

bulky big, heavy, and difficult to carry or handle: *a bulky parcel.*

colossal extremely big in size or amount (usually even bigger than 'enormous'): *a colossal statue as tall as a house.*

considerable quite large in amount: *a considerable sum of money.*

enormous extremely big in size or amount: *an engagement ring with an enormous diamond.*

extensive wide and, often, varied: *She has extensive experience in all aspects of publishing.*

gigantic extremely large in size: *A dinosaur was a gigantic reptile of prehistoric times.*

great large in degree or intensity: *a great sense of achievement.*

huge extremely big in size or amount: *a huge mansion standing in acres of land.*

immense very great in size, degree, or intensity: *They took immense pride in their children's achievements.*

large above average in size or amount – also used to describe a size of commercial products: *This T-shirt comes in small, medium, and large sizes.*

massive very great in size, degree, or intensity: *There has been a massive explosion in the city.*

spacious having a lot of space inside: *a spacious sitting-room.*

vast extremely large, especially in extent: *the vast desert.*

blame *verb*

to say that someone is guilty of a bad action or responsible for something bad that has happened: *Scott blamed his little sister for scribbling on the wall.*

accuse to say that you think someone has done something wrong: *The teacher accused Sophie of cheating in the test.*

censure (*formal*) to express disap- proval of a person or their behaviour: *Dr Thomas was officially censured for inappropriate behaviour.*

condemn to express severe disapproval of a person or a practice: *The model was condemned for setting a bad example to young girls by using hard drugs.*

criticize to express disapproval of a person, their work, or their behaviour: *She was fed up with being constantly criticized by her parents.*

blemish *noun*

a visible mark that spoils the appearance of something, especially a person's skin: *She has soft smooth skin with no blemishes.*

defect an imperfection in something, such as a body part or a machine, that means that it fails to function properly, and that may be in it from the beginning or develop later: *The optician says I have a slight defect in my left eye.*

fault a defect in something such as a machine, a system, or a garment: *I took the CD player back to the shop because there was a fault in it.*

flaw an imperfection that is in something, especially a natural material or an argument or theory, from the beginning: *I think I've discovered a flaw in their argument.*

imperfection a mark or other fault that stops something from being perfect: *an antique table with a slight imperfection in the wood.*

mark a visible imperfection that spoils the appearance of something, such as a garment or a piece of furniture: *He had a greasy mark on his tie.*

spot a usually round mark or blotch that spoils the appearance of something, especially a small raised area on the skin: *a teenage boy with spots all over his face.*

boast *verb*
say things that show that you think that something you own, have done, or are associated with makes you really special or better than other people: *He is always boasting about how much he earns.*

blow your own trumpet (*informal*) to tell people how good or successful you are: *Tariq's a clever guy but he's always blowing his own trumpet.*

brag to boast: *She liked to brag about her two university degrees.*

crow (*informal*) to make it obvious that you take pleasure in the fact that you have an advantage over someone else: *I couldn't help crowing when I beat Ewan at bowling.*

show off to act in a boastful way, especially by demonstrating to other people how well you can do something: *Stop showing off, you're not the only one who can ride a bike with no hands.*

sing your own praises to tell people about how clever, talented, etc., you are: *I got fed up with Shane singing his own praises all the time.*

See also **proud.**

bold *adjective*
easily noticed, especially through having strong colours and a definite outline: *Bold patterns are in this season.*

bright having a strong shining quality, not pale or dark: *The living room was painted in bright blues and oranges.*

loud extremely bright and lacking subtlety: *He was known his loud ties.*

startling having a strong and somewhat surprising effect: *a rather startling close-up photograph of Picasso.*

striking making a strong impression: *a very striking portrait of the Queen.*

strong not weakened or diluted, but intended to convey a definite and powerful impression: *a strong shade of pink.*

vibrant very bright and, sometimes, appearing to glow: *Diana's wardrobe is full of dresses in vibrant colours.*

vivid very bright in an attractive way: *a vivid painting of a rainbow.*

See also **brave.**

border *noun* a real or imaginary line
marking the edge of something or where two things meet: *Carlisle is close to the border between England and Scotland.*

borderline the division, often indistinct, between two places or two things, such as activities or emotions: *the borderline between dislike and hatred.*

boundary a line where two areas of land or property meet: *There is a hedge marking the boundary between our garden and our neighbours'.*

edge a line or area forming the outermost part of something beyond which there is usually space: *There is a slight gap between the edges of the wallpaper.*

frontier the border between two countries: *the Iran–Iraq frontier.*

limits the edges of a particular area, especially a city: *A taxi ride will cost a lot more if you go outside the city limits.*

margin a strip at the edge of something, such as an area of land or a leaf: *the margin of the forest.*

perimeter the outer edge of an area of land, especially of a large military or civil installation such as an airport: *The guard walked round the perimeter of the compound.*

rim the outside edge of a circular or curved object: *He wore glasses with a gold rim.*

boring *adjective*
not interesting or exciting: *The lecture was so boring I almost fell asleep.*

dreary lacking colour and excitement and rather depressing: *a dreary drama about domestic violence.*

dull lacking brightness and colour, or not providing any excitement or entertainment: *I don't know what Susan sees in her new boyfriend; he is so dull.*

flat not, or no longer, exciting or excited, usually because the lively element has been taken away: *The party was really flat after the young people left.*

humdrum very ordinary and with little variety: *a little light relief in her humdrum existence.*

monotonous boring because the same thing happens or you have to do the same thing again and again: *Working on an assembly line can get very monotonous.*

stale uninteresting because not new or original: *He told a stale old joke that I had heard a dozen times before.*

tedious boring, especially because of going on too long: *a tedious journey involving several changes of bus.*

tiresome not simply boring but also annoying: *Her constant chatter is so tiresome.*

uneventful in which nothing exciting or remarkable happens, though this is often a relief and not necessarily boring: *Our journey home was entirely uneventful.*

brave *adjective*
having or showing admirable courage either in taking action or enduring suffering: *Nobody was brave enough to stand up and tell the boss he was wrong.*

bold showing not only courage but also a willingness to take the initiative and take risks and often an imaginative quality as well: *It was a typically bold move, intended to take the enemy completely by surprise.*

courageous brave, usually in taking action rather than in endurance: *a courageous attempt to rescue the hostages.*

daring showing a willingness to take risks that other people would not take: *a daring raid into the heart of enemy territory.*

fearless having or showing no fear in the face of danger: *a fearless military leader.*

gutsy (*informal*) showing courage and determination: *a gutsy marathon runner who kept going despite aching legs.*

have-a-go (*informal*) brave enough to tackle a criminal who is committing a crime: *Have-a-go pensioner, Nancy Smith, single-handedly thwarted a raid on her local post office.*

heroic showing great courage, especially in putting your own life in danger to help or rescue other people: *The way that James risked his own life to save a child from drowning was heroic.*

intrepid (*formal*) acting in a daring or fearless manner: *an intrepid explorer.*

plucky (*informal*) showing courage in difficult or challenging situations: *a plucky little girl who refused to let her disability rule her life.*

valiant showing courage and

determination, often in a situation where you ultimately fail: *They made a valiant attempt to fight the fire, but it was out of control.*

See also **bold.**

break

1 *verb* to damage something so that it is no longer whole or no longer functions: *Ben broke his new toy gun within an hour.*

crack to damage an object so that a narrow gap or gaps appear in it: *This cup is cracked.*

fracture to break a bone in your body: *I fell off the wall and fractured my arm.*

sever to cut something, especially a body part, off completely: *My uncle severed his little finger in an industrial accident.*

shatter to break something, especially something made of glass, completely, so that it falls into many small pieces: *A small stone hit the windscreen and shattered it.*

smash to break or shatter an object,

usually through some deliberate violent action: *She used her shoe to smash the window.*

snap to break sharply at a single point with a cracking or popping sound: *The plastic fork snapped as soon as I put pressure on it.*

splinter to break a hard substance such as wood or stone into many small sharp

pieces: *The cannonball splintered the timbers in the ship's side.*

split to divide something into two or more parts: *The woodcutter struck the log with an axe, splitting it in two.*

2 *noun* a short time away from work or study, for rest or recreation: *The children played tag during the morning break.*

breather (*informal*) a short period of

rest: *After a hard morning's graft, the lads took a breather.*

respite a period of time spent away from a difficult situation, such as being a carer for a family member who is elderly or ill: *The social services arranged for Bridget to have a week's respite from looking after her disabled daughter.*

rest a short period of time in which you rest: *We had been working non-stop for five hours and badly needed a rest.*

tea break a short period of time during which workers are allowed to stop working in order to drink tea: *At work we have a ten-minute tea break every morning.*

See also **holiday**.

brief *adjective*

1 lasting a relatively small length of time, i.e. a few minutes, hours, days, years, etc.: *a brief trip to London to see a show.*

ephemeral (*formal*) existing only for a short time and not important or having a lasting effect: *Much teenage slang is too ephemeral to be entered in a dictionary.*

fleeting happening quickly and last-

ing only for a very short time (usually when you would prefer it to last longer): *I just caught a fleeting glimpse of her before she disappeared into the building.*

momentary affecting someone or happening for only a very short time: *Kemal suffered a momentary loss of confidence.*

short not long (more often used with the word 'time' than is 'brief'): *We've got a lot to do and only a very short time to do it in.*

transitory not permanent, lasting a short time and then passing on: *Her feelings of resentment towards her sister were merely transitory.*

2 using few words: *I left a brief note saying I'd gone to the post office.*

concise expressing something precisely but using few words: *a concise description of the local attractions.*

pithy short, clever, and often witty: *Peter's pithy comments make him an ideal dinner guest.*

short consisting of comparatively few words: *Pat wrote a short article on violence in the workplace.*

succinct expressing something very

aptly but using few words: *a succinct summing-up of the points discussed at the meeting.*

bright *adjective*
shining strongly or having a strong light colour, not dull or dark: *a bright light; a bright green.*

brilliant radiating intense light or colour: *The sun was shining in a brilliant blue sky.*

colourful brightly coloured or having many different colours: *clowns in colourful costumes.*

dazzling so bright as to make you temporarily unable to see: *The dazzling headlights of the oncoming car caused me to swerve.*

glowing shining and usually having a colour associated with fire or heat: *glowing reds and yellows.*

luminous giving off light, especially

so as to be clearly seen in the dark: *The children wear luminous armbands so that motorists will be able to see them on dark winter mornings.*

See also **bold**; **clever**.

build

1 *verb* to make a building or a similar fairly permanent structure using strong materials: *Our house was built in 1901.*

assemble to make something, such as

furniture or a model, by fitting together the parts: *a computer chair that you have to assemble yourself.*

construct to build something, such as a structure or a machine: *The Eiffel Tower is constructed from wrought iron.*

erect to build something upright, such as a tall building or a monument: *A statue of the prime minister was erected in the city centre.*

fashion to form something with care (and often artistic skill) or over a period of time: *Her skilful fingers fashioned the lump of clay into a tall elegant pot.*

form to create something by giving a material form or shape: *The children formed the plasticine into animal shapes.*

put together to build something from different parts or materials: *Tony put together a bookcase from leftover lengths of wood.*

put up (*informal*) to build something such as a wall or another structure that may be either permanent or temporary: *The new block of flats was put up very quickly.*

2 *noun* the size and shape of a person's, especially a man's, body: *He has an athletic build.*

body a person's body with reference to its appearance or physical fitness: *He likes to look after his body by going to the gym four times a week.*

figure the size and shape of a person's, especially a woman's, body: *a woman with a very shapely figure.*

form a person's body, with reference to shape: *He is an admirer of the female form.*

frame the structure and size of a person's body: *The coat looked huge on her slight frame.*

physique a person's, especially a

man's, body, with reference to muscularity: *a boxer with a powerful physique.*

shape the outline of a person's, especially a woman's, body: *a tight-fitting dress that shows your shape to good advantage.*

See also **make.**

business *noun*

1 activities or work involved in the buying and selling of goods or services: *She gave up teaching for a career in business.*

commerce the buying, selling, and distribution of goods or services, especially on a large scale: *commerce between America and Asia.*

dealings business transactions with a person or a company: *We have had dealings with this company in the past.*

industry the production of goods, especially in factories, or a particular branch of manufacturing: *the steel industry.*

trade the buying, selling, and

exchange of goods or services, or a particular area of trading: *There has been a backlash against the fur trade in some countries.*

2 an organization, large or small, concerned with the production or the buying and selling of goods or services: *Stephen has his own plumbing business.*

big business very large and important companies considered as a group: *the alleged corruption of politics by big business.*

company a group of people organized as a business, especially a corporation: *the chairman of an insurance company.*

concern (*formal*) a business: *The*

company is a small family concern, but very successful.

corporation a business organization that is recognized in law as having a separate existence, rights, and responsibilities from the individuals who make it up: *The company has grown into a huge multinational corporation.*

enterprise a business, especially a small one: *She runs a small knitwear enterprise from her own home.*

establishment (*formal*) a shop or other business and the premises that it occupies: *We expect the highest standards from the staff in our establishment.*

firm a company: *The supermodel has a contract with one of the large cosmetics firms.*

outfit (*informal*) a business organization: *He got involved with a dodgy money-lending outfit.*

busy *adjective*

1 working hard or having a lot of work to do: *I have been busy all day cleaning the house.*

diligent working hard and conscientiously: *The detective was diligent in his search for clues.*

engaged not free to speak to someone because you are speaking to someone or doing something else: *Mike is engaged at the moment. Shall I ask him to phone you when he's free?*

In British English a telephone line is said to be *engaged* when someone is speaking on it; in US English, it is said to be *busy*.

engrossed having your attention totally occupied by an activity: *I was so engrossed in my work that I didn't notice it was lunchtime.*

occupied having your time and attention taken up by an activity: *Can you keep the children occupied while I cook dinner?*

rushed off your feet (*informal*) extremely busy, with no time to rest: *We've been rushed off our feet all day in the café.*

2 filled with work or activities: *I have had a very busy day looking after my sister's five children.*

eventful in which a number of important events take place: *With the wedding and the football match, it was a very eventful weekend.*

full in which you have little spare time because you have so many things to occupy you: *We have a very full schedule between now and the end of November.*

hectic extremely busy and rushed: *During exam time things get pretty hectic in the departmental secretary's office.*

tiring involving so much work as to cause you to feel tired: *After a tiring day at the office, I like to put my feet up when I get home.*

3 not quiet or empty, but full or people or activity: *This road is very busy at rush hour.*

bustling full of people who are very busy and energetic: *There is a wide variety of stalls in the bustling marketplace.*

crowded filled with so many people that it is difficult to move about or be comfortable: *It's easy to get lost in the crowded streets of central London.*

swarming crowded with people who, you feel, make the place unpleasant to be in: *Don't go during the festival, the city's bound to be swarming with tourists.*

teeming containing great numbers of people, animals, or things (which may be either a good thing or a bad thing): *In summer the resort is teeming with holidaymakers, and the hotels do really good business.*

vibrant full of interesting activity and excitement: *New York is such a vibrant city.*

See also **active**.

buy *verb* to get something, usually in a shop, in exchange for money: *Melanie bought a jacket with the money she got for her birthday.*

acquire to gain possession of something, often by buying it: *Over the years I have acquired every single Beatles album.*

come by to buy or obtain something, often after searching for it: *Exotic foods are hard to come by if you live in a village.*

obtain (*formal*) to gain possession of something, sometimes by buying it: *Neil succeeded in obtaining a first edition of Seamus Heaney poetry.*

pick up to buy something that you happen to find on a casual shopping trip, rather than after looking specifically for it: *I wandered round the market and managed to pick up a few bargains.*

procure (*formal*) to buy something that is difficult to obtain: *The country's army is trying to procure the special equipment needed to build nuclear weapons.*

purchase (*formal*) to obtain some- thing in exchange for money: *A home is the most expensive item that most people will ever purchase.*

calculate *verb*
to discover the answer to a sum by using mathematics: *Will someone calculate how much each person's share of the bill is?*

assess to work out the amount or size of something, such as a payment or damage, either by calculating or estimating: *My accountant has assessed the amount of income tax I am liable to pay.*

compute to calculate an amount or figure mathematically or using a computer: *The votes have been counted, and we're just computing the percentage share of the vote gained by each candidate.*

count to add up a number of things, people, or figures: *I counted the number of people ahead of me in the queue.*

estimate to make an approximate calculation of a figure or amount: *The garage mechanic estimated that the repair would cost about £90.*

gauge to work out an approximate figure, often involving some guesswork: *I would gauge the crowd to have numbered about 2000.*

reckon to add up roughly a number of things, people, or figures: *I reckon the bill will come to about £60.*

work out to calculate something by thinking it through carefully: *I'm trying to work out whether I have enough money to go to the club and take a taxi home.*

calm *adjective*

1 quiet and normal in manner and behaviour, not worried, angry, or excited: *He stayed calm in the face of danger.*

composed in control of your emotions in difficult situations: *The prime minister must remain composed in a crisis.*

cool in control of your emotions, or not showing an emotional reaction when one would normally be expected: *The murderer stayed cool even when questioned by the police.*

laid-back (*informal*) having a very relaxed and nonchalant attitude or a relaxed and informal atmosphere: *Mary is so laid-back, nothing seems to worry her.*

placid having an even temper, not easily upset or angered: *She was a very placid child, unlike her brother,* who demanded constant attention.

relaxed being at ease and feeling no tension: *A good hostess knows how to make her guests feel relaxed.*

serene at peace with yourself, and often detached from what is going on around you: *The bride remained serene and gracious throughout the ceremony.*

unflappable (*informal*) always in control of your emotions, however serious the situation is: *My mum is unflappable – even when we bring friends to stay without warning, it doesn't bother her.*

2 undisturbed by noisy or violent activity on the part of nature or human beings: *The sea was as calm as mill pond.*

peaceful calm and quiet, usually through a comparative lack of human activity: *a peaceful village in the Scottish Highlands.*

still not moving at all: *The wind died away, and suddenly everything was still.*

tranquil (usually used to describe natural settings) peaceful: *We had a picnic in a tranquil spot by the lake.*

See also **patient.**

capture *verb*

to take someone or something by force and keep them under your control: *He was captured by enemy soldiers and made a prisoner of war.*

apprehend (*formal*) said about the police: to catch and arrest someone suspected of committing a crime: *The police apprehended the suspect as he was about to board the ferry to Ireland.*

arrest said about the police: to catch someone suspected of committing a crime and take them to the police station: *The motorist was arrested for drink-driving.*

catch to get a person or an animal under your control, especially after chasing or hunting them: *We went fishing and I caught three trout.*

nick (*informal*) to arrest someone suspected of committing a crime: *Jamie got nicked for joy-riding.*

seize to capture or arrest someone: *The drug smugglers were seized at the airport.*

take captive to capture someone and keep them as a prisoner or a hostage: *The gunman took a little girl captive and held her for five hours.*

trap use a trap to catch an animal, or to put a person in a position from which they cannot escape: *We were trapped in the lift for two hours when the power failed.*

careful *adjective*

1 taking sensible precautions and not taking risks: *Be careful when crossing the road.*

cautious being very careful to avoid danger or harm, especially by moving slowly or only taking action when you have checked that it is safe to do so: *a cautious driver.*

chary nervous about doing something in case it causes you problems: *I would be chary of actually meeting up with someone I only knew through contacting them on the Internet.*

prudent wise and careful, especially with money: *She made a prudent investment with her redundancy payment.*

vigilant (*formal*) watchful and alert because you expect that there might be danger or problems: *Be vigilant in the city – there are lots of pickpockets.*

wary careful and suspicious: *Helen has been wary of door-to-door salesmen ever since she was robbed by one.*

watchful making sure that you keep your eyes open and look carefully so that you do not miss any signs of danger or trouble: *The invigilator keeps a watchful eye on the students in case they try to cheat during the exam.*

2 paying attention so that you do not miss anything or make any mistakes: *a careful examination of the facts.*

fastidious paying great or sometimes excessive attention to detail, especially to make sure that everything looks right: *She is fastidious about always wearing matching lipstick and nail polish.*

meticulous paying very close attention to every small detail to make sure that what you are doing is done perfectly: *The painter was meticulous about showing every line on the old man's face.*

painstaking done in a very careful way and with an extra effort to get it right (not usually used to describe people): *a painstaking search for clues.*

particular very careful to make sure that everything is just as you want it to be: *She is very particular about eating meat with no fat whatsoever on it.*

punctilious (*formal*) very careful to make sure that you always behave correctly and that other people behave cor-

rectly too: *punctilious about timekeeping.*

thorough very careful to make sure that when a piece of work is done it is properly finished and there are no mistakes in it: *Lesley is very thorough – she always checks and rechecks her work.*

careless *adjective*

not paying enough attention to what you are doing, or caused by someone not paying enough attention to what they are doing: *Misspelling 'separate' was just a careless mistake.*

hasty done too quickly and without taking sufficient care: *a hasty decision.*

inaccurate not conforming to fact, reality, or the actual state of affairs, or containing mistakes about facts, measurements, etc.: *His estimate of how long the job would take to finish was wildly inaccurate.*

lax not taking enough care to make sure that you or other people obey rules or maintain proper standards: *The canteen staff are very lax about food hygiene.*

offhand doing something, or done, in a way that suggests that you do not care about it very much or about what people think of it: *His speech was delivered in an offhand manner.*

slapdash doing something, or done, very quickly and casually, without enough attention to getting it right: *Ethan is so slapdash in his attitude that his work is always full of mistakes.*

slipshod done badly, without proper care and attention: *The refurbishment of the shop was a slipshod job.*

sloppy (*informal*) showing little care or commitment, especially by being untidy or inaccurate: *He's a very sloppy dresser – his clothes never seem to fit, and they're usually dirty.*

carry *verb*

to move something or someone from one place to another, especially by lifting then holding them: *The old lady was struggling up the hill carrying a heavy bag.*

bear (*formal or literary*) to carry something or someone: *The Magi came bearing gifts for the infant Jesus.*

bring to move something or someone from another place to here: *I've brought you this book, I thought you might like to read it.*

cart (*informal*) to carry something heavy or awkward: *I carted this Tvall the way home, and it doesn't even work!*

convey (*formal*) to move people or things from one place to another in a form of transport: *A luxury limousine will swiftly convey you from the airport to your hotel.*

lug (*informal*) to carry or drag something heavy or awkward: *The taxi didn't turn up, so I had to lug my suitcase all the way to the station.*

take to move something or someone from here to another place: *Will you take your grandmother home after dinner?*

transport (*formal*) to move people or things from one place to another in a form of transport: *Pupils are transported from outlying areas in the school bus.*

cause

1 *noun* something that makes something else happen: *The cause of death was heart failure.*

grounds circumstances that provide someone with an acceptable reason for believing something or doing something, especially taking legal action: *Unreasonable behaviour is grounds for divorce.*

justification a fact that justifies a course of action: *There is no justification for a man hitting a woman.*

motivation something that causes you to want to do something: *His only motivation for wanting the job is to earn more money.*

motive a person's reason for doing something, especially for committing a crime: *Jealousy was her motive for murdering her husband.*

occasion (*formal*) a cause for doing something, especially a provocation for a bad action (usually used with a negative): *You had no occasion to be rude to her.*

origin something, often an event, in the past that has caused or created something: *The origin of the industrial dispute was the unfair dismissal of an employee.*

reason an explanation for why someone does something or believes something, or for why something happens: *My reason for going to Paris is to study art.*

root the basic cause, which is not always obvious at first, of an unpleasant situation: *The root of her discontent is a thwarted ambition to be an actress.*

source something or someone that is the starting point from which something developed: *We're trying to trace the problem back to its source.*

2 *verb* to make something happen, or make someone do something: *The customer caused a fuss because the steak was too well done.*

bring about to take action that causes a particular situation to exist: *She brought about a reconciliation between her husband and his father.*

create to cause something, such as a feeling or situation, to exist: *Angela's promotion has created tension among her colleagues.*

effect (*formal*) to take action that causes something, such as a change or development, to take place: *The Women's Movement effected major changes in women's rights.*

generate to create or produce something abstract, for example discussion, excitement, or interest: *Chat-show appearances by the stars generated a lot of interest in the film.*

produce to cause something, such as a reaction or a result, to happen or exist: *You can never be quite certain that an action will actually produce the effect that you intended.*

provoke to produce a particular reaction in people, usually a strong or an adverse one: *The management's decision to have a pay freeze provoked an angry response.*

trigger to be the direct cause of

 something happening: *Her father's death triggered a bout of depression.*

See also **basis**.

chance *noun*

a possibility that something may happen, or that you will be able to do something: *Sean stands a good chance of winning the contest.*

break (*informal*) a piece of luck, especially one that gives you an opportunity to show your abilities: *She got her first big break when she was invited to exhibit her work at the Tate Gallery.*

likelihood the degree to which it is

 possible that something may happen: *There is little likelihood of snow this weekend.*

occasion a situation that enables you to do something: *I had hoped to ask Maria for some advice, but the occasion didn't arise.*

opening an opportunity to achieve something or to show your abilities: *Claire was asked to take over while her boss was away on sick leave, which gave her an opening to show her organizational skills.*

opportunity a situation that enables you to do something that you want to do or to make progress: *I have been given the opportunity to work in Paris for six months.*

possibility the fact that something might happen, although it is equally likely that it might not happen: *There's a possibility that the president will visit the scene of the disaster.*

probability the fact that something is more likely to happen than not to happen: *There's a probability that you will need an operation.*

prospect the fact that something is quite likely to happen in the future: *The family faced the prospect of losing their home.*

change

1 *noun* an instance of becoming different or making something different: *There has been a change in the weather.*

adjustment a minor alteration or rearrangement: *The computer technician made a few adjustments to my settings, and that fixed the problems.*

alteration a change, especially a change made to something such as a garment or figures: *The bride's dress needed some alterations after she lost weight.*

amendment a small change that

 improves something, especially a written document: *I have made an amendment to your bill to correct the error.*

conversion a major change to the form or function of something, such as a building: *The builders are working on a barn conversion.*

makeover a set of major changes that are intended to improve the appearance of something, especially a person or a room: *After she had a makeover, the Tv presenter's career was revived.*

modification a minor change to make something work better or more efficiently: *I have made modifications to the filing system which speed up the process considerably.*

reversal a change in something that makes it the opposite of what it was before: *The Minister has had a complete reversal of opinion on local taxation.*

revolution a major change, for example in working methods, that means that everything is done in a new way: *The introduction of computer technology brought about a revolution in animated films.*

transformation a major or complete change in the appearance or nature of something or someone: *There has been a transformation in Tony's appearance since he got married.*

2 *verb* to become different or to make something different: *I've decided to change the time of the meeting.*

adjust to make a minor alteration or

rearrangement to something: *I adjusted my watch so that it showed the same time as the clock on the town hall.*

alter to change, especially to make changes to something such as a garment or figures: *I altered the 'a' to an 'e' and the 'v' to an 'r', so that the word reads 'here' instead of 'have'.*

amend (*formal*) to improve something, especially a written document, by making usually small changes to it: *I have amended the final paragraph to make it easier to read aloud.*

convert change something so that it has a new form or function: *I have converted amounts in zlotys to amounts in Euros.*

modify to make minor changes to something so that it works better or more efficiently: *They modified the design of the exhaust system to reduce the emission of harmful gases.*

reverse to change something, for example a decision, so that it becomes the opposite of what it was before: *A higher court may reverse a judgment made in a lower court.*

revolutionize to change a way of doing something completely, and usually for the better: *The advent of the computer revolutionized the way in which data is stored.*

transform to cause a major or complete change in the appearance or nature of something or someone: *By sheer hard work and business skill they transformed a failing company into a highly successful enterprise.*

character *noun*
the collection of psychological and moral qualities that makes someone the kind of person that they are: *He is not a bad man, but there is a weakness in his character.*

disposition a person's usual frame of

mind: *The little girl has such a sunny disposition that she always makes us smile.*

image the nature of a person, organization, or commercial product as it is presented to, or perceived by, the public: *The Minister likes to play up to his image as a family man.*

make-up the collection of qualities that are seen by other people as being typical of a person's character: *Jealousy is not in her make-up.*

nature the basic character of a person, especially the traits that they are born with, which determines how they behave: *It is not in his nature to forgive and forget.*

persona (*formal*) the version of your character that you present to other people: *Often a celebrity's public persona is quite different from his true personality.*

personality a person's character, especially with regard to whether they are lively and interesting: *What he lacks in looks he makes up for in personality.*

temper the kind of nature that a person has, particularly with regard to how easily they become angry: *Juliet has a very even temper; nothing much seems to bother her.*

temperament the kind of nature that a person has, with regard to how emotional or calm their reactions are: *This film is not suitable for people of a nervous temperament.*

characteristic *noun* one of the qualities that, combined, make up the nature of a person or thing: *Kieron's sincerity is his most attractive characteristic.*

attribute a quality that someone or something has, especially a positive quality: *One of the main attributes of his paintings is his vivid use of colour.*

 feature a distinctive aspect of a person, thing, or place: *The Eiffel Tower is Paris's most easily recognizable feature.*

idiosyncrasy an unusual character trait or habit: *Wearing a bow tie is one of his little idiosyncrasies.*

peculiarity a distinctive or unusual feature: *Cartoonists pick out peculiarities of their subjects and exaggerate them.*

quality a distinguishing characteristic, especially a positive one: *Ahmed has all the qualities needed to be a good doctor.*

quirk a slightly strange character trait or habit: *She found some of her husband's quirks very hard to live with.*

trait one of the qualities that make up someone's personality: *Arrogance is a trait he seems to have inherited from his father.*

cheap *adjective*
not costing a lot of money to buy or use, although often not of very good quality: *You can't expect top-quality service in a cheap hotel.*

affordable (usually used to describe commercial goods and services) within a price range that most people can afford: *'Three-piece suites at affordable prices.'*

budget (usually used to describe commercial goods and services) designed to be sold at a relatively low price: *a company that deals in budget holidays.*

dirt-cheap (*informal*) costing very little indeed: *I bought this watch at the flea market – it was dirt-cheap!*

economical (usually used to describe machines and vehicles) not costing much to use: *an economical car with low petrol consumption.*

inexpensive not costing a lot of money (often used to avoid the possible negative sense of 'cheap'): *an inexpensive family restaurant.*

low-cost (used only in business contexts) costing comparatively little: *low-cost car hire.*

no-frills (*informal*) not expensive because only a basic service is offered: *We flew with a no-frills airline, which does not offer in-flight meals.*

on special offer sold for a limited period of time at a lower price than usual, often with specific conditions: *Melons are on special offer: buy one, get one free.*

reasonable being offered at a price

that seems very fair: *a shop that sells designer clothing at reasonable prices.*

cheat *verb*

to behave in a dishonest way to prevent someone from getting something that they ought rightfully to have: *Philip cheated me out of my share of the money.*

con (*informal*) to trick someone or steal from someone after gaining their trust: *A couple posing as charity workers conned people into giving them donations.*

deceive to make someone believe in something that is false or unreal, usually in order to gain an advantage over them: *We were deceived by his honest appearance and professions of good faith.*

defraud (*formal*) to get money from someone by dishonest or illegal means: *The singer was defrauded by his agent, who took a huge percentage of his earnings.*

dupe to fool someone into believing

something that is not true: *We were all duped into believing her sob story about being robbed.*

rip off (*slang*) deliberately overcharge someone or cheat them out of money: *The hotel tried to rip us off by charging for the minibar, which we hadn't used.*

swindle to get money from someone by dishonest or illegal means: *Many people were swindled in unreliable pension schemes.*

trick to use clever, amusing, or dishonest means to deceive someone or make them do something that puts them at a disadvantage: *Computer users can be tricked into giving away personal information that can be used in crimes against them.*

check *verb* to make sure that something is as it should be: *Always check your spelling before you post a letter.*

double-check to check your work and then check it again: *Chris is very meticulous; she double-checks every document before she files it.*

examine to look carefully at something or someone to check whether they are all right: *The doctor examined the girl's foot to see if there was a broken bone.*

give the once-over (*informal*) to look someone or something over quickly but carefully: *He gave the new girl the once-over and liked what he saw.*

investigate to examine facts in order to discover the truth about something, such as a crime: *The police are investigating a bank robbery.*

scrutinize to examine something or

someone very closely, often in order to discover information about them: *I scrutinized his face for signs of distress.*

test to try something or someone out in order to discover information about them: *New drugs must be tested thoroughly before they can be licensed for use.*

verify to check the truth of some information: *You must always verify your facts before you publish them.*

See also **inspect**.

choose *verb*

to decide that you want something or someone (or a number of different people or things) when there are various alternatives on offer: *Would you like to choose a dessert from the trolley?*

elect to choose someone to hold an official position, for example as an MP or a chairperson, by voting for them: *Tony Blair was elected leader of the Labour Party in 1994.*

go for (*informal*) to choose something (usually one particular thing): *I'd go for the chicken korma, if you want a curry that's not too hot.*

opt to choose one thing, such as a

particular course of action, in preference to other options: *Given the choice of driving or walking, we opted to walk.*

pick to choose something or someone (or a number of different things or people), especially to choose something that you can take in your hand or to select the members of a team: *Pick a card, look at it, but don't tell anyone what card it is.*

plump for (*informal*) to choose one person or thing, usually after careful consideration: *We weighed up the pros and cons of a holiday in Spain or Italy and in the end we plumped for Spain.*

select to make a careful choice from among several options, especially to choose the people who are going to make up a team: *He's been selected to be in the national squad for the World Cup.*

settle on to come to a decision about whom or what you are going to choose, usually after spending a lot of time considering various alternatives: *They have finally settled on a date for the wedding.*

single out to choose one person or thing from a group for special attention: *The other students were resentful because Kimberley appeared to have been singled out for special treatment.*

See also **decide.**

clean *adjective*
free from dirt: *She put clean sheets on the bed.*

hygienic very clean and free from

anything that might be dangerous to health: *It's important for kitchen staff to work in hygienic conditions.*

immaculate extremely clean, with no trace of dirt: *He was wearing an immaculate white shirt.*

pristine (*formal*) extremely clean or in very good condition, as if new: *'One microwave for sale, in pristine condition.'*

pure free from contamination, or not having anything else mixed with it: *pure spring water.*

spick and span (*informal*) very clean and neat: *Make sure you leave the apartment spick and span.*

spotless kept very clean: *They may be poor, but their house is always spotless.*

sterile absolutely clean and treated with something that kills all germs: *Surgical operations must be performed in sterile conditions.*

clear *adjective*
easy to see, perceive, or understand: *It was clear to me that the man was lying.*

apparent able to be perceived or

noticed: *It soon became apparent that she was totally unsuitable for that kind of work.*

blatant (used to describe something bad or immoral) obvious, often because no attempt is made to hide it: *He said he had found the wallet in the street, but that was a blatant lie.*

conspicuous standing out from its surroundings and so able to be easily seen: *a conspicuous landmark.*

evident that can be seen by the evidence, for example by somebody's facial expression or body language: *With evident distaste he changed the baby's nappy.*

obvious very easy to see, perceive, or understand: *It's obvious from the way he looks at her that Tom is attracted to Jane.*

patent (*formal*) (used to describe behaviour or abstract things) obvious: *For the Minister to preach about family values while cheating on his wife was patent hypocrisy.*

plain clear and leaving no room for doubt: *I thought I had made my feelings on this subject plain.*

clever *adjective*
having or showing above average intelligence or skill: *a clever plan.*

astute having a sharp mind and wise judgment: *an astute judge of character.*

brainy (*informal*) very intelligent and knowledgeable: *You're brainy; will you help me with my homework?*

bright quick to learn and having lots of ideas: *Melanie is a very bright pupil but lacks concentration.*

brilliant extraordinarily intelligent: *a brilliant scientist.*

gifted born with a high degree of skill or intelligence: *a school for gifted children.*

ingenious showing an unusual kind of cleverness and originality: *an ingenious invention.*

intelligent having or showing an ability to learn, think, or understand effectively, especially with relation to serious subjects: *an intelligent conversation.*

shrewd having or showing practical intelligence based on experience of life and people's behaviour: *a shrewd assessment of their chances of success.*

smart (*informal*) having or showing intelligence and quick thinking: *a smart answer.*

Smart is very commonly used to describe people who are clever in US English, but is less commonly used about people in British English.

See also **able; shrewd**.

climb *verb*
to move towards the top of something by using your feet or your hands and feet: *The boys amused themselves by climbing trees.*

ascend (*formal*) to move upwards, or to go up something: *They ascended the staircase to the bedroom.*

clamber to use your hands and feet to get up something that is usually quite low and easy to climb: *The children clambered all over the climbing frame in the park.*

mount to climb onto something that you are going to ride, such as a horse or a motor cycle, or to go up something, such as steps or a hill: *The cowboy mounted his horse and rode off.*

scale to climb to the top of something high, such as a wall or a hill: *Sir Edmund Hillary scaled Mount Everest in 1953.*

scramble to climb with difficulty or awkwardness: *We scrambled up the sand dunes on our hands and knees.*

shin up to climb up something narrow and tall, such as a rope or a pole, by using your hands and knees: *When I locked myself out, I had to shin up the drainpipe and climb in through the bedroom window.*

swarm up to climb quickly up something, such as a rope or a mast, by gripping with the knees and pulling yourself up by the hands: *The sailor swarmed up the mainmast.*

See also **rise**.

close

1 *adjective* (to rhyme with *dose*) a short distance away: *Our house is very close to the church.*

adjacent (*formal*) right next to something, but usually not joined to or touching it: *Our premises are located on a prime site adjacent to the city centre.*

adjoining right next to something and usually joined to or touching it: *a suite of adjoining rooms.*

handy (*informal*) situated conve-niently close to something: *My office is very handy for the station.*

near a short distance away in space or time: *in the near future.*

nearby situated a short distance away from where you are: *We could see a light in the window of a nearby cottage.*

Not used with *more* or *most.*

neighbouring (usually used to describe buildings or large areas) right next to each other: *Spain and Portugal are neighbouring countries.*

nigh (*old-fashioned*) close in time: *I saw a man with a placard saying 'The end of the world is nigh'.*

on your doorstep (*informal*) very close to your home: *When we lived in the city, we had shops, restaurants, and cinemas right on our doorstep.*

2 *verb* (to rhyme with *doze*) to move something, such as a door or a window, so that it is no longer open: *Close the gate so that the sheep don't escape.*

bolt to fasten a door securely with a bolt: *I locked and bolted the doors before I went to bed.*

fasten to close a belt, buckle, or other fastening device: *Fasten your seat belts.*

push to to push a door or a gate so that it is almost closed: *Push the door to, but don't shut it, in case the cat wants to come in.*

seal to close something, such as an envelope or a container, very tightly: *The jam is put in jars, which are then sealed so that they are airtight.*

secure to close or fasten something tightly, for example with a rope or a lock, to prevent it from moving or being opened: *He moored the boat and secured it with a rope.*

shut to move something, such as a door or window, so that it is no longer open: *Don't shut the window, we need some fresh air in here.*

slam to close a door or window with a loud bang, often because you are angry: *She stormed out in a temper, slamming the door.*

clumsy *adjective*
moving about or doing things in way that is not graceful or coordinated, so that you often drop things or bump into them: *Phil is very clumsy, always knocking things over.*

awkward not graceful in the way you move or position your body and not skilful in handling objects, but unlikely to cause damage: *His jacket was too tight for him, and every time he moved his arms he looked awkward and uncomfortable.*

bungling (*informal*) irritatingly clumsy and inefficient: *You bungling idiot! You've ruined our plan!*

gauche (*formal*) not good at talking to or dealing with people in social situations, because of inexperience or shyness: *a gauche young man who always seems to say the wrong thing.*

ham-fisted (*informal*) very clumsy or incompetent: *Some ham-fisted mechanic had broken the fan belt while attempting to tighten it.*

heavy-handed using or showing too much force or effort and too little skill: *his heavy-handed attempts at humour.*

lumbering large, heavy, and moving awkwardly: *a lumbering giant.*

uncoordinated moving awkwardly and without smoothness, especially unable to use two or more parts of your body together in a smooth and rhythmic way: *He is too uncoordinated to be a dancer.*

ungainly showing a lack of grace in movement: *an ungainly walk.*

cold *adjective*

having a low temperature: *a cold drink.*

biting (used mainly to describe the wind) so cold as to cause a biting or stinging sensation on the skin: *a biting wind.*

bitter (used to describe the weather or temperature) very cold: *The poor dog was left out in the bitter cold.*

chilly rather cold: *It's a bit chilly now that the sun has gone down.*

cool slightly cold, often pleasantly so: *The sun was beating down, but there was a lovely cool breeze.*

freezing extremely cold: *The hall was freezing, as the radiators were off.*

frosty so cold that frost has formed on the ground, trees, and other surfaces: *I have to scrape the car windscreen on frosty mornings.*

frozen feeling extremely cold: *We were frozen by the time the bus arrived, half an hour late.*

icy so cold as to feel like ice: *Come indoors, your hands are icy.*

See also **unfriendly.**

comfortable *adjective*

which makes you feel at ease or relaxed: *a comfortable bed.*

comfy (*informal*) comfortable: *I always wear my comfy shoes for trudging round the shops.*

cosy warm and comfortable, because in a small, enclosed space that brings people close together: *a cosy little cottage.*

relaxing causing you to feel at ease: *a relaxing warm bath.*

restful causing you to feel rested: *a nice restful evening in front of the TV.*

snug small, warm, and comfortable: *a snug little corner by the fire.*

spacious comfortable because containing a lot of room to move around in: *a spacious apartment.*

complain *verb*

make negative comments about something or someone: *They complained to the manager about the food in the restaurant.*

bellyache (*informal*) to complain in a bad-tempered way: *Jim is bellyaching about having to do the washing-up.*

gripe (*informal*) to complain moodily: *Stop griping and just get on with the task!*

grumble to mutter about something in a dissatisfied manner: *Joe was grumbling about the noise of the children playing outside.*

make a fuss (*informal*) to complain loudly in a way that attracts attention to you: *It's only a tiny scratch, there's no need to make a fuss.*

moan to complain about something in a bad-tempered way: *Brenda is always moaning about the weather.*

protest to object, often formally, to something, such as a plan or a course of action: *Local people protested about plans to open a massage parlour.*

whine to complain about something in a moody or self-pitying way: *Instead of whining to me about your boss, why don't you talk to him about your grievances?*

whinge (*informal*) to complain in a moody or childish way: *I'm fed up listening to you whingeing all the time.*

complete *adjective*

1 with no parts missing: *the complete works of Shakespeare.*

entire all of something, such as a time or a place: *the entire universe.*
Only used before a noun.

full with all the space inside taken up, or with no parts missing: *a full pack of cards.*

intact not broken or damaged: *The framed picture you sent me arrived intact.*

unbroken not broken or interrupted: *an unbroken run of success.*

whole including every part: *I ate the whole bar of chocolate.*
Mainly used before a noun.

2 (used mainly with negative words, but also with some positive words like *success*) in every respect: *Their marriage was a complete disaster.*

absolute (used with negative and positive words) to the very highest degree: *It was an absolute pleasure to meet my sporting hero.*

outright (used mainly with words like *success* or *victory*) clear and leaving no doubt about the result: *an outright victory.*

thorough (usually used with negative words) being a strong example of something: *They made a thorough mess of trying to organize a party.*

total (used with negative and positive words) in every respect: *The child went off with a total stranger.*

unmitigated (used with negative words) having no good or redeeming features: *The man is an unmitigated scoundrel.*

unqualified (used with positive words) having no bad or doubtful features: *The party was an unqualified success.*

utter (used mainly with negative words) to the very highest degree: *We stared at the scene in utter disbelief.*

See also **achieve; finish**.

complicated *adjective*
(used mainly to describe things, systems, or processes) difficult to understand or deal with because of having many different elements that do not link up or relate to one another in a straightforward way: *Carol's life is very complicated, with a full-time job, a family to look after, and her charity work.*

complex (used mainly to describe states or situations, but also people and living things) difficult to understand or deal with as a whole, because made up of many different, sometimes conflicting, elements: *Jack was a very complex man – capable of great sensitivity, but also of the most appalling brutality.*

difficult causing problems or requiring a lot of effort to deal with or understand: *a difficult crossword puzzle.*

elaborate made or planned in a complicated way with a great many, often too many, details: *A rebel group hatched an elaborate plot to assassinate the president.*

86

fiddly (*informal*) difficult to handle or accomplish because of involving many small or delicate parts: *It was a fiddly job to disentangle the fine chain.*

intricate (used mainly to describe things with a pattern or sequence) made up of many parts or stages that are linked together in a complicated way: *an intricate dance routine.*

involved made annoyingly difficult to follow or to do because of being unnecessarily detailed or complicated: *She told us a long involved story about various mishaps that occurred on her way to work to explain why she was late.*

knotty difficult to resolve: *a knotty problem.*

See also **difficult.**

confident *adjective*
feeling or showing that you are sure of your own worth or abilities and that you are likely to be able to do something well: *After studying hard for months, Shereen felt confident of passing her exams.*

assertive firmly stating your opinions or wishes: *You will have to be more assertive or people will take advantage of you.*

cocky (*informal*) excessively confident to the point of being irritating: *Luke got a little cocky after all the teachers praised him.*

poised sure of yourself in a calm and dignified way: *While the other acts were in a state of nerves, the star of the show was perfectly poised.*

positive tending to expect a favourable outcome: *Joel's success owes a lot to his positive outlook on life.*

secure feeling no anxiety or self-doubt: *The woman stood for election, secure in the knowledge that she had her family's support.*

self-assured feeling or showing that you have no doubts about your ability to do something: *The singer gave a smooth self-assured performance.*

self-possessed calm and confident: *When the school went on fire, the teacher remained self-possessed and calmly steered the children to safety.*

sure of yourself feeling no doubts about your ability to do something: *David is remarkably sure of himself for a beginner.*

See also **sure.**

conflict *verb*
(said about things such as opinions or ideas) to be opposed to or in disagreement with something or with each other: *The interests of the business sometimes conflict with the interests of the family.*

be at odds (said about people and ideas, etc.) to disagree with someone, or to conflict with something or each other: *Joan is always at odds with her mother-in-law on the subject of child care.*

clash to disagree and have a violent argument with someone, or (said for example about colours) to be incompatible with each other: *The two co-presenters of the show frequently clashed in private.*

contradict to say something that disagrees with somebody else's account of something and suggests that the other account is wrong: *Your version of events contradicts Jenny's.*

differ to be different from each other, or to hold a different or opposing point of view: *I think we should just agree to differ on this point, because neither of us will change the other's mind.*

go against (said about actions, ideas, statements, etc.) to be contrary to or contradict something: *This policy goes against everything that the party is supposed to stand for.*

See also **disagree; fight; oppose; quarrel**.

consider *verb*
to have a particular idea or image of someone or something, based on your experience of them, that you are reasonably sure is a true one: *I consider myself to be a good judge of character.*

believe to have a particular idea or image of someone or something, based on your experience of them, but without being entirely sure that it is a true one: *I always believed her to be a good mother, but, of course, you know her better than I do.*

deem (*formal*) to think of something or someone in the specified way, especially to think about something in terms of how it affects your dignity and status: *I would deem it an honour to be invited to your wedding.*

judge to form an opinion about someone or something based on evidence: *Anna was judged to be the best candidate for the job.*

rate to think of someone or something in terms of whether they are good or bad, successful or unsuccessful: *The band's comeback concert was rated a huge triumph.*

reckon to have a particular idea or

image of someone or something, especially as regards their quality or status: *Gordon is reckoned to be the best table-tennis player in the youth club.*

regard as to have a very definite idea of someone or something, usually because of long experience of them: *I have always regarded you as one of my dearest friends.*

think to have an opinion about someone or something, which may be based on little evidence or formed very quickly: *You may think me paranoid, but I prefer not to disclose any personal details over the Internet.*

See also **think.**

continuous *adjective*
happening without interruption over a period of time: *5 hours' continuous rain.*

constant happening repeatedly, sometimes to the point of irritation: *I'm fed up with his constant nagging.*

continual happening repeatedly, usually at short intervals: *continual interruptions.*

endless lasting a long time or happening very often, and therefore tedious: *her endless boasting about her children's achievements.*

incessant never stopping or pausing, and irritating or tiring because of that: *their incessant chatter.*

nonstop (*informal*) proceeding at a fast pace and never stopping, which may seem energetic or exciting: *a nonstop round of social engagements.*

solid (used to describe a length of

time) continuing without a break: *We queued for tickets for three solid hours.*

uninterrupted continuing without any interruptions: *Parents of young babies rarely have a full night's uninterrupted sleep.*

control *verb*

to have power to make someone or something do what you want: *There was a strong police presence to control the crowd.*

command to be in a position of authority over a group of people, especially in the armed forces: *The admiral commanded a destroyer patrol force during the war.*

conduct to organize and carry out something, such as an enquiry or a study: *The commissioner conducted an enquiry into alleged corruption in the police force.*

direct to be in charge of a group of people or an activity: *The agency directed an advertising campaign for the Dairy Council.*

head to be the highest-ranking person in something, such as a business or a department: *Mr Murphy heads the Accounts Department.*

lead to be the person directly responsible for telling or showing a group of people what to do in any sphere of activity from government to business or sport: *The captain led his team to victory in the championship.*

manage to organize and be in charge of a business, or part of a business, or the work of a group of people: *She manages a fashionable restaurant in the city.*

organize to plan something, such as a social occasion or other activity, and be responsible for making sure that it happens according to plan: *I am organizing a concert for charity.*

oversee to be in charge of an activity or task to make sure that the work is done satisfactorily: *Your role as Managing Editor is to oversee the work of freelance proofreaders.*

run to be in overall charge of a business or an activity: *He runs the family business almost single-handedly.*

supervise to be in charge of a group of people or an activity, especially to be present and watch people to make sure they do what they are supposed to do: *A teacher must be present to supervise the students who are in detention.*

convincing *adjective*

that makes you believe something, especially something that you did not previously believe: *Sarah is a very convincing liar.*

believable realistic enough to appear to be true: *The star put in a believable performance as a tough detective.*

cogent (*formal*) that makes you believe that something is true or correct by presenting strong reasons: *a cogent argument.*

compelling capable of influencing someone's thoughts or opinions: *The defence lawyer made a compelling case for her client's innocence.*

credible reasonable enough to be believed: *It was hardly credible that such an unattractive man would have such a beautiful wife.*

persuasive that persuades you to do something or to believe something: *Michael can be very persuasive when he really wants you to do something for him.*

plausible reasonable enough to be believed: *a plausible excuse.*

See also **persuade; sure.**

copy *noun*
something made to look like or reproduce something else: *Karen gave me a copy of her notes, as I missed the lecture.*

duplicate an exact copy of something, such as a document, often an unnecessary copy: *You can discard this page, as it is just a duplicate of page 5.*

fax a copy of a document sent electronically from one fax machine to another: *I sent a fax of my Cv to various prospective employers.*

forgery a copy of something, such as a painting or a banknote, intended to deceive people into thinking that it is an original not a copy: *The painting believed to be by Picasso turned out to be a forgery.*

imitation something that is made using something else as a model and tries to be like it: *This song is just a poor imitation of a Beatles song.*

photocopy a photographic copy of a document or a picture made on a photocopier machine: *I need to make a photocopy of my phone bill for my tax records.*

replica a copy of something three-dimensional: *a replica of an Art Deco statuette.*

reproduction a copy of something of historic or artistic value: *a reproduction of the Book of Kells.*

See also **imitate**.

cowardly *adjective*
lacking in courage: *a cowardly decision.*

chicken (*informal*) afraid to do something daring: *Come on, don't be chicken - let's go on the rollercoaster!*

craven (*literary*) shamelessly cowardly: *a craven neglect of her duty.*

faint-hearted nervous about taking action and easily discouraged by difficulties or failure: *Liam was too faint-hearted to approach the girl he was interested in.*

gutless (*informal*) completely lacking in courage or strength of character: *He's a gutless coward, picking on somebody half his size.*

lily-livered (*literary*) timid and cowardly: *The lily-livered knave abandoned the ladies to the mercies of the bandits.*

spineless lacking in courage or strength of character: *Daniel is too spineless to stand up for himself.*

timid lacking in courage and self-confidence and nervous about taking action: *The little boy was too timid to let go of his mother's hand.*

wimpish (*informal*) having or showing weak character: *Everyone thought he was wimpish for not sticking up for himself.*

yellow (*informal*) very cowardly: *He showed his yellow streak when he didn't back me up against the bullies.*

See also **afraid**.

crawl *verb*
to go somewhere slowly and, sometimes, with difficulty: *The roads were jammed with holidaymakers, so we were just crawling along.*

creep to go somewhere with slow quiet movements: *He crept into the bedroom, trying not to wake his wife.*

ease to move, or to move someone or something, into a place slowly and carefully: *The nurse gently eased the patient into a sitting position.*

edge move in a particular direction with small careful movements: *I had to edge gradually into a tight parking space.*

glide to move slowly and smoothly: *The model glided along the catwalk in an elegant evening gown.*

inch to go somewhere with small gradual movements: *The timid child slowly inched towards the cat and eventually stroked it.*

worm to make your way somewhere in a slow, indirect, and perhaps devious, manner: *He slowly wormed his way through the crowd right to the front.*

wriggle to move into or out of a narrow space by making a series of small twisting movements: *The boy wriggled through the gap in the fence.*

criticize *verb*
to express disapproval by saying that someone has behaved badly or that something is bad or faulty: *The singer was widely criticized for miming during her stage shows.*

cast aspersions on (*formal*) to make unfavourable remarks about someone or something, especially attacking their honour or integrity: *How dare you cast aspersions on my family's honour!*

denounce to make a public statement expressing your strong moral disapproval of a person or their actions: *He stood up in court and denounced the proceedings as a travesty of justice.*

disparage (*formal*) to make remarks that show that you have a low opinion of someone or something, often in an unkind way: *You shouldn't disparage his efforts, when he's obviously trying his best to please you.*

run down (*informal*) to make critical remarks about someone or something in an unkind or humiliating way: *She is always running down her husband, but he's actually quite a nice man.*

slag off (*informal*) to make very critical and insulting remarks about someone: *The two rival bands are always slagging each other off.*

slam (*informal*) to criticize a person or their actions severely: *The manager's team selection was slammed by all the sports journalists.*

See also **attack 2; blame**.

cruel *adjective*
deliberately causing pain or distress: *the cruel taunts of the bullies.*

brutal using physical violence or harsh methods to hurt people or achieve your aims: *a brutal beating.*

callous having or showing no compassion for others: *a callous disregard for other people's feelings.*

harsh very severe and unpleasant: *her harsh treatment of her ex-husband.*

heartless without mercy or compassion: *You would have to be heartless not to be moved by the newsreels of the starving children in Africa.*

nasty extremely unpleasant in the way you treat someone: *nasty spiteful remarks.*

sadistic taking pleasure in making others suffer: *He takes a sadistic pleasure in making his girlfriend jealous.*

vicious deliberately intending or intended to cause a lot of harm: *a vicious attack on a defenceless old lady.*

cry *verb*
to have tears coming from your eyes and, often, make distressful noises because you feel sadness or some other emotion: *The woman cried with relief when her missing child was returned safely.*

bawl (*informal*) to show distress by crying and making loud noises: *Vicky is bawling in her room because she is grounded.*

blub or *blubber* (*informal*) to cry excessively: *For goodness sake, stop blubbing, you've only got a small scratch!*

howl to cry violently and make loud and long noises: *The little boy was howling because he couldn't find his mother.*

snivel to cry quietly, with a lot of sniffing, in a way that others might find annoying: *Ken lost patience with his girlfriend because she was constantly snivelling.*

sob to make distressful noises while taking loud gulps of air: *I heard someone sobbing in the next room.*

wail to make a loud long vibrating noise to show sadness or pain: *The mothers of children who had been killed in the earthquake were wailing in their grief.*

weep to shed tears: *My husband caught me weeping at a sad film.*

whimper cry with soft muffled sounds, often because you are afraid: *When the police took the gunman away, the hostages were whimpering in the corner.*

custom *noun*
something that is done habitually by a person or in a particular society: *First-footing is a Scottish custom in which it is considered good luck if the first person to cross your threshold at New Year is a tall dark stranger.*

convention a way of doing something that is traditionally accepted as being correct: *It's a convention that the bride's father gives her away at her wedding.*

habit something that a person does regularly: *Brian has a bad habit of biting his nails.*

norm the usual way of doing something: *Large families used to be the norm in this country, but now they are quite unusual.*

practice an established way of doing something: *The practice of cremating dead bodies is common in many societies.*

ritual an established pattern of behaviour that a person or members of a particular society or religion follow: *Hara-kiri is the ritual of suicide by disembowelment that was practised by Japanese samurai warriors.*

routine a pattern of behaviour that you follow regularly: *A pre-breakfast jog is part of my morning routine.*

tradition an established pattern of behaviour that has been followed for a long time: *There is a long tradition of conflict between the two tribal groups.*

cut *verb*
to separate something, split it into pieces, or damage it, with a sharp implement: *Cut the meat into small pieces before cooking it.*

carve to cut a cooked joint of meat into slices or to form a piece of wood into a shape or design: *Father traditionally carves the turkey.*

chop to cut something into small pieces with heavy blows, especially using an axe or cleaver: *We chopped the logs into smaller pieces for the fire.*

dice to cut food into small cubes: *Dice the vegetables and add them to the pan.*

gash to injure a part of your body by making a long deep cut in it: *The boy gashed his knee playing football.*

lacerate (*formal*) to make many cuts in a part of your body: *The assault victim's face was badly lacerated and required 18 sutures.*

slash to make a long cut in something, such as fabric or skin, with a swift stroke from a blade: *The vandals slashed the curtains and painted slogans on the walls.*

slice to cut something, especially food, into flat pieces: *The fishmonger sliced the smoked salmon finely.*

slit to make a small narrow cut in something, such as a piece of fabric or a piece of meat: *Slit the chicken breast in two places and insert a garlic clove in each.*

snip to cut something such as hair or a plant with short quick strokes: *Snip the ends off the flowers before you put them in a vase.*

trim to neaten something, such as hair or a hedge, by cutting a little off the edges: *Bob has a small pair of scissors for trimming his moustache.*

See also **share; shorten.**

D

damage *verb* to cause harm or injury that has a bad effect on the appearance of something or makes it work less well, but does not necessarily make it completely unusable: *My car was badly damaged when another car drove into the back of it.*

deface to deliberately spoil the appearance of something, especially by writing or drawing on it: *Vandals have defaced the war memorial with red paint.*

destroy to make something completely unusable: *The old barn was destroyed by a fire.*

harm to have a bad effect on someone or something: *Revelations about the candidate's private life may harm his political prospects.*

hurt to cause someone physical pain or emotional distress: *These new shoes hurt my feet.*

injure to physical harm to someone or to a part of their body: *Darren was injured in a car crash.*

ruin to damage something, especially a building, beyond repair, or to spoil something completely: *The guests arrived very late, by which time the dinner was ruined.*

spoil to make something less pleasant to experience than it should have been: *The constant arguments spoilt the holiday for me.*

vandalize to damage something, especially a building, for example by breaking windows and writing graffiti on it, for no reason except the fun of doing it: *Every single telephone box in the main square had been vandalized.*

wreck to damage something, especially a

ship or vehicle, beyond repair, or to spoil something completely: *The scandal wrecked her chances of becoming party leader.*

See also **bad 2; destroy; hurt.**

danger *noun*
a situation, or a particular thing, that could easily cause harm to a person or thing: *The air-traffic controller guided the aircraft out of danger.*

hazard a particular thing that is likely to have a harmful or deadly effect: *the health hazards associated with passive smoking.*

menace (*often humorous*) something or someone that is likely to cause harm: *She's a menace to all other road users the moment she gets behind the wheel of a car.*

peril (*formal*) danger: *The journey through the mountains was filled with peril.*

risk the possibility of something harmful happening: *The firefighter put his own life at risk by going into the burning building to rescue a child.*

threat the prospect of something frightening or worrying happening: *The threat of redundancy was hanging over their heads.*

See also **dangerous.**

dangerous *adjective*
likely to cause harm, or able to be used to cause harm: *a dangerous weapon.*

dodgy (*informal*) unsafe, unreliable: *Watch out for that dodgy rung on the ladder!*

hairy (*informal*) dangerous and frightening: *It was a bit hairy when we skidded on that hairpin bend.*

insecure dangerous because unsteady or not properly fixed: *We had to make our way across an insecure rope bridge.*

perilous (*formal*) involving serious danger: *a perilous voyage in a lightweight craft.*

precarious dangerous because there is a strong chance of falling: *Be careful on that footpath - the footing is precarious!*

risky involving the possibility of harm or failure: *a risky business venture.*

treacherous dangerous to move on
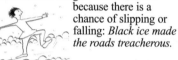
because there is a chance of slipping or falling: *Black ice made the roads treacherous.*

See also **danger.**

dark *adjective*

1 with little or no light, as during the night time: *We want to be home before it gets dark.*

dim with little light, so that it is difficult to see things clearly: *a dim corridor.*

dingy unpleasantly dark and rather dirty: *a dingy basement.*

gloomy with little light and a depressing atmosphere: *a gloomy winter's day.*

murky difficult to see clearly in or through: *the murky waters of the pond.*

shady cool and dark because shaded from the sun: *We found a shady spot under some trees.*

unlit having no artificial light: *an unlit room.*

2 not pale or bright in colour: *dark hair.*

black of the darkest possible colour: *a black taxi.*

dusky having a fairly dark shade: *a dusky pink.*

swarthy having dark skin and dark hair: *a swarthy stranger.*

dead *adjective*
no longer alive: *a dead body.*

deceased (used mainly in official documents) having died, especially recently: *The deceased woman's son collected her belongings from the hospital.*

defunct (not used to describe peo-

ple) no longer in existence: *the now-defunct Whig party.*

departed (*euphemistic or literary*) having died, especially recently: *the funeral of her dear departed husband.*

extinct (not used to describe people) no longer having any members still living: *The dodo is an extinct species of bird.*

gone (*informal*) having just died: *I rushed to the hospital but my Dad was already gone.*

inanimate (not used to describe people) never having had life: *A still life is a painting of inanimate objects.*

late (used before someone's name or a word describing them) who has died, especially recently: *My late mother was a nurse.*

lifeless (*literary*) dead: *The murder victim's lifeless body lay in the street.*

decent *adjective*
morally acceptable, especially in relation to sex or the way people present themselves in public: *Frankly, the way she was dressed was scarcely decent.*

decorous (*formal*) conforming to

accepted standards of correct behaviour: *A lady should conduct herself in a decorous manner at all times.*

honourable showing honesty, respect, and fairness to other people: *Owning up to your mistake would be the honourable thing to do.*

proper conforming to accepted standards of correct behaviour, especially on formal occasions: *the proper way to address the Queen.*

respectable regarded as deserving respect because of moral behaviour or social standing: *She comes from a very respectable family background.*

upright behaving in a moral and lawful manner: *an upright citizen.*

well-brought-up taught by your parents or guardians to have good morals and good manners: *a well-brought-up young man who treats everyone with respect.*

worthy (*formal*) regarded as deserving respect because of moral behaviour: *a worthy member of the local community.*

decide *verb*
to arrive at a particular idea or choice regarding something after thinking about it: *After careful consideration, I decided to accept the job offer.*

choose to take a particular course of action after thinking about various alternatives: *Lisa chose to stay at home to look after the baby, rather than go back to work.*

conclude to find what you think is the right answer or course of action after considering evidence or various alternatives: *They concluded that their elderly mother needed a home help.*

determine (*formal*) to work out what the answer to a problem is or what course of action should be taken: *My friends' support helped me to determine how I should proceed.*

elect (*formal*) to choose: *Gareth elected to do the driving for the evening out.*

fix on to agree on or settle on a particular arrangement: *We fixed on 10 December for our next meeting.*

make up your mind to make a firm decision about something after a period of uncertainty: *Once John has made up his mind about something, you will never dissuade him.*

resolve (*formal*) to make a firm decision to do something: *David resolved to stop smoking in the New Year.*

rule to make or announce a formal decision about something: *The government ruled that pubs could serve alcohol up to 24 hours a day.*

decrease *verb*
become fewer in number or less in size, intensity, etc.: *The programme's viewing figures have decreased significantly over the last few weeks.*

abate (said about something violent) to become less intense: *The storm gradually abated.*

diminish to become smaller or less effective: *Her intellectual powers sadly diminished with old age.*

drop off (*informal*) to become fewer in number or less in amount: *Sales of videos dropped off after DVDs were introduced.*

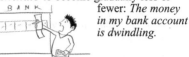

dwindle to become gradually less or fewer: *The money in my bank account is dwindling.*

lessen to become less, or make something less: *The new law lessens the opportunities for companies to avoid paying tax.*

lower to bring something to a lower height or level: *The age limit for membership of the club has been lowered to 18.*

reduce to become, or to make something smaller in size, number, price, etc.: *All dairy goods have been reduced to half price.*

shrink to become, or to make something, especially a piece of clothing, smaller in size, often accidentally: *My sweater has shrunk in the wash.*

subside to become less intense: *I took some medicine, and the pain gradually subsided.*

defeat *noun*
the act of beating a person, team, or country in a contest, fight, race, etc., or the fact of being beaten: *the defeat of the French fleet by Admiral Nelson at the Battle of the Nile.*

beating the act of defeating a person or team soundly in a contest, race, etc.: *The local darts team suffered a thorough beating at the hands of their nearest rivals.*

conquest the act of beating an enemy in a war or battle and taking control of their country: *the Spanish conquest of Mexico.*

fall the loss of power by a leader or government: *Losing a vote of confidence brought about the fall of the government.*

overthrow the removal of someone from power by an act of violence: *the overthrow of a tyrannical regime.*

rout an overwhelming defeat of an army: *the rout of the Persian army by the Arabs.*

thrashing (*informal*) a comprehensive

defeat of a person or a team in a game or contest: *I gave Derek a thrashing at squash.*

trouncing (*informal*) a comprehensive defeat of a person or a team in a game or contest: *The school football team got a right trouncing on Saturday.*

See also **beat 2**.

defend *verb*

to take action to prevent someone from being harmed or captured when they are attacked: *He defended his wife's good name against attacks in the media.*

champion to speak in support of a cause or a person: *She championed the cause of women's rights.*

guard keep someone or something safe from harm, especially by being physically present to fight off an attacker: *They have a large dog guarding the house.*

protect to keep someone or something safe from harm: *Use a high-factor sun screen to protect your skin from the harmful rays of the sun.*

safeguard (*formal*) to take action to keep something safe from harm: *Safeguard your computer files by backing up regularly.*

shield to protect someone from

something, such as a physical threat or unwanted attention: *The film star shielded her children from the press photographers.*

speak up for to defend or support someone verbally: *Danielle spoke up for me when all the others said I was wrong.*

stick up for (*informal*) give someone strong support: *Although the brothers argue constantly, they will always stick up for each other against an outsider.*

support to express agreement with a person, their point of view, or their aims: *The committee supported the chairman's proposal.*

See also **help; support.**

delay *verb*

1 not to do something when you had planned to, but to wait until later: *If you delay posting your job application, you may miss the closing date.*

adjourn to have a break in proceedings

and begin again later: *I propose that we adjourn the meeting until after lunch.*

defer to delay an action, such as paying a bill, until a later time: *They always defer payment of bills for as long as possible.*

postpone to cancel an arrangement and rearrange it for a later time: *I had to postpone my driving test because I was unwell.*

procrastinate (*formal*) to keep putting off doing something that you have to do, often because you do not really want to do it at all: *Kerry keeps procrastinating when she knows she should be revising for her exams.*

put off not to do something when you should but to wait until later: *Tim put off going to the doctor because he was afraid.*

reschedule to cancel an arrangement and rearrange it for a later time: *I would like to reschedule my dental appointments because I am going on holiday.*

shelve to cancel a planned project completely or postpone it until a much later time: *We had to shelve our plans to build an extension because we ran out of funds.*

2 to cause someone to be late for something, such as an appointment: *Sorry I'm late - I was delayed by a last-minute phone call.*

detain to hold someone back, for example by talking to them: *I was detained by a client who stayed longer than I had expected.*

hold up cause someone to be late: *We were held up for an hour in a traffic jam.*

set back slow down someone's progress: *When Richard's computer crashed, it set his schedule back considerably.*

delicious *adjective*
tasting or smelling very pleasant: *a delicious curry.*

appetizing looking or smelling as if it would taste good: *the appetizing smell of freshly brewed coffee.*

delectable (formal) tasting very pleasant indeed: *delectable strawberries.*

luscious tasting very sweet and pleasant: *luscious chocolate truffles.*

scrumptious (informal) tasting very pleasant indeed: *Mmm, that dinner was really scrumptious!*

succulent juicy and sweet-tasting: *succulent peaches.*

tasty having a fairly strong, pleasant, usually savoury, flavour: *The lentil soup is very tasty.*

yummy (informal) tasting very pleasant: *I had a cup of tea and a nice cream cake.*

destroy *verb*
to damage something to the extent that it is completely unusable or worthless, or no longer exists: *Much of the city was destroyed in the war.*

annihilate to destroy something, such as a place or military force, completely: *The army was annihilated in the battle.*

demolish to destroy something, such as a building, by knocking it down: *The block of flats where I lived as a child has been demolished.*

knock down to destroy something, such as a building or other structure, by toppling it: *They're going to knock down all the old houses to make way for the new motorway.*

ruin to damage something, especially a building, beyond repair, or to spoil something such as a social occasion: *The bride's uncle ruined the wedding by getting drunk and starting a fight.*

smash to break or shatter an object or a vehicle, sometimes through some deliberate violent action: *The thief smashed the car window and stole the CD player.*

spoil to greatly reduce the value, quality, or appearance of something: *The rain spoilt her elaborate hairdo.*

wreck to damage something, especially a ship or vehicle, beyond repair, or to spoil something completely: *A serious car accident in his teens wrecked Peter's career as a footballer.*

See also **damage.**

deteriorate *verb*
to become worse or weaker: *The patient's condition has deteriorated rapidly.*

decline to become gradually worse: *The former president's health has declined over the last few years.*

degenerate become worse, for example in quality or in strength: *The discussion degenerated into a slanging match.*

ebb to become gradually less and less: *Her husband undermined her confidence until it gradually ebbed away completely.*

go downhill (*informal*) to become worse, weaker, or less successful: *The old lady had a stroke last year and has gone downhill since then.*

wane to become gradually less suc-

cessful: *The actor's career has waned since he reached middle age.*

weaken to become gradually weaker: *Her singing voice has weakened over the years.*

worsen to become gradually worse: *The standard of his school work has worsened every year as he appears to have lost interest.*

determined *adjective*

having made a firm decision to do something and showing the courage and will-power needed to do it: *She was determined to finish the marathon even though she was exhausted.*

dead set on (*informal*) having a partic-ular aim or plan that no one will be able to persuade you to give up: *dead set on going to university.*

focused concentrating your mind and efforts on a particular aim or subject: *To be a tennis champion, you have to be really focused.*

hell-bent (*informal*) recklessly deter-mined to do something: *He was hell-bent on winning, no matter what it took.*

intent having made up your mind to do something: *She seemed to be intent on causing trouble.*

resolute showing courage and firmness in keeping to a decision that you have made: *He was resolute in his refusal to get involved in petty arguments.*

unflinching firm and strong despite

difficulties or opposition: *her unflinching support for her husband.*

development *noun*

the way that something or someone progresses: *a child's development into an adult.*

evolution slow gradual change, espe-

cially in species of plants and animals over a very long period of time: *In the evolution of apes, there is a trend of increase in size.*

formation the process of developing something, such as an idea or plan: *They are working on the formation of a new marketing strategy.*

growth the process of becoming gradu-ally larger, more fully developed, or more successful: *There has been a marked population growth in this area over the last ten years.*

progress the process of developing and moving forward: *We have been very impressed with Stacy's progress at school this year.*

devoted *adjective*

very loving and loyal towards someone: *a devoted wife.*

caring showing kindness or compassion towards people in general: *a kind and caring neighbour.*

committed having made a statement or promise of your support for a person, a religion, or a cause, and showing loyalty to them: *a committed Christian.*

dedicated giving a great deal of time and effort to a cause or an activity: *a dedicated athlete.*

doting excessively fond of someone, often to the point of being blind to their faults: *His doting parents had spoiled him somewhat.*

faithful unfailingly loyal and supportive: *a faithful companion.*

fond having a liking or affection for someone or something: *I was very fond of my first car.*

loving showing love for someone or for each other: *a loving couple.*

loyal able to be relied on to support someone or something: *Loyal fans of the singer supported him throughout his court case.*

See also **faithful; reliable.**

difference *noun*
the fact of being unlike someone or something else: *I can't tell the difference between the twins.*

contrast a marked difference between two people or things resulting from their being opposites or near opposites: *The contrast between yesterday's wind and rain and today's bright sunshine is remarkable.*

discrepancy a difference between two reports or two sets of figures that suggests that one must be wrong: *There is a discrepancy between the two boys' accounts of last night's events.*

disparity (*formal*) a point of difference or an inequality between two things: *There is disparity in the earnings of men and women.*

dissimilarity (*formal*) a difference or difference: *The dissimilarities between the two sisters' characters are more noticeable than the similarities.*

distinction something that enables the difference between two people or things to be perceived: *There is a clear distinction between teasing and bullying.*

diversity the fact of existing in many different forms or of consisting of many different elements (usually used in serious contexts): *Religious and ethnic diversity enriches the culture of the nation.*

variation a slight difference: *We found a variation in prices between the supermarkets.*

variety the fact of existing in many different forms or offering a choice of different alternatives: *We have a variety of entertainments on offer.*

difficult *adjective*
not easy to do or to understand: *The exam was really difficult.*

awkward requiring great tact or diplomacy: *an awkward situation.*

demanding requiring a lot of effort over a long time: *She has a very demanding job in the City.*

exacting requiring a lot of effort and care: *Restoring a painting is exacting work.*

formidable difficult to do because of the size and nature of the task: *Retrieving the bodies from the collapsed building was a formidable task.*

gruelling putting a very great strain on your physical or mental strength: *a gruelling trek through the mountains.*

hard difficult, especially because of demanding a lot of physical or mental effort: *hard labour.*

laborious requiring a lot of effort, especially physical effort, and usually boring or repetitive: *Stripping the wallpaper is a laborious job.*

tiring making you feel tired: *a long tiring journey.*

troublesome causing problems: *troublesome neighbours.*

trying annoying and difficult to deal

with: *I've had a very trying day looking after six five-year-olds.*

uphill very difficult because presenting a lot of resistance: *It's an uphill struggle trying to make conversation with Tom.*

See also **complicated; stubborn.**

dirty *adjective*
not clean, because covered or marked with soil, mud, stains, etc.: *My hands were dirty after gardening.*

dusty covered in a layer of dust, or full of dust: *Wipe the top of the table, it's dusty.*

filthy very dirty indeed: *The boys came home filthy after playing football.*

grimy having a layer of dirt or soot on the surface: *a grimy windowsill.*

grubby dirty and shabby: *a grubby old raincoat.*

messy (*informal*) untidy and dirty: *It's a bit messy in here, because I haven't had time to clear up.*

mucky (*informal*) covered in dirt, especially mud: *Take those mucky boots off before you come in the kitchen.*

muddy covered in mud, or full of mud: *The path's very muddy after the rain we've had.*

polluted containing waste or harmful chemicals: *polluted water.*

soiled (*formal*) marked with soil, mud, or stains: *soiled bedclothes.*

squalid dirty and unpleasant: *a squalid basement flat.*

disagree *verb*
to have a different opinion from someone else, or think or say that what someone else says is wrong: *I disagree with his political views.*

argue to express an opposing opinion to someone, especially in an angry way: *We always argue about where to go on holiday.*

differ to hold different opinions or a different opinion from someone else: *On that point we differ.*

dispute to say that a statement or allegation is wrong: *I'm not disputing the fact that you did a good job.*

squabble to argue over something trivial: *The children were squabbling over whose turn it was to use the computer.*

take issue with to express objections to what someone has said: *I must take issue with your views on capital punishment.*

See also **conflict; fight; oppose; quarrel.**

disappear *verb*
to cease to exist or stop being visible: *Her anxiety disappeared as soon as she saw that her children were safe.*

cease (*formal*) to stop occurring or stop doing something: *Ten years have elapsed since the country ceased to be an independent nation.*

die out to gradually stop: *Interest in the band has died out over the last few years.*

evaporate to become weaker and cease to exist completely: *His self-confidence evaporated the moment he stepped on stage.*

fade to become gradually weaker: *Hopes of finding the missing girl alive are now fading.*

melt away to become weaker or cease to exist: *Her anger with her boyfriend melted away when he apologized sincerely.*

pass gradually stop existing: *Your uncertainty will soon pass as you get used to driving on the right-hand side of the road.*

slacken (off) to become less intense or busy: *Business slackened off after the holiday period.*

vanish to be no longer in evidence; to stop existing: *When the business tycoon lost all his money, the support of his friends vanished too.*

disapprove *verb*
have or express an unfavourable opinion of something or someone: *Her parents disapprove of her smoking.*

deplore (*formal*) to disapprove strongly of something or someone: *They deplore the enormous waste of food in the West.*

frown on to consider a practice to be wrong or unacceptable: *The teacher frowns on pupils chewing gum in class.*

look down your nose at (*informal*) to consider someone or something to be inferior: *She looked down her nose at him because he was a manual worker.*

object to feel that something is wrong, often on moral grounds, and be unwilling to do it: *He objects to having to tip taxi drivers.*

take a dim view of (*informal*) to dis-

approve of something: *He takes a dim view of people who arrive late for their appointments.*

take exception to to disapprove of or be offended by someone's words or actions: *She took exception to being addressed as 'Miss'.*

See also **criticize**.

disaster *noun*
an event, such as an explosion or an earthquake, that brings death, suffering, or hardship to many people, or something that goes very badly wrong: *The whole village was in mourning after the mining disaster.*

accident an unexpected event that usually has harmful effects: *She was injured in a road traffic accident.*

adversity a situation in which things go very badly for you and you have to deal with difficulties, hardship, or suffering: *They showed great courage in the face of adversity.*

calamity (*usually humorous*) an event
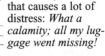
that causes a lot of distress: *What a calamity; all my luggage went missing!*

cataclysm (*formal*) an event, such as an earthquake or a tidal wave, that causes great destruction and loss of life: *The tsunami was a cataclysm with devastating effects.*

catastrophe an unexpected event that causes a lot of damage and distress, or something that goes badly wrong: *Bird flu could threaten to be a major global catastrophe.*

misfortune bad luck, or an event that has bad consequences for you: *She has had her share of misfortune.*

setback an event that spoils your plans or slows down your progress: *Losing a key member of staff was a bit of a setback.*

tragedy a very sad event: *Her sudden death at such an early age was a great tragedy.*

discourage *verb*
to make someone lose their enthusiasm for something or their wish to do something: *The miserable weather discouraged us from going out.*

demoralize to destroy someone's confidence and make them feel that their actions have no purpose: *The threat of redundancy had the effect of demoralizing the staff.*

deter to make someone not want to do something: *Many people believe that stiffer sentences are needed to deter violent criminals.*

disappoint to make someone feel sad because something is not as good as they had hoped: *Stephen's exam results disappointed him, as they were not good enough to qualify for the course that he wanted to do.*

dishearten to make someone feel sad because their actions have not had the effect they hoped for or because they are making no progress: *The teacher was disheartened by her pupils' lack of enthusiasm.*

disillusion to make someone realize that someone or something is not as good in reality as they imagined them to be: *I hate to disillusion you, but she's not as pretty in the flesh as she looks in the photograph.*

dissuade to persuade someone not to do something:

Harriet's friend dissuaded her from having a tattoo.

put off to make someone not want to do or have something: *The thought of all the crowds puts me off going to a rock festival.*

talk out of to persuade someone not to do something by talking to them about it: *Jeremy's wife talked him out of resigning from his job.*

discussion *noun*

the act of talking about a subject, exchanging opinions on it, and sometimes reaching a decision: *We had a family discussion about where to go on holiday.*

chat an informal conversation, often with a friend: *The two girls had a cosy chat about boyfriends.*

confab (*informal*) a casual conversation:
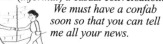
We must have a confab soon so that you can tell me all your news.

conference a formal or serious discussion, often of an academic, political, or business nature: *a conference to discuss climate change.*

conversation a situation in which two or more people are talking to one another: *I had an interesting conversation with my neighbour about his childhood in India.*

debate a discussion, usually a formal one, in which people give their views on a particular subject, often in the form of speeches: *a debate on the subject of debt relief.*

dialogue a conversation or discussion between two or more people or groups, especially between people or groups who are opposed to one another: *It's important to get a dialogue going between the two opposing sides.*

talk a conversation, usually one which has a particular subject or purpose: *Barry had a talk with his son about his exam results.*

disgrace *noun*

loss of honour or of respect because lots of people know that you have done something bad: *His thuggish behaviour has brought disgrace on the family.*

degradation a very low and miserable state in which nobody respects you and you usually have no self-respect either: *This film is a grim portrayal of hopeless addiction and degradation.*

discredit damage to your reputation: *It's to her discredit that she let her colleague take the blame for her mistake.*

dishonour loss of honour or reputation:

There is no dishonour in coming second out of 1000 contestants.

disrepute a state in which the general public has a low opinion of something: *The players' drunken antics has brought the game into disrepute.*
Usually used in the phrase *to bring something into disrepute.*

humiliation a deeply embarrassing feeling or state and a loss of self-respect that results from people knowing that you have done something bad or have been treated badly: *She suffered the humiliation of her husband being pictured in the newspapers with another woman.*

infamy (*formal*) the state of being well known for shameful reasons: *He achieved infamy after his involvement in a plot to assassinate the president.*

scandal a shockingly immoral incident or situation: *a scandal involving a government minister and a call girl.*

shame a feeling of embarrassment and humiliation: *They left the area because they could not live with the shame of their son's conviction for rape.*

disgusting *adjective*
extremely unpleasant or offensive, usually to the physical senses, but sometimes also to your sense of morality: *disgusting personal habits.*

foul extremely unpleasant to the senses of smell or taste: *a dark, damp, foul-smelling room.*

ghastly (*informal*) extremely unpleasant or unattractive, or in very bad taste: *He was wearing a ghastly Hawaiian shirt.*

gross (*informal*) nauseating, usually because of some disgusting physical action: *That film was so gross, especially when the alien burst out of the guy's chest!*

nauseating extremely unpleasant, almost to the point of causing you to feel that you want to vomit: *a nauseating smell.*

offensive causing people to feel upset because their feelings of what is right and proper have been attacked: *offensive language.*

off-putting unattractive, making you not want something or not want to be with someone: *A price increase is likely to be off-putting for many customers.*

repugnant (*formal*) morally unacceptable or offensive: *I found their racist attitude repugnant.*

repulsive extremely unattractive in appearance or nature: *She found her colleague's advances quite repulsive.*

revolting extremely unpleasant to the senses: *a revolting bright blue ice lolly.*

sickening causing you to feel disgusted, usually morally rather than physically: *a sickening display of greed.*

dishonest *adjective*
not acting or done in a way that is morally right: *dishonest politicians.*

corrupt dishonest, especially in being open to bribery: *a corrupt police officer.*

crooked (*informal*) dishonest, corrupt, or likely to break the law: *a crooked lawyer.*

deceptive giving a false impression, whether consciously intending to deceive or not: *Her youthful looks are deceptive.*

deceitful giving a false impression, with the intention to deceive: *He is sneaky and deceitful and I don't trust him.*

false not true or genuine: *She gave a false impression of being wealthy.*

fraudulent intentionally deceiving people, especially indulging in illegal practices to make money from other people: *fraudulent benefits claims.*

mendacious (*formal*) telling lies, especially habitually: *I found him to be mendacious and totally untrustworthy.*

untrustworthy not able to be trusted or believed: *an untrustworthy witness.*

untruthful not consistent with the truth, or not telling the truth: *an untruthful statement.*

See also **illegal.**

dislike *noun*

a feeling of not finding someone or something pleasant or appealing: *She couldn't hide her dislike of her sister's new boyfriend.*

animosity a very strong feeling of hostility and dislike between two people or groups: *The animosity between Trevor and his ex-wife was clear to see.*

antipathy (*formal*) a deep-rooted feeling of dislike or opposition to something or someone: *I must confess to having an antipathy to people who like dogs.*

aversion a very strong dislike of something or someone, which makes you want to avoid them as far as possible: *I have a deep aversion to public speaking.*

distaste the fact of finding something or someone unpleasant or disgusting: *The corners of his mouth turned down in distaste.*

hatred a very powerful and active dislike of someone or something, strong enough that it may make you want to harm or destroy them: *In that moment her dislike of him turned to absolute hatred.*

hostility an openly unfriendly attitude towards someone: *There is a lot of hostility between the two rival gangs.*

loathing intense hatred: *I had never felt* *such a strong loathing for anyone as I did for Louis at that moment.*

See also **disapprove; hate.**

dismay *noun*

a usually mild feeling of fear, disappointment, and sadness when something unpleasant happens: *Much to my dismay, the cup slipped out of my hands spilling coffee all over my hostess's best carpet.*

alarm a feeling of anxiety or fear caused by impending danger: *Try to evacuate the children from the school without causing alarm.*

disappointment a feeling of sadness because something is not as good as you had hoped: *Amy could not hide her disappointment when she opened her birthday present.*

distress sorrow or mental suffering: *It was painful to see the distress of those who had lost loved ones in the incident.*

sadness a feeling of unhappiness: *It* *is with sadness that I have to announce that my father passed away this morning.*

shock a strong sense of surprise and anxiety caused by something that has happened or been said: *It was such a shock to find that we had been burgled.*

surprise the feeling you have when something happens unexpectedly, whether welcome or unwelcome: *Imagine my surprise when my Australian cousin turned up without warning!*

upset mental or emotional pain caused by something that has happened or been said: *It took the children a long time to get over the upset of their father leaving.*

See also **frighten; sad; shock; surprise.**

disobedient *adjective* not doing as you are told: *a disobedient child.*

defiant showing that you do not care that someone has said you have done something wrong or opposes you: *He remained defiant, refusing to apologize to the referee.*

headstrong stubbornly determined to do what you want in spite of warnings against it: *his headstrong insistence on driving despite dangerous weather conditions.*

mischievous badly behaved in a playful way: *The mischievous children hid from their parents when it was time to go home.*

naughty badly behaved, but not in a serious way: *The naughty schoolboy threw a snowball at his teacher.*

rebellious refusing to do what people in authority tell you to do: *a rebellious teenager.*

unruly difficult to control: *an unruly crowd.*

wayward behaving badly and being disobedient, but usually in a forgivable way: *Their wayward son came home begging for forgiveness for his past misdemeanours.*

wilful always doing what you want even if that means disobeying other people or ignoring their advice: *Sophie was always wilful, even as a child.*

disorder *noun*
lack of organization or of tidiness in a place: *The burglars had ransacked the house and left it in complete disorder.*

chaos a state of complete confusion and disorganization, sometimes with a jumble of noise: *The teacher left the class for five minutes and returned to find the room in chaos.*

confusion a state in which things are uncertain or disorganized, sometimes because something unexpected has happened: *After the bomb went off, the streets were in a state of confusion, with people running in all directions.*

disarray a state of disorganization, confusion, or untidiness: *The managing director's unexpected resignation has left the company in disarray.*

disorderliness (*formal*) an untidy state, or a state in which things are not where they should be: *The disorderliness of the patient's appearance suggested that she might have been attacked.*

mess a very untidy, jumbled, or dirty state: *My teenage son's bedroom is usually in a dreadful mess, with dirty clothes and old pizza boxes all over the floor.*

untidiness lack of neatness or order, especially in a place: *The untidiness of the storeroom makes it difficult to find what you are looking for.*

See also **illness; trouble 2.**

distant *adjective*
being a long way away, either in space or in time: *in the dim and distant past.*

far distant, or situated in the extreme part of a place, in any particular direction: *the Far East.*

faraway being a very long way away and usually having an interesting exotic or romantic quality: *a faraway country.*

far-flung (*literary*) being a long way away or spread widely in different places: *a far-flung empire.*

far-off faraway: *strangers from far-off lands.*

outlying being a long way from the centre of a city, country, etc.: *mail for outlying districts.*

remote being a long way away and very difficult to reach: *a remote part of Tibet.*

See also **unfriendly.**

disturb *verb*
to stop someone from continuing with, or concentrating on, what they are doing: *I'm sorry to disturb you when you're working, but would you mind helping me for a moment?*

bother to disturb someone in an annoying way or repeatedly, especially about something that seems trivial to them: *Stop bothering me, I've got a very important letter to write.*

butt in (*informal*) to interrupt someone by saying something when they are speaking: *I'm trying to explain something to Jane, and he keeps butting in.*

disrupt to cause trouble and prevent something from happening in an orderly manner: *Protesters tried to disrupt the meeting.*

distract to draw someone's attention to something other than what they are supposed to be concentrating or working on: *I was distracted by something that was happening further along the street and didn't notice her.*

interrupt to stop something from continuing or to stop someone continuing with something, especially to stop someone from continuing to speak by saying something: *Please don't interrupt, I'll answer your questions when I've finished what I have to say.*

intrude to come into or be in a place where you are not wanted, or disturb someone who wants to be private: *You're intruding on a private conversation.*

pester to disturb someone deliberately and repeatedly in order to get them to do something or pay attention to something: *She keeps pestering me to write to the council about the state of the pavement outside our house.*

trouble to disturb someone, usually by asking them to do something: *Sorry to trouble you, but would you mind shutting the window, there's a terrible draught.*

See also **affect 2; hinder; interfere.**

doubtful *adjective*
not able to be known definitely, or not feeling sure about something and tending to have negative feelings about it: *It's doubtful whether this birthday card will be delivered on time.*

debatable about which people may have differing opinions: *It's debatable whether Jill's presence was a help or a hindrance.*

dubious feeling doubtful about something, or questionable: *I'm dubious about whether the painting is worth the price they are asking for it.*

questionable causing you to feel doubt and ask questions, especially as to whether something is good, reliable, or trustworthy: *of questionable morals.*

uncertain doubtful, or not able to make up your mind about something: *I'm uncertain whether to go or stay.*

unlikely to be expected not to happen rather than to happen: *It's unlikely that I will be able to go to the party.*

draw *verb*
to produce a picture of someone or something, using a pencil or pen: *The little girl drew a picture of a snowman.*

depict (*formal*) to represent a subject in a painting or drawing: *The painting depicts a castle on a hillside.*

design to draw a detailed plan of something that is yet to be created, such as a building, a garment, or a publication: *We're designing a simpler and cheaper model that will appeal to the mass market.*

doodle to draw absent-mindedly, often while doing something else: *Jim always doodles while talking on the phone.*

illustrate to provide pictures to appear in a book or other publication, especially pictures that show things described in the text: *This book is expensive because it is illustrated in full colour.*

portray to represent a subject, especially a person, in a drawing or painting: *The cartoonist portrayed the party leaders as different animals.*

scribble to draw or write untidily, as a young child does: *When Sally was two years old, she scribbled all over the wall in crayon.*

sketch o make a quick and often incomplete drawing of someone or something: *Keith quickly sketched Amber while she was reading her book.*

trace make a copy of a picture by placing thin transparent paper over it and drawing over the lines with a pencil: *The boy traced a picture of a dinosaur from his book.*

dream *noun*

pictures that you see in your mind while you sleep: *I had a dream about falling off a cliff last night.*

daydream an instance of imagining pleasant events in a dreamlike way while you are awake: *Julie was having a daydream about travelling to Russia.*

fantasy an instance of imagining a pleasant situation that you would like to happen but which is unlikely to happen: *Grant had a fantasy about being a professional footballer.*

hallucination an instance of seeing something that does not really exist, caused by illness or drugs: *At the height of his fever he was having hallucinations.*

nightmare a frightening or very unpleasant dream that you have while you sleep: *The little boy woke up crying because he had been having a nightmare.*

reverie (*formal*) an instance of

imagining pleasant events in a dreamlike way while you are awake: *My reverie was interrupted by loud banging on the door.*

vision an instance of seeing something that other people cannot see, sometimes caused by mental illness or drugs: *The woman claims to have had a vision of Christ.*

drink *verb*

to take a liquid into your mouth and swallow it: *I drank a cup of tea at breakfast time.*

down (*informal*) to drink all of something, often quickly: *He can down a pint of lager in one go.*

gulp drink something hastily swallowing large amounts at a time: *We had to gulp down our drinks before the pub closed.*

guzzle (*informal*) to drink something greedily: *teenagers guzzling cheap cider.*

knock back (*informal*) to drink something quickly, usually in one gulp: *Come on, knock it back in one!*

quaff (*old-fashioned or humorous*) to drink an alcoholic drink often in large amounts: *They spent the whole night quaffing wine.*

sip to drink something in small mouthfuls: *delicately sipping sherry.*

slug (*informal*) to take a large mouthful of an alcoholic drink: *slugging whisky from a hip flask.*

swallow to pass liquid from your mouth into your throat and down into your stomach: *Wine tasters don't swallow the wine – they spit it out.*

swig (*informal*) to drink something quickly and in large amounts: *The boys were swigging cans of cola.*

drunk *adjective*
whose behaviour and thinking are affected by having consumed a lot of alcohol: *He was so drunk that he couldn't walk in a straight line.*

inebriated (*formal*) affected by having drunk a lot of alcohol: *Everyone was rather inebriated by the end of the office party.*

intoxicated (*formal*) affected by having drunk a lot of alcohol: *The Tvpresenter appeared to be intoxicated.*

legless (*informal*) extremely drunk, so that you are unable to walk: *He was absolutely legless and had to be helped home.*

over the limit having drunk more alcohol than is legally permitted if you are going to drive: *I will have to leave the car here and take a taxi home because I am over the limit.*

paralytic (*informal*) extremely drunk so that you are unable to move: *Kevin got paralytic and fell asleep at the bar.*

smashed (*informal*) extremely drunk: *A group of teenage girls staggered out of a club, absolutely smashed.*

tiddly (*informal*) tipsy: *My aunt was quite tiddly after a couple of glasses of sherry.*

tipsy slightly drunk and usually feeling very cheerful as a result: *We had wine with lunch and I felt a little tipsy.*

duty *noun*
something that you are obliged to do, often as part of your work: *Ordering stationery for the department is one of my duties.*

assignment a task that you are given to do, often as part of your work or studies: *We have to hand in our History assignment tomorrow.*

burden a responsibility that is difficult to cope with: *If Anne gets a part-time job, it will ease the family's financial burden a bit.*

chore a task that has to be done regularly, especially in the home, and that you find tedious: *Cleaning the bathroom is the least favourite of my household chores.*

commission a job, often something creative, that someone has asked you to do for them: *The artist has a commission for a set of six paintings for the new concert hall.*

function the main duty of a person in a particular job: *The function of a teacher is to educate children.*

job a task or duty that you are asked to perform: *The old lady next door wants me to do a couple of little jobs around the house for her.*

responsibility a task that you must do and that you can be blamed or punished for not doing: *It's the caretaker's responsibility to lock up the building for the night.*

task a piece of work that you have to do: *My first task for today is to weed the garden.*

eager *adjective* wanting very much to do or to have something: *I was eager to go home.*

agog expecting or watching something in a state of great excitement: *The children were all agog, waiting for Santa Claus to arrive at the party.*

Only used after a verb.

anxious wanting very much to do or to have something and slightly nervous in case you cannot: *She was anxious to make a good impression on her boyfriend's parents.*

avid very enthusiastically involved in an activity: *She is an avid reader.*

enthusiastic having or showing a great interest in something and very positive feelings about it: *enthusiastic about golf.*

keen wanting very much to do or to

have something: *She is keen to go to university.*

passionate caring very much about a subject or activity: *a passionate skier.*

raring to go (*informal*) very excited about something you are going to do and anxious to start doing it: *I've got my train tickets and now I'm just raring to go.*

zealous strongly committed to a particular cause or religion: *a zealous campaigner for animal rights.*

earn *verb* to receive money in return for work: *He earns £30,000 a year.*

clear (*informal*) to receive a specified amount of money, usually a large sum that you are pleased about, after deduc-tions have been made from your earnings or takings for tax, etc.: *With over-time, I cleared £500 that week.*

gross (usually used in a business

context) to earn a specified amount of money before deductions have been made for tax, etc.: *The film grossed $100 million worldwide.*

make to receive a certain amount of money in wages or salary, or as profit, or when you sell something: *I made a lot more money this year than I did last year.*

net (usually used in a business context) to receive a specified amount of money in profit after deductions have been made for expenses, etc.: *She didn't net enough to have to pay income tax last year.*

take home to receive a specified amount of money after deductions have been made from your earnings for tax, etc.: *The amount he takes home is not enough to support a family.*

easy *adjective*
not difficult to do or to understand, especially because requiring little effort: *That was an easy question.*

cushy (*informal*) that does not involve hard work: *a cushy job.*

effortless carried out with no effort: *He gave a seemingly effortless performance.*

elementary requiring little knowledge and ability to understand, or relating to the most basic facts and principles of a subject: *an elementary course in human biology.*

foolproof impossible or difficult to get wrong: *I'm trying to devise a foolproof method of calculating how much income tax a person owes.*

simple not difficult to do or to understand, especially through not being complicated: *simple arithmetic*.

straightforward not complicated or difficult: *I was worried about finding my way to the hospital, but it was quite straightforward.*

uncomplicated straightforward and easy to do or to understand: *an uncomplicated recipe.*

undemanding requiring little effort to do, understand, or appreciate: *an undemanding film.*

eat *verb*
to put solid food into your mouth and swallow it: *Vegetarians don't eat meat.*

bolt (down) to eat something quickly, especially by swallowing it without chewing it: *Don't bolt your food; you will get indigestion!*

chew to crush food with your teeth: *Some people find that chewing gum helps them to concentrate.*

consume (*formal*) to eat, drink, or use up something: *Members of staff should not consume alcohol while on company premises.*

devour (*formal*) (usually said about an animal or someone who eats like an animal) to eat something greedily: *The lions devoured the carcass of a zebra.*

gobble to eat something quickly and

greedily: *The children were so hungry that they gobbled their food up in no time.*

munch to eat something noisily: *Adam was munching a packet of crisps.*

nibble to take small dainty bites of something: *Kirsty nibbled her sandwich while she worked.*

scoff (*informal*) to eat a large quantity of food quickly and greedily: *I thought I*

had made too much food for the party, but the kids scoffed the lot.

swallow to pass food from your mouth into your throat and down into your stomach: *Some people find it difficult to swallow pills.*

wolf (*informal*) to eat a large quantity of something quickly and greedily: *I felt sick after wolfing a whole box of chocolates.*

eccentric *adjective*
(usually only used about people) rather unusual in behaviour or appearance: *an eccentric old lady who lives with thirty cats.*

idiosyncratic being an unusual trait that a particular person has, but no other person does: *her idiosyncratic style of singing.*

odd different from what is considered normal or ordinary: *His behaviour has been rather odd since his illness.*

peculiar odd: *He has a peculiar way of swinging his arms while he walks.*

quirky unusual in an amusing or interesting way: *a comedian with a quirky outlook on life.*

unconventional not sticking to the ways of doing things that are usual in society: *Maria is unconventional, which is probably why she decided to get married in a red dress.*

wacky (*informal or humorous*) very unusual, or crazy: *All the kids have had problems at school, and some of them are pretty wacky.*

weird very strange, in a puzzling or alarming way: *This way he looked at me was distinctly weird.*

See also **strange**.

empty *adjective*
having nothing or no-one inside: *My glass is empty.*

bare (usually used to describe an enclosed space such as a room, or a shelf) having nothing in it or on it: *The cupboards were bare.*

blank not written on: *a blank page.*

deserted in which there are no people: *a deserted car park.*

hollow having an empty space inside: *a hollow mould.*

unfurnished containing no furniture: *I rented an unfurnished flat.*

uninhabited in or on which no one lives: *an uninhabited island.*

unoccupied not being used or lived in by anybody: *an unoccupied room.*

vacant unoccupied: *This flat is vacant.*

endanger *verb*
to put someone or something in a dangerous position: *People who drink and drive are endangering their own lives and the lives of others.*

compromise to expose something, such as your safety or your beliefs, to danger or damage: *I refuse to compromise my principles in order to fit in with the crowd.*

expose leave someone or something open to danger or harm: *You should not expose your skin to the harmful rays of the sun.*

imperil (*formal*) to put someone or something in danger: *I urge you not to do anything that might imperil the lives of the troops under your command.*

jeopardize (*formal*) to make something likely to fail: *Raymond's infidelity is jeopardizing his marriage.*

put at risk to put someone or something in danger of harm or failure: *By*
smoking during pregnancy, you put your unborn child's health at risk.*

risk to deliberately put yourself or something, such as your life, in danger in order to do something: *The man risked his own life to pull a child out of the way of an oncoming car.*

threaten to put something, such as a relationship, at risk of failing or being harmed: *Andy feels his relationship with Pam is threatened by her obsession with work.*

See also **threaten.**

enemy *noun*
a person who dislikes you and wishes to cause you harm, or a person or force that is opposed to another: *The police discovered that the murdered man had several enemies.*

adversary someone who opposes you in a fight, contest, debate, etc, or something that acts against you: *Ian was less than pleased to see his old adversary from university at the interview.*

antagonist a person who is your adversary, often someone who represents the opposite values to your own: *In certain religions, the Devil is the antagonist of God.*

foe (*literary*) an enemy: *Dictatorship is the foe of democracy.*

opponent someone playing against you in a sporting contest or opposing you in a situation similar to a sporting contest: *The heavyweight champion defeated his opponent in the third round.*

the opposition the people, or sometimes the person, opposing you, especially a party opposing a government in a parliament: *Before entering any contest, you should try to gauge the strength of the opposition.*

rival someone with whom you compete for something: *Ewan and Jamal are rivals for Abbie's affections.*

entertain *verb*

to do something that makes people laugh or something that gives them pleasure, such as singing or dancing: *A group of children went to the nursing home to entertain the residents.*

amuse to make someone laugh or keep them occupied in an enjoyable way: *There was a clown at the party to amuse the children.*

delight to give someone pleasure or enjoyment: *The speaker delighted the audience with her tales of life as a cabaret singer.*

divert (*old-fashioned*) amuse someone: *The company was diverted by the ladies playing the piano and singing.*

enthral to hold someone's attention and interest for a long time in an enjoyable way: *The actress's great beauty enthralled the audience.*

interest to attract someone's attention and give them something to think about: *I found an article in the newspaper that might interest you.*

regale to provide people with something, especially interesting and enjoyable stories: *The old sailor regaled us with tales of his naval exploits.*

tickle (*informal*) to make someone laugh: *Your sense of humour really tickles me.*

See also **game; interesting.**

err *verb* (*formal*)

to make a mistake, or to do wrong: *He admitted that he had erred in the past.*

be mistaken to be wrong about something: *I thought the last train was at 11 pm, but I was mistaken.*

blunder make a stupid mistake: *I really blundered this morning when I called Tim's new girlfriend by his ex-wife's name.*

boob (*informal*) to make a stupid mistake: *Oops, I've boobed again; that was the wrong number I gave you.*

go wrong to make a mistake and arrive at a bad result, for example in trying to solve a problem or in dealing with people: *Parents whose children end up in serious trouble often ask themselves where they went wrong.*

miscalculate to count or estimate something incorrectly: *I miscalculated how long it would take to drive to Newcastle.*

misunderstand to take the wrong meaning out of what someone has said: *You misunderstood me. I wasn't arguing with you; I am on your side.*

slip up (*informal*) to make a silly or unimportant mistake: *Chris slipped up when he posted his application form without signing it.*

escape *verb*

to get away from a place, especially from captivity: *A lion has escaped from the zoo.*

abscond (*formal*) to leave a place, often after committing a crime or to avoid arrest: *The company treasurer absconded with the funds.*

bolt to run away quickly and suddenly: *Someone opened the front door, and the dog bolted.*

break out get away from a place where you are being kept as a prisoner or are surrounded by enemy forces: *A convicted murderer has broken out of prison.*

flee to run away, especially from an unpleasant situation: *Sally fled to her parents' house to escape an abusive marriage.*

113

get away to leave a difficult or unpleasant situation: *Graham joined the army to get away from a boring job.*

leg it (*informal*) to run away fast: *Here come the cops – quick, leg it!*

run away to leave a place by running, or to escape from a threatening or unpleasant situation: *Lisa ran away from home to avoid an unhappy environment.*

See also **avoid**.

eternal *adjective*
lasting for ever: *a quest for eternal life.*

ceaseless (*formal*) going on for a long time without stopping: *his ceaseless complaining.*

everlasting lasting for ever, or for the rest of your life: *everlasting love.*

immortal living for ever, never dying: *A god is an immortal being.*

infinite having no end or no limits: *infinite time.*

limitless having no limits or no restrictions: *for a limitless period.*

perpetual lasting for ever, or going on for a long time without stopping: *perpetual youth.*

undying (usually used to describe a feeling) never ceasing or lessening: *undying admiration.*

unending going on for a long time without coming to an end: *a subject of unending fascination.*

See also **continuous**.

event *noun*
something that happens, especia lly something important: *a momentous event in history.*

episode an event or a period of time occurring in the course a longer period: *That was a shameful episode in my past.*

experience something that happens to you: *The train crash was a terrifying experience.*

happening something that happens, especially something unusual: *Police asked local residents if they had been aware of any unusual happenings in recent weeks.*

incident something that happens at a particular time, especially something unpleasant: *a violent incident.*

occasion an organized event, especially a celebration of some kind: *a grand occasion, like a coronation.*

occurrence something that happens, usually something quite ordinary that may be repeated: *Mislaying my keys is practically an everyday occurrence.*

examination *noun*
a test of someone's knowledge or skill, especially in school, college, or university: *I failed my history examination.*

assessment a judgment of someone's progress, for example on a course of study: *Instead of an end-of-term exam we have continuous assessment of classwork.*

exam (*informal*) an examination: *I passed all my exams!*

interrogation a situation in which someone, especially someone acting in an official capacity, for example a police officer, asks someone else a series of probing questions: *The police conducted an interrogation of the murder suspect.*

oral (*informal*) a spoken, rather than written, examination: *We have our Spanish oral tomorrow.*

paper a piece of paper with questions on it, as part of an examination: *The first maths paper was easy but the second one was difficult.*

quiz a set of questions and answers, usually spoken, to test people's knowledge, as a competition: *The local pub holds a quiz night every Thursday.*
In US English a *quiz* often means a *test* of school students' knowledge of a particular subject.

test a method of assessing someone's knowledge or skill: *I am practising for my driving test.*

excellent *adjective*
extremely good: *We had an excellent meal at the new restaurant.*

brilliant (*informal*) extremely good or enjoyable: *I had a brilliant holiday.*

exceptional of an unusually high standard: *an exceptional athlete.*

exemplary setting a good example for other people: *The conduct of the police officers dealing with the incident was exemplary.*

fantastic (*informal*) extremely good or enjoyable: *Lorraine has got a fantastic new job.*

first-rate of the highest possible standard: *a first-rate crime writer.*

great (*informal*) extremely good or very enjoyable: *I had a great time at the party.*

marvellous (*informal*) extremely good or enjoyable: *a marvellous singer.*

outstanding of exceptionally high quality: *an outstanding performance.*

terrific (*informal*) extremely good or enjoyable: *We had a terrific time at the wedding.*

wonderful extremely good or enjoyable: *a wonderful painting.*

excited *adjective*
full of a lively, bubbly, happy feeling, often because of something good that is going to happen: *The little boy was so excited about meeting his soccer hero.*

animated acting, talking, or done in a lively and excited way: *After a couple of glasses of wine, Jill became very animated.*

exhilarated feeling very happy and as if you have much more life and energy than you usually do: *I felt quite exhilarated when we reached the top of the mountain.*

high (*informal*) exhilarated or in a dreamlike happy state, usually as a result of taking drugs or alcohol: *They were high on Ecstasy.*

hyper (*informal*) overexcited and very active, sometimes as a result of a medical condition or of taking drugs or alcohol: *Little Scott was totally hyper yesterday, running around and yelling nonstop.*

overwrought extremely nervous and out of control of your emotions: *Please excuse Alison's behaviour last night – she was a little overwrought.*

thrilled very happy and excited: *I was thrilled to visit the Parthenon.*

worked up extremely nervous and overemotional: *She tends to get all worked up about animal rights.*

exclusive *adjective*
restricted to rich people or people of high social standing: *an exclusive yacht club.*

classy (*informal*) having or showing good taste and sophistication: *She was wearing a simple but classy black suit.*

elite belonging to a group of people considered special or privileged: *elite troops.*

fashionable stylish and favoured by people of high social standing: *a fashionable area.*

high-class of superior quality: *a high-class establishment.*

posh (*informal*) smart and expensive: *a posh frock.*

select specially chosen: *just for the select few.*

up-market intended for people who are rich or of high social standing: *an up-market restaurant.*

See also **fashionable.**

expect *verb*
to be fairly certain that something is going to happen or that you are going to get something: *I am expecting a parcel in the post.*

anticipate to realize that something is likely to happen: *Joe had not anticipated such a strong negative reaction to his proposal.*

await to wait for something to happen: *I await confirmation of the booking.*

bank on to be confident that something is going to happen: *I am banking on getting your support.*

hope for to want something to happen or to get something: *The farmers are hoping for rain.*

look forward to to be happy about something that is going to happen: *We are really looking forward to going on holiday.*

See also **hope.**

explain *verb*
to give information about something that makes it easier to understand: *Ray explained the filing system to the new member of staff.*

clarify to make a statement clearer by giving further information: *Can you clarify what you meant in this first paragraph?*

define to describe the meaning of a word or phrase: *This dictionary defines over 100,000 words.*

describe to state what someone or something is like: *This author has often been described as a genius.*

elaborate to give further details about something, such as a proposal or a statement: *Can you elaborate on this suggestion?*

enlighten (*formal*) to make someone understand something better by giving more information: *Will someone please enlighten me as to how to operate the fax machine?*

interpret to explain the underlying meaning of something, such as a statement or a work of art, as you understand it: *I interpreted Matthew's words as a threat.*

shed light on to make something easier to understand by giving more information: *Can you shed any light on how the DVD player got broken?*

F

fail *verb*
to be unsuccessful in an examination or an endeavour: *If you don't work hard, you will fail your exams.*

bomb (*informal*) to be extremely unsuccessful, especially in the theatre: *The play bombed in the West End.*

collapse fail suddenly and completely: *The pay negotiations collapsed when neither side would concede anything.*

come to grief to end in disaster: *The*

boating trip came to grief when the boat capsized.

fall through to fail to be achieved: *Our plans for a skiing holiday fell through.*

flop (*informal*) to be unsuccessful: *The band's first single flopped.*

flunk (*informal*) fail an examination or test: *Kay flunked her driving theory test.* Common in US English, but not very common in British English.

founder to end unsuccessfully: *Their marriage foundered after only 6 months.*

go pear-shaped (*informal*) to go disastrously wrong: *United were in the lead but it all went a bit pear-shaped in the second half and they ended up 3-1 down.*

fair *adjective*
treating people properly and equally: *If I pay for lunch today and you pay tomorrow, that will be fair.*

dispassionate not affected by your own emotions: *As a jury member, you must be dispassionate when reaching your decision.*

even-handed treating everyone equally: *Teachers must be even-handed in their treatment of the children.*

impartial without bias: *an impartial judge.*

just morally right and proper: *a just punishment.*

kosher (*informal*) generally considered to be right or acceptable: *a kosher excuse.*

objective not affected by personal feelings, preferences, or prejudices: *an objective opinion.*

reasonable sensible and proper: *a reasonable solution.*

right in accordance with justice, morality, or good treatment of other people: *You shouldn't make fun of people because of their disabilities: it's just not right.*

unbiased not affected by your own interests: *an unbiased account of events.*

faithful *adjective*
not changing your feelings towards someone or doing anything that will have a harmful effect on the good relationship you have with them: *a faithful friend.*

constant (*literary*) remaining the same, especially in your love or friendship for someone: *constant in his loyalty.*

loyal faithful, especially in your friendship with someone or in the support you give to a superior or a cause: *Her Majesty's loyal subjects.*

staunch never wavering in your support: *a staunch supporter of feminism.*

steadfast firmly loyal and supportive, especially in difficult situations: *steadfast support.*

true faithful or loyal: *The party remains true to the principles established by its founders.*
Usually used after a verb in this sense.

unswerving (*literary*) never changing its nature, or never changing your feelings, whatever happens: *unswerving loyalty.*

See also **devoted; reliable; true**.

fall *verb*
to move downwards towards the ground or a lower level, or to go from a standing position to a position on the ground, usually accidentally: *The old man fell down the stairs.*

collapse to fall down, especially in a faint: *The heat and lack of air in the shop caused a girl to collapse.*

drop to move downwards, especially suddenly: *The apple dropped off the tree.*

plunge to fall fast and dramatically, usually from a considerable height, either towards the ground or into water: *I heard a shot and saw a bird plunge towards the ground.*

sink to move downwards quite slowly, either towards the ground or under water: *A stone hit the boy in the head and he sank to the ground.*

topple to become unsteady and fall over: *The vase toppled over and smashed on the floor.*

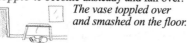

trip to stumble over an object or an unevenness in the ground and, sometimes, fall over: *Granny tripped over a toy car and broke her hip.*

tumble to fall in an untidy way or head over heels: *The child tumbled down the stairs and landed on her head.*

false *adjective*
not true or not correct, often deliberately changed from what is true or correct in order to deceive people: *false information.*

deceptive giving a false impression, sometimes deliberately: *a deceptive smile.*

erroneous (*formal*) incorrect: *an erroneous translation of a Hebrew word.*

inaccurate not conforming exactly to fact, reality, or the actual state of affairs: *an inaccurate description.*

incorrect containing or based on a mistake: *an incorrect answer.*

misleading encouraging people to believe something that is untrue or incorrect: *a misleading statement.*

mistaken involving a failure to understand or recognize what something or someone really is: *a case of mistaken identity.*

untrue not true or not factual: *The story he told me about his father being a millionaire proved to be untrue.*

wrong different from the one that you should have chosen, taken, etc.: *We took the wrong turning off the motorway.*

See also **artificial; dishonest**.

famous *adjective*
known to a lot of people now, or still remembered, for being very good at something or very successful or extraordinary: *a famous pop star.*

celebrated well-known and admired, especially for being very talented: *a celebrated concert pianist.*

distinguished greatly admired and respected: *a distinguished military career.*

eminent important and highly respected, especially in a certain type of work: *an eminent neurosurgeon.*

great very well known and highly respected: *the great Surrealist painter, Salvador Dali.*

illustrious (*formal*) (used mainly to refer to people whose fame or good reputation has survived for a long time) famous: *a member of an illustrious Italian family.*

infamous well-known for a very bad reason: *the infamous Acid Bath Murderer.*

legendary having been extremely well-known for a long time: *the legendary reggae star Bob Marley.*

notable important or interesting because of a certain characteristic: *Venice is notable for its canals.*

noted well-known because of a certain characteristic: *He is noted for his dry sense of humour.*

notorious well-known for a bad reason: *a notorious womanizer.*

renowned (*formal*) well-known and admired for a certain skill or characteristic: *a renowned story-teller.*

well-known known to a lot of people: *a well-known television personality.*

See also **popular**.

fashion *noun*
a style of dress or behaviour that is popular at a particular time: *the fashion for shoulder pads in the 1980s.*

craze something that is extremely popular with a great many people, but whose popularity only lasts for a short time and which may not be a very sensible idea: *Why is there this sudden craze for riding tricycles?*

fad a particular activity, product, etc., that is very popular, but usually only for a short time, and often because people think that it is good for them: *the latest fad in diets.*

style a manner of dress, furnishings, etc., that is considered elegant or is popular at a particular time: *She is always dressed in the latest style.*

trend a style of dress or an activity that is in the process of becoming popular or widespread: *The trend is for more and more people to take two holidays a year.*

vogue a style of dress, music, etc., that is popular at a particular time: *Punk rock was in vogue in the late 1970s.*

fashionable *adjective*
popular at a particular time: *a fashionable nightclub.*

all the rage (*informal*) very fashionable for a short time: *Reality Tv is all the rage these days.*

chic fashionable, elegant and tasteful: *a chic trouser suit.*

cool (*informal*) considered stylish and attractive, especially by young people: *He was wearing cool shades.*

designer made by a fashionable designer: *She wouldn't be seen in anything other than designer clothes.*
Only used before a noun.

elegant attractive, stylish, and tasteful, whether or not it is fashionable by current standards: *She was wearing an elegant ivory silk evening dress.*

hip (*informal*) conforming to the latest fashions for young people in clothing, music, etc.: *a hip new band.*

in (*informal*) currently very popular and fashionable: *the in thing in sportswear.*

modern in a style that is currently popular and that looks up to date: *a very modern kitchen.*

sharp (*informal*) very smart and elegant: *a businessman in a sharp suit.*

stylish having or showing a sense of style and elegance: *Alison is a very stylish woman – whatever she wears always looks just right.*

trendy (*informal*) conforming to the latest fashions: *I've got a trendy new watch.*

See also **exclusive.**

fast *adverb*
at great speed: *I ran as fast as I could.*

briskly at a fairly vigorous pace: *Walking briskly is very good exercise.*

hastily fast because you have little time in which to do something or because you realize that something is urgent: *I hastily packed my bags and ordered a taxi to take me to the airport.*

hurriedly hastily and sometimes carelessly: *I hurriedly wrote a covering letter and posted it, forgetting to enclose the cheque.*

like a shot (*informal*) very fast, or without delay: *Alan will be out of there like a shot if you ask him to help with the washing-up.*

promptly without delay: *Thank you for replying so promptly to my letter.*

pronto (*informal*) quickly, or immediately: *Go to your room and do your homework - pronto!*

quickly fast or in a very short time: *The children finished their breakfast quickly so that they could go out to play.*

rapidly (usually used when describing processes that continue or develop over a period of time) at a fast speed or rate: *I am rapidly going off him.*

swiftly (usually used when describing movement) fast: *moving swiftly on to the next topic.*
See also **quick.**

fat *adjective*
having too much flesh on your body: *If you eat too much, you will get fat.*

chubby (*informal*) slightly fat and rounded: *chubby cheeks.*

flabby (*informal*) having a lot of soft, loose excess flesh: *I'm getting flabby since I stopped going to the gym.*

obese (often used to describe people whose weight causes medical problems for them) extremely fat: *He is so obese that he can't walk far without a rest.*

overweight weighing too much relative to your height: *The doctor said I was a little overweight and he's put me on a diet.*

plump slightly fat and rounded: *the baby's plump little arms.*

podgy (*informal*) having a lot of excess flesh: *He's looking a bit podgy around the middle.*

rotund (*formal*) having a very fat, rounded body: *a rotund elderly gentleman.*

stout having a fat and rather solid body: *a stout matronly figure.*

tubby (*informal*) having a fat body: *You wouldn't think Dave was once a tubby teenager.*

favourite *adjective*
that you like best: *my favourite film.*

beloved (often used humorously and usually about other people) that someone is very or excessively fond of: *He won't go anywhere without his beloved pipe.*

best that you are fonder of than any other: *my best friend.*

chosen singled out for special attention: *The other members of staff think Kate is the manager's 'chosen one' because she seems to get privileges that they don't get.*

dearest that you are very fond of or want more than anything else: *It has always been my dearest wish to see you happily married.*

pet that someone is particularly or excessively interested in: *You've got him started on his pet subject again.*

preferred that you always or usually use when you have a choice: *E-mail is my preferred method of communication.*

special that you are particularly fond of: *Dorothy is a very special friend of mine.*

fear *noun*

an unpleasant feeling caused the sense that you are in danger or might be hurt: *Isabelle always travels by train because she has a fear of flying.*

awe a feeling of wonder or great respect, mixed with fear, caused usually by someone or something much bigger or more powerful than you: *Most of the children were in awe of the head teacher.*

dread a strong feeling of anxiety about something that may happen: *Elizabeth was filled with dread at the prospect of her in-laws coming to stay.*

fright a sudden feeling of intense fear: *I got such a fright when a face suddenly appeared at the window.*

horror a feeling of fear mixed with strong dislike: *Mark has a horror of clowns.*

panic an acute feeling of fear and anxiety, often one that spreads through a number of people and makes them act uncontrollably: *The explosion caused panic in the streets.*

phobia an unreasonable and uncontrollable fear of something: *a phobia about spiders.*

scare (*informal*) a fright, or something that causes people to feel frightened: *Sylvia had a cancer scare last year, but the lump turned out to be benign.*

terror extreme fear: *The villagers gazed at the monster in sheer terror.*

See also **afraid; anxiety**.

feeling *noun*

a sensation inside you that may be definable as, for example, love or anger or may be vague: *He couldn't hide his feelings of frustration.*

emotion a definite feeling, such as love or anger, that is usually quite strong: *Jealousy is a very destructive emotion.*

instinct a strong feeling that seems to arise spontaneously and is not easy to explain in rational terms: *I just had an instinct that he was not to be trusted.*

intuition an idea or insight that seems to arise spontaneously and is not the result of conscious thought: *I had an intuition that all was not well in their relationship.*

passion strong emotion: *She always sings with passion.*

sense a feeling of something or that something is the case: *Jenny felt a sense of loss when her best friend emigrated.*

sentiment a particular feeling towards someone else that someone expresses: *The sentiments expressed in the card touched my heart.*

See also **opinion.**

few *adjective*
not many: *Very few people applied for the job.*

infrequent which does not happen often: *our infrequent phone calls.*

insufficient not enough: *an insufficient number of votes to win the election.*

meagre small or insufficient in quantity: *meagre rations.*

precious few very few indeed: *Precious few people offered to help.*

scarce in short supply: *Bananas were scarce during the Second World War.*

sparse small in number and spread out: *sparse trees.*

thin on the ground (*informal*) sparse, or existing in small numbers only: *Television sets were thin on the ground in the early 1950s.*

fight *noun*
a struggle, either physical or verbal, between people, groups, or armed forces: *There was a fight between supporters of the rival teams.*

battle a fight between armed forces during a war, or an attempt to do or achieve something that involves overcoming opposition of some kind: *They won the battle but lost the war.*

bout an organized fight between two contestants in a sport such as boxing or wrestling: *the heavyweight title bout.*

brawl a disorganized physical struggle in which people hit and kick each other: *a drunken brawl.*

fisticuffs (*old-fashioned or humorous*) a physical struggle in which people punch each other: *The argument ended in fisticuffs.*

scrap (*informal*) a minor physical fight:

two boys having a scrap in the playground.

scuffle a physical fight of short duration: *A scuffle broke out outside the nightclub.*

skirmish a minor battle during a war: *There were several border skirmishes between the two countries over disputed territory.*

See also **argument; disagree; oppose; quarrel**.

fill *verb*
to make something, such as a container or a room, full: *We filled our water bottles from the stream.*

cram to force a lot of things into a tight space, or to fill a space with more things than it can comfortably hold: *I crammed my bag full of books.*

gorge to overfill yourself with food: *The children gorged themselves on party food.*

jam to force something into a space or container that is really too small for it: *She tried to jam even more clothes into her already bulging suitcase.*

load to put objects into a container or a vehicle: *I loaded the boot with rubbish to be taken to the dump.*

pack put clothes and other belongings into a container, such as a suitcase or bag, before you travel somewhere: *I packed some essentials into an overnight bag.*

replenish (*formal*) to restock something, such as a food cupboard or a refrigerator: *After our house guests left, we had to replenish our food stocks.*

stock to put goods into a shop to be sold, or into something such as a cupboard for storage: *The stationery cupboard is fully stocked.*

stuff to put large quantities of something into a container or your mouth: *Kyle stuffed a handful of peanuts into his mouth.*

find *verb*

to come upon someone or something that is lost, either by accident or after looking for them: *I found my other sock in the laundry basket.*

come across to find someone or something by chance: *I was looking for my birth certificate and came across my old school photographs.*

detect to discover the presence of something, such as an illness or radiation, by using sensitive equipment or a test: *The cervical smear test is used to detect precancerous cells.*

discover to find something, such as a place or scientific information, especially something that has not been previously known or that has been hidden: *Christopher Columbus is said to have discovered America in 1492.*

ferret out (*informal*) to discover

something by searching hard for it, especially in places where you might not usually look: *A journalist ferreted out the names of the politician's former lovers.*

locate (*formal*) to discover the whereabouts of someone or something: *Police are trying to locate the owner of a blue car that was seen near the scene of the crime.*

stumble across to discover something by accident, often while looking for something else: *I stumbled across your phone number while looking for the health centre's number.*

track down to find someone or something by searching thoroughly: *Melanie would not rest until she had tracked down her birth mother.*

uncover to discover something, especially information that has been hidden or kept secret: *The police have uncovered vital evidence that may lead to the identification of the murderer.*

finish *verb* to bring something to an end, or reach the end of something: *Have you finished your homework yet?*

close to bring an action or an event to a formal end: *We shall close the service with a hymn.*

complete to bring something to an end after doing all that has to be done: *I have almost completed my first novel.*

conclude bring an event or an action to an end, or to be the final item in something: *They concluded the concert with a song performed by the whole cast.*

end to stop something from continuing, or to show that something is finished or complete: *You should end a formal letter with 'Yours faithfully'.*

finalize to put something such as a plan or arrangement into its final and definite form: *We have finalized the wedding arrangements.*

round off (*informal*) to bring something to to a satisfying end in a specified manner: *We rounded off the party with a good old singsong.*

terminate (*formal*) to bring something, such as an action or agreement, to an end: *The team manager's contract has been terminated.*

wrap up (*informal*) to complete

something, such as a meeting or an agreement: *I'm hoping we can wrap up the meeting quickly, as I want to leave early today.*

See also **stop**.

fix *verb*
to work on something that is broken or not functioning properly in order to bring it back into a satisfactory condition: *The heating engineer fixed our central heating.*

correct to put right an error or a fault: *Would you read over my letter and correct any spelling mistakes before I post it?*

mend to make a usually small repair to something, especially something in the home, that is broken or torn: *Richard's mother mended the split in his trousers.*

overhaul check something thoroughly and make large-scale repairs or changes to something so that it functions properly: *It's no good tinkering with the system, it needs to be completely overhauled.*

patch to mend a hole or a worn part in a garment by putting a small piece of material over it: *I have patched the hole in my sleeve.*

patch up (*informal*) to repair something hastily or temporarily: *I've patched up the heating system so that it will work for the rest of the winter, but it actually needs a complete overhaul.*

rectify (*formal*) put right a mistake or an injustice: *Your name had been left off the list, but that error has now been rectified.*

renovate to repair and redecorate an

old building so that it meets modern standards: *Now the block of flats has been renovated, the residents* have to pay a higher rent.

repair to work on something that is broken or not functioning properly in order to bring it back into a satisfactory condition: *I have taken my car into the garage to have the suspension repaired.*

restore to return something, usually something valuable such as a historic building or an old piece of furniture, to its former condition: *The French polisher*

restored the old scratched table so that it looked as good as new.

See also **decide**.

follow *verb*
to go after a person or vehicle, in the same direction: *Follow that car!*

chase to run after someone in order to try to catch them: *The man chased the thief and caught him.*

hound to follow someone openly, persistently, and in a way that makes them feel harassed, usually in order to get information from them: *The press hounded the couple constantly.*

pursue (*formal*) to go after someone in order to try to catch them or track them down: *After pursuing him for several years, the police finally tracked down the terrorist.*

shadow to follow someone in secret: *The detective shadowed the murder suspect in the hope of gathering evidence.*

stalk to harass someone by following

them persistently: *A man was arrested for stalking his ex-girlfriend.*

tail (*informal*) to follow someone who is under suspicion in order to watch what they do: *She had a private investigator tail her erring husband.*

track to try to find a person or an animal by following their tracks: *The hunters tracked the lion by its prints.*

See also **observe; understand.**

fool *noun* a person who lacks intelligence or common sense: *He was a fool to believe she would change her ways.*

buffoon (*old-fashioned*) a person whose behaviour is ridiculous: *The man is a blustering buffoon.*

clown (*informal*) a stupid or ineffectual person: *Those clowns at the dry-cleaners ruined my best suit!*

dunce someone who is unintelligent generally or who is not good at a particular subject: *I'm such a dunce when it comes to computers.*

idiot (often used humorously) a stupid or foolish person: *Don't be an idiot; of course you're not in the way!*

ignoramus (*formal*) an ignorant person: *She is such an ignoramus; she thought Paris was the capital of Spain.*

imbecile a very stupid or foolish person: *Only an imbecile would shoot himself in the foot.*

laughing stock someone that people laugh at because of their foolish or strange behaviour: *He has made himself a laughing stock with his obsessive behaviour.*

moron (often used as a very rude insult) a very stupid or worthless person: *Some moron has desecrated my father's grave.*

twit (*informal*) a rather stupid or fool-

ish person: *I've been a bit of a twit and locked my keys inside the car.*

forgive *verb*
set aside feelings or anger or resentment towards someone who has upset you or done something wrong; not hold something against someone: *She never forgave her mother for having her adopted.*

absolve to declare that someone is not to blame for some wrongdoing, or to declare that someone's sins have been forgiven: *The social-work department was absolved of all blame for the child's tragic death.*

condone to find nothing wrong with an action that most other people regard as being wrong: *If you don't speak out*

against their actions, it may look as if you condone them.

excuse not to blame someone for doing wrong or condemn their wrongdoing, or to provide an explanation for someone's wrongdoing that makes it seem less bad: *I know she was upset about splitting up with her boyfriend, but that doesn't excuse her terrible behaviour.*

exonerate (*formal*) to declare that

someone is not guilty of any wrongdoing: *The pedestrian's death was declared an accident and the driver was completely exonerated.*

let off to decide not to punish someone for something wrong that they have done: *The police let the boy off with a caution since it was the first time he had been in trouble.*

overlook to decide not to punish something wrong that someone has done: *I'm prepared to overlook your lateness this time, but don't let it happen again.*

pardon to forgive someone for some wrongdoing, or, more specifically, to officially declare that someone who has been found guilty of a crime will not, or will no longer, be punished for it: *Pardon my rudeness; I should have introduced you two.*

turn a blind eye to to pretend not to notice someone's wrongdoing, perhaps in order to avoid having to do something about it: *Marion seems to be prepared to turn a blind eye to her husband's affairs as long as he comes home to her.*

See also **mercy.**

fortunate *adjective*
having good luck: *They are in the fortunate position of having no money worries.*

fortuitous (*formal*) happening by chance, and usually having beneficial results: *Our meeting again after so many years was completely fortuitous.*

happy happening by good luck: *a happy coincidence.*

lucky having or bringing good fortune: *the lucky winner of the prize draw.*

opportune giving someone an opportunity to do something: *He just happened to appear on the scene at an opportune moment.*

privileged having certain advantages over other people, especially those of wealth or social standing: *She was in the privileged position of being able to choose whether she wanted to work or not.*

providential (*formal*) happening by chance and having very beneficial results: *the providential discovery of some ancient artifacts.*

See also **happy.**

frank *adjective*
speaking openly and honestly: *a frank admission of guilt.*

blunt honest and open, almost to the point of rudeness: *Many people find Colin's blunt manner off-putting.*

candid speaking openly, especially about private or intimate matters: *a candid autobiography.*

direct going straight to the point: *The interviewer was very direct in his line of questioning.*

forthright saying what you think openly and forcefully, even if it may hurt another person's feelings: *My best friend is very forthright but I know I can rely on her to tell me the truth.*

open not holding back information: *The actress gave a very open and honest interview about her breakdown.*

outspoken expressing your opinions freely and forcefully: *She is very outspoken on the subject of benefits cheats.*

straightforward direct and without being evasive: *a straightforward reply.*

up-front (*informal*) very open and direct in expressing your views or intentions: *He is very up-front about the fact that he is motivated by money.*

See also **sincere.**

free

1 *adjective* costing nothing: *a free gift with the magazine.*

complimentary which you do not have to pay for: *complimentary tickets for the game.*

on the house offered free by a business such as a pub or restaurant: *These drinks are on the house.*

unpaid done without being paid in return: *unpaid voluntary work.*

2 *adverb* without paying anything, or without charging anything: *My bus pass allows me to travel free.*

for nothing (*informal*) free, especially without being paid: *You can't expect the man to work for nothing.*

gratis (*formal*) free: *Refreshments are provided gratis to members of the club.*

without charge without expecting to be paid: *The gardener offered his services without charge to his elderly neighbour.*

See also **release.**

friend *noun*
someone that you like and have a close relationship with: *Becky and Sapna have been friends since university.*

acquaintance someone that you know, but not very well: *He is not so much a friend of mine as a passing acquaintance.*

ally someone who is on your side when there is difference of opinion: *Andrew was my only ally when all the others ganged up against me.*

buddy (*informal*) a friend, especially a senior school pupil who befriends and looks after a younger pupil: *Rachel has been asked to be a buddy to one of the first-year girls.*

chum (*old-fashioned*) a close friend: *I'm going to visit an old school chum.*

companion a person who is with you when you go somewhere or do something: *Those two are constant companions.*

comrade a friend or companion, especially one with whom you have shared a difficult experience: *The two old men were army comrades in the Second World War.*

mate a friend or companion, especially a male friend of a man: *Adam's at the pub with his mates.*

pal (*informal*) a close friend: *He's acting as if he is my best pal, just because he wants me to do him a favour.*

frighten *verb*
to make someone feel afraid: *The big dog that lives next door frightens me.*

alarm to make someone feel worried or afraid, usually about something that might happen in the future: *I don't want to alarm you, but we are almost out of petrol and it's a long way to the next filling station.*

intimidate to deliberately make someone feel afraid, usually so that they will do what you want: *They try to intimidate the younger children by threatening to beat them up after school.*

panic to make a person or a group of people act uncontrollably because they are afraid: *The sound of gunfire panicked the crowd into fleeing in all directions.*

petrify to make someone feel so afraid that they are temporarily unable to move: *The sight of a snake in the house completely petrified me.*

scare to make someone feel suddenly afraid or worried: *The sound of fireworks scares cats and dogs.*

startle cause someone to be surprised and mildly afraid: *Oh, you startled me! I didn't realize you were in the room till you spoke*

terrify to make someone very afraid: *Rollercoasters terrify me.*

See also **afraid; fear.**

full *adjective*
having all or most of the space inside taken up: *a full carton of milk.*

chock-a-block (*informal*) completely filled with people or vehicles so that it is very difficult to move about: *The shops were chock-a-block during the sales.*

crowded filled with many people so that it is quite difficult to move about in: *crowded streets.*

jam-packed (*informal*) absolutely packed: *The assembly hall was jam-packed for the school concert.*

loaded carrying a full load: *The loaded tanker was low in the water.*

occupied being used, or having people inside: *All the rooms in the hotel are occupied.*

packed filled with as many people as it can hold: *a packed theatre.*

See also **busy; complete**.

funny *adjective*
that makes you laugh, either intentionally or unintentionally: *a funny story.*

amusing quite funny, usually making you smile rather than laugh loudly: *an amusing anecdote.*

comical unusual in way that is amusing or funny: *She has a comical way of talking.*

droll witty in a slightly unusual way: *He has a very droll sense of humour.*

facetious light-hearted and intended to be amusing: *a facetious comment.*

hilarious extremely funny: *That was the most hilarious film I have ever seen.*

humorous written or performed in a style designed to make people laugh: *a humorous article.*

side-splitting that makes you laugh a lot: *a side-splitting comedy routine.*

witty amusing through using words or describing things in a clever way: *a very witty speaker.*

See also **strange; unusual.**

game *noun*
an activity that people, especially children, take part in for fun, especially one that has rules or involves make-believe: *The children were playing a game of knights and dragons.*

amusement something such as a game that is organized or provided to give people, especially children, some fun: *The hotel doesn't really provide any amusements for the children.*

diversion (*formal*) something that amuses you: *His chief diversion was teasing his workmates.*

entertainment something provided to give people enjoyment: *We set out to see what entertainments the town had to offer.*

hobby an activity that you do for enjoyment in your spare time: *Alan collects stamps as a hobby.*

pastime an activity that you do for enjoyment in your spare time: *Bowling is my favourite pastime.*

play the activity of taking part in games for fun: *We watched the children at play.*

recreation something that you do for amusement or relaxation: *My father's chief recreation is fishing.*

sport a physical activity with rules in which individuals or teams compete against each other: *Taking part in sports keeps you fit.*

gather *verb*
to come together, or to bring people or things together: *A small crowd gathered round the speaker.*

accumulate to acquire a large quantity of something gradually, or to build up into a large quantity gradually: *Over the years they accumulated an impressive art collection.*

amass to acquire a large quantity of something, especially money, gradually: *He amassed a fortune in property development.*

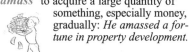

assemble to come together or bring people or things together in an orderly or organized way: *When the fire alarm sounded, the staff evacuated the building and assembled in the car park.*

collect to gather, especially to try to acquire a large number of things of the same type that you have a special interest in: *Brian collects foreign coins.*

congregate (said about people) to come together in one place: *Crowds congregated in the town square to launch the demonstration.*

hoard to build up a store of something, such as food or money, just for yourself: *David is hoarding sweets in a shoebox under his bed.*

round up (*informal*) to gather together a group of people: *Can you round up some parents to help out on the school trip?*

stockpile to build up a store of something, such as food or ammunition, for future use: *The country has been stockpiling chemical and biological weapons.*

general *adjective*
relating to or applied to everything or everyone, not simply to individuals: *There has been a general improvement in exam results this year.*

all-purpose having many uses: *an all-purpose cloth.*

broad covering a wide range of things or ideas: *He's a friend in the broad sense of the word.*

common widely known or shared: *It's common knowledge that their marriage is in trouble.*

comprehensive covering every aspect of something: *a comprehensive survey.*

overall taking everything into account: *My overall impression of him is a good one.*

sweeping applied to all without discrimination: *a sweeping generalization.*

genuine *adjective* exactly what it seems or is supposed to be, and not false or fake: *a genuine Picasso painting.*

authentic genuine, especially in being able to be proved to be what it is supposed to be: *I know it's signed 'Picasso', but is the signature authentic?*

bona fide that can be accepted as a genuine example of the thing specified: *a bona fide rock star.*

legitimate justifiable, or for which there is a good reason: *a legitimate complaint.*

original as it was when it was made, not changed and not a copy: *still in its original condition.*

real actual or genuine, as opposed to apparent or false: *I still don't think we know the real reason why he left.*

true being an excellent example of the thing specified: *He is a true gentleman.*

See also **sincere; true**.

get *verb*
to come into possession of something, either by buying it, finding it, or being given it: *I got a new dress for the party.*

acquire to get something that you did not have before: *I seem to have acquired a red pen – did you leave it on my desk?*

gain to get something that you did not have before or to get more of something that you already have: *Matthew gained a lot of respect when he admitted he had a drink problem and sought help.*

obtain (*formal*) to get something, usually by making an effort: *You can obtain a copy of this leaflet in your local library.*

procure (*formal*) to get something,

usually with difficulty and by making a special effort: *My father has somehow procured tickets for the Cup Final.*

receive to be given something: *I have received a cheque in the post.*

secure (*formal*) to manage to get something, such as a job or a business deal, through effort: *Olivia has secured a place at Birmingham University.*

See also **achieve; buy; understand**.

ghost *noun*

the spirit of a dead person that some people believe they can see: *The Blue Lady is a ghost that is believed to haunt the castle.*

apparition something that appears in a ghostly or spiritual shape: *The girl claimed to have seen an apparition of the Virgin Mary.*

ghoul an evil spirit believed to steal dead bodies from graves and eat their flesh: *a scary film about flesh-eating ghouls.*

phantom a ghost or a ghostly vision: *I woke up in the middle of the night and thought I saw a phantom in the doorway.*

poltergeist a supernatural being that appears to cause disruption, by moving objects or making noises: *My friends moved home because they believed there was a poltergeist in their old house.*

spectre a ghost or a ghostly vision, or an idea or situation that haunts or worries you: *The spectre of death hangs over the starving people.*

spirit a ghost or a supernatural being: *They called in a priest to exorcize their house from evil spirits.*

spook (*informal*) a ghost or a ghostly figure: *The children dressed up as spooks for Hallowe'en.*

gift *noun*

1 something that you give another person, usually for a special occasion, or something that you receive and do not have to pay for: *We all clubbed together to buy a gift for our colleague who was leaving.*

bequest (*formal*) a sum of money or some property that someone leaves to another person when they die: *He made a generous bequest to the niece who had looked after him.*

bonus an additional payment made by an employer, for example to an employee who has done especially good work: *The workers were offered a bonus if they could finish their work ahead of schedule.*

contribution a sum of money that you

give, along with other people, to pay for something: *All the staff made a contribution towards a retirement present for their boss.*

donation a sum of money that you give to a charity: *The singer made a large donation to cancer research.*

grant a sum of money that the government or another organization sometimes gives to help people to pay for something: *The tenants are hoping to get a council grant to help with the cost of their new windows.*

gratuity (*formal*) a tip: *Gratuities are at the discretion of the customer.*

legacy a sum of money or some property that is left to someone in somebody's will: *My grandmother left me a legacy of £1000.*

present a gift given to another person, usually for a special occasion: *I gave my sister a book as a birthday present.*

reward something that you are given in return for a good deed or an achievement: *The boy received a £20 reward for his honesty when he handed in the purse he had found.*

tip a small sum of money that you may give to someone such as a hairdresser or taxi driver, to show that you appreciate what they have done for you: *We gave the taxi driver a good tip because he had helped us with our luggage.*

2 a natural ability to do something very well, especially something artistic or entertaining: *A gift for comedy makes you really popular at school.*

ability the fact of being able to do something, especially to do it well: *Ali has an ability to get on well with most people.*

aptitude an ability to do something easily that many people find difficult: *David has an aptitude for learning languages.*

flair an ability to do something well and with style, especially something artistic: *She has a flair for flower arranging.*

talent an ability to do something very well, especially something artistic, entertaining, or sporty: *Val has a talent for imitating people.*

See also **reward 1.**

give *verb*
to hand or present something to someone: *Dan gave his girlfriend a diamond ring.*

contribute to give something, especially a sum of money, to a common fund: *Would you like to contribute to Jeremy's wedding present?*

donate to give something, such as money or blood, to help other people in need: *Hospitals depend on members of the public donating blood for transfusion to patients.*

furnish (*formal*) to supply someone with what they need for a particular purpose: *I feel unable to comment on this matter until I have been furnished with all the facts.*

hand to put an object that you are holding into someone else's hand: *Would you hand me the remote control, please?*

pass to hand an object to someone across a space: *Please pass the salt.*

present to give someone a gift or an award, especially in a formal presentation: *The band was presented with an award for Best Album.*

provide to make something, especially an essential such as food or shelter, available to someone: *Michael's landlady provides all his meals.*

supply to give someone something that they need, such as materials or equipment: *This catering company supplies many pubs in the city with food.*

go *verb*
to move away from the place where you are, or to move or progress to a particular place or in a particular direction: *Go right at the traffic lights!*

advance to move forward, or to move or progress towards a person or place: *The police marksmen slowly advanced on the besieged building.*

journey (*formal*) to travel a long distance: *Roald Amundsen journeyed from Norway to the South Pole.*

make your way to move towards a particular place: *Please make your way to the dining hall, where refreshments will be served.*

move to change position and progress to a particular place or in a particular direction: *We moved from the back of the cinema to the middle to get a better view.*

pass to move in a particular direction, or from one place or position to another: *We caught a glimpse of the singer as he passed from the hotel into the waiting car.*

proceed (*formal*) to move to a particular place or in a particular direction, especially forwards: *If the fire alarm sounds, proceed in an orderly manner to the nearest fire exit.*

progress (*formal*) to move onwards or forwards: *As we progressed along the coast road, we passed through several picturesque fishing villages.*

travel to go on a journey, usually a fairly long one: *The group of students travelled across Europe by train.*

walk to go somewhere on foot, usually at a fairly leisurely pace: *As it was a beautiful day, I left the car at home and walked to work.*

See also **travel; work 3.**

good *adjective*

1 having or showing high moral standards: *good deeds.*

moral committing acts that are generally considered morally right: *Ian is a very moral man, who always tries to do the right thing.*

noble having or showing honour and generosity of spirit: *Sharing the prize with his helpers was a noble gesture.*

virtuous having high moral values, especially in sexual matters: *a virtuous young woman.*

2 having or likely to have positive results, for example for your health: *Eating lots of fruit is supposed to be good for you.*

advantageous likely to help you do or get what you want: *It would be very advantageous to you to have him on your side.*

beneficial improving your position or your health: *the beneficial effects of exercise.*

favourable likely to help you or bring positive results: *You'll never get a more favourable opportunity to put your plan into action.*

propitious (*formal*) likely to bring positive results in the future: *The circumstances seemed propitious for the launch of a new commercial venture.*

rewarding giving you a sense of satisfaction: *a rewarding job.*

See also **appropriate; decent; excellent; kind 1; nice.**

grand *adjective*
large and splendidly decorated so as to seem suitable for very solemn or high-class occasions: *the grand staircase.*

imposing impressive through being tall or high up and making you feel rather small in comparison: *There was a very imposing archway at the entrance to the house.*

impressive having a strong effect on you and making you admire it: *The singer made an impressive debut.*

magnificent impressive in scale or beauty: *a magnificent view.*

majestic very impressive and dignified in appearance or manner: *That big black horse is a really majestic animal.*

palatial large and luxurious, like a palace: *a palatial home.*

regal noble and dignified, like a king or queen: *The mayor has a very regal air about her.*

splendid impressively beautiful and usually quite colourful and showy: *a splendid array of flowers.*

stately moving in a slow, graceful and dignified manner: *The royal couple continued their stately progress up the aisle of the cathedral.*

See also **beautiful**.

grateful *adjective*
knowing that someone has done for you and having friendly feelings towards them and wanting to thank them: *We were very grateful to the doctors and nurses who took care of our father.*

appreciative showing that you like or approve of something that someone has done for you or given to you: *an appreciative audience.*

beholden feeling that you owe someone something because they have done something to you, and often resenting the fact: *I won't accept his help because I don't want to be beholden to him.*

glad pleased and thankful: *I'm just glad to be out of that terrible situation.*

indebted owing a debt of gratitude to someone: *We are indebted to everyone who has supported us through this difficult period.*

obliged (*formal*) grateful to someone for something that they have done for you: *I am much obliged to you for all your assistance and support.*

thankful pleased about something that someone has done for you or something good that has happened to you: *Let's just be thankful that the snowstorm was less severe than predicted.*

greedy *adjective*
wanting to have more of something, especially money or food, than you need: *Don't be greedy with your sweets – share them with your sister.*

acquisitive excessively concerned with acquiring material possessions: *Many young people today are too acquisitive – they see something they like and feel they have to have it.*

avaricious excessively concerned with getting money or possessions and keeping them for yourself: *Tony is too avaricious to give to charity.*

covetous wanting to have something that belongs to someone else: *Will is very covetous of his friend's sports car.*

gluttonous inclined to eat too much and too fast: *It would be gluttonous to eat the whole packet of biscuits.*

grasping acquisitive in a nasty way that usually involves taking things away from other people: *Most people's image of a tax collector is of someone who is mean and grasping.*

insatiable having an appetite for something, especially food or drink, that is almost impossible to satisfy: *You've eaten a whole chicken? You are insatiable!*

materialistic more concerned with having money or material possessions than with spiritual matters or human relationships: *Judy is so materialistic – she only goes out with rich men.*

miserly reluctant to part with any money: *Eric is so miserly, he never buys a round of drinks.*

group *noun*

a number of people or things gathered together or classed together: *A group of children were throwing snowballs at each other.*

band a number of people acting together: *a band of robbers.*

bunch a number of things clustered 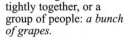 tightly together, or a group of people: *a bunch of grapes.*

class a number of people or things that are regarded as being in the same category because of shared physical, social, or other characteristics: *a member of the upper classes.*

clique a small group of friends or associates who exclude other people: *Megan is lonely at her new school because there are already established cliques and she feels left out.*

gang a group of people who associate together, sometimes for criminal purposes: *A gang of youths ran rampage through the town centre, causing thousands of pounds' worth of damage.*

pack a group wild animals that live together: *a pack of wolves.*

set a number of people, especially people of high social standing, who associate together: *the polo set.*

squad a group of people who work together, especially in the army or police force, or a group of players from whom a team is selected: *the vice squad.*

team a group of people who work together or who play together in a competitive sport: *the international rugby team.*

guard *noun*

someone who is employed to protect people or a place or to prevent a prisoner from escaping: *A woman was stopped by a security guard for shoplifting.*

bodyguard someone who is employed to protect the life of an important person: *The president was accompanied by four huge bodyguards.*

escort someone whose job is to accompany and protect an important person: *The prime minister arrived at the airport with a police escort.*

lifeguard someone who is employed to look after the safety of members of the public at a swimming pool or a beach: *The lifeguard dived in and saved the child from drowning.*

lookout someone who keeps watch, especially while their accomplices are doing something wrong: *One man acted as lookout, while the others broke into the shop.*

night watchman someone who is employed to guard a building, such as a shop or an office building, during the night: *The night watchman caught two men trying to break into the building.*

sentinel (*old-fashioned*) a guard or lookout: *A sentinel was posted at the door of the embassy.*

sentry a soldier who is on duty guarding a particular area, especially the entrance to a building or place: *The sentry prevented an intruder from entering the palace.*

warder someone who is employed to supervise the inmates in a prison: *The warders went round locking the cells up for the night.*

See also **defend**.

guess *verb*

to form an opinion about something, or state what you think is the answer to a question, without having enough information to know for sure: *Guess how much these boots cost.*

assume to suppose that something is the case, without proof: *I just assumed that you two had met before.*

conjecture (*formal*) to guess: *We can only conjecture as to the cause of the accident.*

estimate to calculate a figure or quantity on the basis of a certain amount of information and often in advance of doing something, but without guaranteeing that the calculation is accurate: *The garage estimated that the repair would cost £200.*

reckon to estimate a figure or quantity roughly: *I reckon it's about five kilometres to the nearest supermarket.*

speculate to say what you think will happen without knowing the full facts: *The newspapers are speculating as to when the prime minister might resign.*

surmise (*formal*) to think that something may be the case, based more on intuition than on facts: *He is rather less keen on the idea, I surmise, than she is.*

guide *verb*

to advise and help someone with something that is new to them or difficult for them: *My friend guided me through the installation of my new computer software.*

advise to tell someone what you think they should do about a problem or difficulty: *I would advise you to get a good night's sleep before your exam tomorrow.*

counsel (*formal*) to give someone advice, especially on a serious problem: *A minister of the church sometimes has to counsel parishioners with marital problems.*

govern to be the factor that controls someone's decisions or actions: *Policies have been established to govern the treatment of prisoners.*

influence to persuade someone to act or think in a particularly, either deliberately or because they admire you: *Teenagers are often influenced by their friends' attitudes.*

lead to be the cause of someone's decisions or actions: *What led him to give away all his money?*

recommend to give someone positive advice on which course of action you think they should take: *The doctor recommended that I stop smoking.*

See also **accompany**.

handle *verb*

to touch, hold, or move an object with your hands: *'Please do not handle the merchandise!'*

feel to touch an object or fabric with your hands: *Feel how soft this sweater is.*

finger to touch something with your fingers, sometimes as a nervous reaction: *He kept fingering his tie nervously during the interview.*

fondle to touch a person affectionately or sexually: *There was a couple kissing and fondling each other on the bus.*

paw (*informal*) to touch someone roughly or in an unacceptably intimate way: *I can't stand the way he paws all the women in the office.*

pick up to lift something, such as food or an ornament, with your hands: *You shouldn't pick up food if you are not going to eat it.*

touch to make contact with someone or something with your hands: *She touched his cheek lovingly.*

wield to hold something, such as a weapon or tool, in your hand or hands and move it about: *The mugger was wielding a knife.*

happiness *noun*

a feeling of pleasure and satisfaction because things are going well for you: *He finally found happiness running his own antique shop.*

bliss a state of extreme happiness: *The young couple are living in wedded bliss.*

cheerfulness a happy and lively quality, especially in a person: *Meena's cheerfulness always lifts the atmosphere in the office.*

contentment a state in which you are happy with the way that something is and have no wish to change it: *He was a man who never achieved true contentment.*

delight a feeling of great pleasure produced by something: *To the delight of her parents, she announced that she was coming home for Christmas.*

ecstasy a state of great happiness, especially a state of such intense happiness that you are no longer in control of your mind or actions: *Chloe was in ecstasy when she met her pop idol.*

elation a state of intense happiness and exhilaration, for example, because you have achieved something: *Skydiving gave me a feeling of sheer elation.*

euphoria a state of great happiness that is often produced artificially or based on an unrealistic assessment of a situation: *Some drugs produce a temporary feeling of euphoria.*

glee delight, often at someone else's misfortune: *The girls laughed in glee as their classmate fell over on the ice.*

joy a feeling of intense happiness: *The joy of the newborn baby's parents was clear for all to see.*

See also **happy.**

happy *adjective*

having a feeling of pleasure and satisfaction, often over a long period, or causing such a feeling: *a happy marriage.*

cheerful happy and lively, with a positive outlook: *a cheerful disposition.*

content happy and satisfied with your circumstances: *Adam is much more content since he gave up his stressful job.*

elated (usually only used to describe people) intensely happy and exhilarated, especially because of an achievement or an exciting experience: *Caroline was elated when she completed her first marathon.*

exuberant (usually used to describe people) happy, enthusiastic, and energetic: *As he grew older, he found it more difficult to cope with children's exuberant behaviour.*

joyful feeling or causing intense happiness: *The wedding was a joyful occasion.*

merry (*old-fashioned*) feeling, showing, or causing cheerfulness or high spirits: *merry laughter.*

satisfied pleased about the quality or standard of something, or about your circumstances in general: *The inspectors were not satisfied with the standard of cleanliness in the hotel.*

smiling (usually used to describe people) showing happiness or friendliness in your facial expression by smiling: *One look at her smiling face told me she had been successful in her job interview.*

See also **fortunate; happiness**.

hard *adjective*
with a rigid surface that does not yield when you press it, and that may be uncomfortable to sit or lie on: *a hard bench.*

firm resisting pressure but not completely rigid: *a firm mattress.*

rigid not able to be bent or not able to move: *rigid plastic.*

solid hard and not hollow inside: *solid rock.*

stiff firm and unable to be bent easily: *stiff cardboard.*

strong made in such a way that it is difficult to break, smash, etc.: *The bridge isn't strong enough to bear the weight of a really big lorry.*

tough difficult to tear or cut, or made to withstand rough treatment: *This meat is very tough.*

See also **difficult; harsh**.

harsh *adjective*
causing, or intended to cause, people to suffer: *living in harsh conditions.*

austere having no comfort or luxuries: *an austere cell.*

hard involving a lot of work and unpleasant conditions and very few pleasures: *a hard life.*

severe very bad, causing difficulties or hardship for people: *severe weather conditions.*

stark with no soft or gentle qualities and very bare: *a stark landscape.*

tough unpleasant and difficult to cope with: *They've been having a tough time recently.*

See also **cruel**.

hate *verb*
have a very strong dislike of someone or something: *My sister really hates rats.*

abhor (*formal*) to hate something or someone intensely: *I abhor prejudice in any shape or form.*

despise to regard someone or something with contempt: *The officer despised weakness in his men.*

detest to hate someone or something intensely: *I really detest liver.*

dislike to find someone or something unpleasant or unappealing: *They moved to the country because they disliked the noise in the city.*

loathe to hate someone or something intensely: *My father loathes modern art.*

See also **dislike.**

healthy *adjective*
in a good physical and mental state, with no illnesses: *a healthy baby boy.*

better having returned to good health after an illness: *I had flu but I am much better now.*

fit in good physical condition, especially as a result of regular exercise: *I go to aerobics to keep fit.*

hale and hearty having good health and lots of energy: *My mother is still hale and hearty in her seventies.*

in the pink (*informal*) feeling particularly well: *Having lost a stone in weight, I feel in the pink.*

raring to go (*informal*) feeling very healthy and energetic: *After a good night's sleep, I am raring to go!*

strong physically fit and powerful: *a strong constitution.*

vigorous strong and energetic: *a vigorous dancer.*

well in good health: *'How are you?' 'I'm very well, thank you.'*

See also **active; vigour.**

heavy *adjective*
weighing a lot: *a heavy bag.*

bulky large and heavy: *a bulky parcel.*

hefty (*informal*) large and heavy: *a hefty woman.*

overweight weighing too much relative to your height: *George is a bit overweight since he stopped playing football.*

substantial consisting of a strong material or solidly made: *It would be better to cover the hole with something a bit more substantial than a piece of cardboard.*

weighty (*informal*) heavy: *weighty boxes.*

help *verb*
to make it easier for someone to do something: *Can you help me with my homework?*

aid (*formal*) to help to achieve something: *To aid recovery, have plenty of bed rest and drink lots of fluids.*

assist to help someone, often in a subsidiary position: *The deputy manager assists the manager.*

do your bit (*informal*) to make a contribution towards a common aim: *The women knitted socks to do their bit for the war effort.*

lend a hand to help someone to do something: *The job would get done faster if you would lend a hand.*

muck in (*informal*) to help each other as a group: *If we all muck in, we can have the room decorated by teatime.*

oblige to do someone a favour: *Would you oblige me by looking after the kids for half an hour?*

rally round to combine to help and support someone, especially someone who is in a difficult situation: *We can rely on our friends to rally round, if Angela has to go into hospital.*

support help and encourage someone: *Stephanie's adoptive parents supported her in her search for her birth parents.*

hesitate *verb* to pause in uncertainty before speaking or acting: *I hesitated before accepting Brandon's invitation.*

dither to waste a lot of time hesitating and thinking about what you ought to do before you act or take a decision: *They dithered so long over the house purchase that someone else got in there before them.*

falter to hesitate in speech or action through lack or loss of confidence or because of feeling strong emotion: *The speaker's voice faltered when he referred to his recently deceased mother.*

pause to stop momentarily in speaking or before acting: *The old lady paused uncertainly at the top of the stairs, but a young man came to help her.*

shilly-shally (*informal*) to keep changing your mind about what you ought to do: *Stop shilly-shallying and make up your mind!*

stumble to make mistakes when speaking, often through nervousness or emotion: *The bridegroom was so nervous about making a speech that he stumbled over his words.*

think twice to pause to reconsider before taking action: *If I were you, I would think twice before spending so much money on a second-hand car.*

vacillate (*formal*) to keep changing your mind about which of various options or decisions you ought to take: *He vacillated between a desire to travel and a duty to his family.*

waver to be undecided or unsure about something: *After wavering, Jamie finally decided to accept the job offer.*

hide *verb* put an object where it cannot be seen, to prevent people from seeing an emotion or a piece of information, or to put yourself in a place where other people cannot see you: *My mother used to hide the biscuits so that we wouldn't eat them all at once.*

bury to put something out of sight under other things, not necessarily deliberately: *I found my phone buried under a pile of dirty socks.*

camouflage to disguise something, such as a military vehicle, so that it blends into the background and is hard to see: *The tanks are camouflaged in greens and browns so that they don't show up against the vegetation.*

cloak (*literary*) (most often used in the passive) to hide or cover something: *The mountains were cloaked in mist.*

conceal to put an object where it cannot be seen or prevent people from seeing an emotion or a piece of information: *He had concealed his criminal record from his employers.*

cover to hide something from view by putting something in front of or on top of it: *The footballer covered his face with a newspaper when he saw the waiting photographers.*

screen to act as a barrier that prevents something from being seen: *A high hedge screens the garden from the road.*

secrete (*formal*) to put something out of sight so that other people will not find it: *He has drugs secreted somewhere on his person.*

stash away (*informal*) to put something away in a secret store: *She has lots of sweets stashed away under her bed.*

high *adjective*
to describe objects or buildings, which may be large or broad, but not people) extending a long way above the ground: *a high wall.*

elevated raised high above the ground: *the elevated railway.*

lofty (*literary*) very high or very tall: *the lofty pine trees.*

soaring rising high up into the air: *a soaring plane.*

steep rising at a very sharp angle: *a steep hill.*

tall (used to describe people and objects or buildings that are fairly narrow) of greater than average height: *a tall dark stranger.*

towering rising a very long way above the ground and usually looking impressive: *towering mountains.*

See also **excited.**

hinder *verb*
to make it difficult for someone to do something or for something to be done: *The severe weather is hindering the rescue operation.*

block to prevent someone from reaching a place or from taking a certain action by putting an obstacle in the way: *There are barriers blocking the entrance to the stadium.*

foil to prevent someone from carrying out a plan, usually a plan to cause harm or destruction: *The police foiled the terrorists' plot to plant a bomb.*

hamper to make it difficult for someone to move or to take action: *The completion of my task was hampered by lack of co-operation by my colleagues.*

impede (*formal*) to slow down the progress or movement of someone: *Our progress up the mountain was impeded by thick mist.*

obstruct to block something or make it difficult to pass along or through something, or to hinder someone: *Your car is obstructing the entrance to my garage.*

prevent to stop something from happening or stop someone from doing something: *Putting the brick there is designed to prevent the car from moving back.*

stymie (*informal*) to make it impossible, or very difficult, for someone to do something: *Jackson was stymied in his attempt to break the world record by a pulled hamstring.*

thwart to prevent someone from
 carrying out a plan: *Leanne's plan to live abroad was thwarted by her mother's illness.*

See also **prevent.**

hit *verb* to come into contact with an object, usually with a lot of force: *The ball hit the window and smashed it.*

bump into to accidentally hit someone or something, usually when they are not moving and you are moving fairly slowly: *I have a big bruise on my knee from bumping into the coffee table.*

collide (said two moving objects,
 especially vehicles) to hit one another accidentally: *A bus has collided with a car.*

crash into to accidentally hit something, usually something that is not moving, when usually in a vehicle that is moving fast or is out of control: *The car skidded off the road and crashed into a wall.*

graze hit the edge or side of something lightly while moving past it, causing little damage: *The bullet grazed my cheek.*

knock hit something, usually with part of your body or part of an object and with a quick or accidental blow, especially to hit a surface in order to produce a loud noise: *Someone's knocking on the door.*

ram to hit another vehicle deliberately: *One car rammed the other from behind, forcing it off the road.*

smash into to crash into something: *The plane went out of control and smashed into a mountain.*

strike to hit something: *Pete swung the bat and accidentally struck Mike on the head.*

See also **beat 1**.

hole *noun*
an opening in something, or an empty space in something with an opening: *There's a hole in the bucket.*

burrow a hollow space dug in the ground, where a small animal lives: *The rabbit popped out of its burrow.*

cavity a hollow space, for example in the body or in a decayed tooth: *The dentist says I have a cavity that needs a filling.*

crater a large hollow made in the ground when something explodes or hits it with enormous force: *a bomb crater.*

crevice a narrow crack: *a crevice in the rock.*

gap an opening in something or a space between two things: *a gap in the hedge.*

pit a very deep hole in the ground, especially one dug for mining: *a coal pit.*

split a long gap in a garment that has been ripped or in material that has cracked: *a split in the wood.*

tear a gap in a garment or in fabric that has been ripped: *There's a tear in your shirt.*

holiday *noun* a period of time away from work or study, for rest, recreation, or travel: *We went to Austria on a skiing holiday.* More commonly used in British English than in US English.

break a short time away from work or study, for rest, recreation, or travel: *I am looking forward to having a break from work next week.*

leave time that you are entitled to have away from work: *We have five weeks' annual leave.*

long weekend a weekend when you have an extra day or two days away from work because of a public holiday: *They are going to Prague for the long weekend at Easter.*

R and R (*informal*) rest and recreation: *I'm off to Greece next week for some R and R.*

sabbatical a fairly long period of time away from work, especially for a university lecturer, often for research or travel: *My tutor is going on a year's sabbatical to the USA.*

time off time away from work or study: *My doctor advised me to take some time off for the sake of my health.*

trip a journey, or some time spent away from home, taken for pleasure: *The kids are going on a school trip to France.*

vacation a holiday: *Where did you go on vacation this summer?* In US English a *vacation* means 'a holiday'; in British English it means specifically a period when normal work stops at a university and the students go on holiday.

honour *noun*
the quality of behaving according to what you believe to be right: *The president was widely respected as a man of honour.*

decency the quality of behaving in a

fair and moral way: *He has always treated me with decency.*

goodness the quality of being kind and compassionate: *She helps at the drop-in centre out of the goodness of her heart.*

honesty the quality of being truthful and trustworthy and doing what is right: *The police commended the girl's honesty when she handed in the purse she had found.*

integrity the quality of being honest and honourable: *The Minister has conducted himself with integrity throughout this ordeal.*

morality the quality of behaving according to what is generally considered to be right: *Many people question the morality of wearing fur.*

nobility (*formal*) the quality of behaving with honour and generosity of spirit: *There is a certain nobility about these villagers who, though they are living in abject poverty, will always share the little they have with strangers.*

hope *noun*
a wish for something to happen and a belief that it might well happen: *What are your hopes for the future?*

ambition something that you hope to achieve in the future: *Calum's ambition is to be an astronaut.*

aspiration a desire for high achievements: *Many young people have aspirations to be famous.*

desire a wish to have something or for something to happen: *I have a great desire to go to Egypt some day.*

dream something that you would very much like to achieve or to have in the future: *My dream is to have my own recording studio.*

expectation something that you believe will happen or that you will achieve in the future: *The joy of parenthood has exceeded all their expectations.*

goal something that you aim to achieve: *Helen has set herself a goal of losing 5 kilograms in weight before her holidays.*

intention something that you plan to do: *I have no intention of resigning.*

plan a method that you have worked out to achieve what you want: *Tina has a plan to open her own business next year.*

See also **expect.**

hot *adjective*
having a high temperature: *a hot bath.*

boiling heated to the temperature at which water turns into steam, or (*informal*) very hot: *Pour boiling water into the teapot.*

burning hot to the touch: *The sick child's cheeks were burning.*

scalding (used to describe liquid) extremely hot so that it will hurt you if you touch it: *She poured a cup of scalding coffee all over me.*

scorching (*informal*) very hot and sunny: *a scorching day.*

sultry hot and humid: *a sultry summer's night.*

sweltering uncomfortably hot: *Come in out of the sweltering heat.*

tropical in or like the regions of the world close to the equator: *a tropical climate.*

See also **warm.**

hungry *adjective* wanting to eat:
Exercise always makes me feel hungry.

empty having an empty feeling in your
stomach because you have not eaten for
a while: *I feel empty; is it lunchtime yet?*

famished (*informal*) very hungry: *We
were famished after
swimming.*

malnourished not having had enough
healthy food for a long time: *The children were so malnourished that their
arms and legs were stick-thin.*

peckish (*informal*) slightly hungry:
If you feel a bit peckish, have an apple.

ravenous very hungry indeed: *After missing lunch, I was ravenous by dinnertime.*

starving (*informal*) very hungry:
'Are you hungry?' 'Yes, starving!'

underfed having eaten a less than
healthy amount for some time: *a poor
little underfed dog.*

voracious very hungry or greedy: *a
voracious appetite.*

hurry *verb* to move quickly: *Lisa
hurried to answer the phone.*

accelerate to make something, especially a vehicle, move faster: *I acceler-
ated to overtake the car in front.*

dash to run or move somewhere
quickly: *Caroline
dashed off to answer
the door.*

fly to go away quickly: *I must fly – I'm
late for an appointment.*

get a move on (*informal*) to start to
move more quickly: *Come on, get a
move on or we'll miss the bus!*
hasten to move or act quickly: *The
nurse hastened to reassure us that there
was no cause for concern.*

rush move quickly or do something too
quickly and, sometimes, without care:
*Lucy rushed through her homework and
made lots of mistakes.*

speed to move very quickly, especially
to exceed the speed limit when driving:
*Darren was caught speeding on his way
home from work.*

See also **run; speed.**

hurt *verb*
to cause pain or physical damage to
someone or part of the body, deliberately
or accidentally, or to make someone feel
sad or offended: *Joe hurt his back lifting
a heavy weight.*

bruise to hit or knock a part of your
body, causing a painful
dark mark to appear: *I
bumped into the coffee
table and bruised my
knee.*

harm to cause pain or physical damage
to a person or an animal, usually deliberately: *What kind of person would harm
an innocent child?*

impair to make something, such as a
person's eyesight or hearing, less good
or effective: *My aunt's eyesight is
impaired since she had a stroke.*

injure to cause someone physical damage: *Three people have been seriously
injured in a road traffic accident.*

maim to cause someone permanent
serious physical damage, such as the
loss of a limb: *Many people were killed
or maimed in the explosion.*

pain (*formal*) to cause someone to feel
disapproval or irritation: *It pains me to
see that you have still not heeded my
warnings.*

wound to cause someone an injury,
especially by breaking the skin: *My
grandfather was wounded in the war.*

See also **damage.**

idea *noun*

something produced in your mind that can be put into words, especially something that is a starting-point for a thinking process or a plan of action, or a belief or opinion: *I have a few ideas for my essay, but I have not started writing it yet.*

brainchild (*informal*) an original idea or invention thought up by the person specified: *The UK National Health Service was the brainchild of Aneurin Bevan.*

brainwave (*informal*) an inspiration:

A student had a brainwave which led to him becoming an Internet millionaire.

concept an idea of what something is: *the concept of democracy.*

inspiration a brilliant or creative idea that suddenly occurs to you: *I was struggling to write my speech and then I had a sudden inspiration.*

notion a usually rather vague idea or belief: *I have a notion that she may have mentioned this before.*

plan something you have thought out carefully as a course of action: *Ruth's plan is to retire to the country.*

suggestion an idea that you offer for consideration: *I would welcome suggestions for the Christmas night out.*

thought the process of thinking, or an idea: *If you have any thoughts on the subject, perhaps you would let me know.*

See also **plan; suggest**.

ignorant *adjective*

having a lack of knowledge, either generally or about a particular subject: *Being ignorant of the dangers of sunbathing can lead to skin cancer.*

inexperienced having a lack of knowledge or experience, especially of a particular activity or subject: *His application for promotion was rejected because he was too inexperienced.*

innocent having a lack of knowledge about how things are done in the world, especially about the more unpleasant aspects of life: *With an innocent childlikeness, Tracy tends to trust everyone she meets.*

unaware not knowing certain infor-

mation or not realizing that something is happening: *He was unaware of the effects of his smoking on his wife and children.*

unconscious not noticing something or not being aware of something: *The children played amidst the earthquake ruins, happily unconscious of the danger they were in.*

ill *adjective*

suffering from a disease or medical condition, feeling that something is physically wrong with you, or generally in poor health: *My father is seriously ill in hospital.* Always used after a verb.

indisposed (*formal*) slightly ill: *James is indisposed after last night's celebrations.*

out of sorts (*informal*) slightly ill: *I'm feeling a bit out of sorts; I think I will have a lie-down.*

poorly (mainly used when speaking to or about children) ill: *The baby is poorly – I think she is teething.*
Always used after a verb.

queasy feeling as if you are going to vomit: *The sight of blood made me feel queasy.*

seedy feeling slightly ill, especially feeling as if you might vomit: *I felt a bit seedy after the long car journey.*

sick (used after a verb) vomiting, or feeling as if you are about to vomit; (used before a noun or after a verb) ill: *Emma has been sick all over the bathroom.*

under the weather (*informal*) slightly ill: *Dad is a bit under the weather this morning; he may be catching a cold.*

unhealthy likely to cause people to become ill: *an unhealthy diet.*

unwell having an illness: *Pat has been quite unwell with pneumonia.* Always used after a verb.

illegal *adjective*
which is forbidden by law: *illegal drugs.*

banned which is officially not allowed: *banned substances.*

black-market bought or sold illegally: *black-market ivory.*

contraband smuggled into or out of a country: *contraband cigarettes.*

criminal which is a crime, or which commits crimes: *criminal activities.*

crooked (*informal*) illegal or dishonest: *crooked dealings.*

dishonest not truthful or trustworthy, or not conforming to what most people think is morally right: *I don't know whether cheating at cards is illegal, but it's definitely dishonest.*

illicit which is forbidden by law or goes against moral conventions, and which is usually done secretly: *She is having an illicit relationship with a married man.*

prohibited which is officially not allowed: *Signs inside the hall said: 'Smoking prohibited'.*

unlawful which is forbidden by law or not recognized by law: *unlawful arrest.*

See also **dishonest.**

illness *noun*
something that affects your physical or mental health and makes your body or mind unable to function normally: *a terminal illness.*

ailment a minor illness: *She is always moaning about her ailments.*

complaint a minor health problem that is troubling someone: *Backache is a very common complaint.*

condition the state of health or ill health of a person, or a problem affecting a particular part of the body: *a serious heart condition.*

disease a particular kind of serious illness that has recognizable symptoms: *a tropical disease such as malaria.*

disorder a problem affecting a particular part of the body or a bodily function: *an eating disorder.*

infection a disease caused by a virus or bacteria: *a throat infection.*

malady (*old-fashioned*) a kind of illness: *a mysterious malady.*

sickness vomiting, nausea, or illness generally: *radiation sickness.*

imitate *verb*
to speak or act like someone else, often in order to amuse others, or to try to look or be the same as something else: *Andrew makes his classmates laugh by imitating the teachers.*

ape to copy the actions of another person, because you want to be like them: *Little Jane apes her older brother.*

copy to do or say the same as someone else, or to make something that is exactly the same as something else: *Babies learn to speak by copying their parents.*

emulate (*formal*) to try to be like someone that you admire or to copy their success: *Kelly's ambition is to be a singer and she wants to emulate the success of her idol, Madonna.*

impersonate to copy a person's speech, actions, or appearance, in order to amuse others or to convince others that you are that person: *He was arrested for impersonating a police officer.*

mimic to copy a person's speech or actions, often to ridicule them or to amuse others: *The school bullies mimicked the new girl's accent.*

parrot to repeat another's person's words or views unquestioningly: *Jonathan's wife just parrots everything he says.*

send up (*informal*) to deliberately speak or act like someone else, usually exaggerating their often in order to ridicule them: *an impressionist who sends up the Prime Minister.*

take off (*informal*) to deliberately speak or act like someone else, often in order to amuse others: *In her act she takes off several singers and actresses.*

See also **copy**.

impatient *adjective*
getting angry or restless if you have to wait for something or someone, or if someone behaves in a way that annoys or inconveniences you: *Many drivers were getting impatient in the traffic jam.*

agitated very anxious or disturbed and unable to rest or be still: *The patient became more and more agitated until eventually he had to be sedated.*

anxious feeling tense and worried about possible harm that may happen to you or to someone or something else: *I started to feel anxious when my daughter didn't come home from school at the usual time.*

nervous being worried and having physical symptoms such as trembling because of something you are about to do: *The best man at the wedding was very nervous about having to make a speech.*

restless feeling bored, impatient, and uncomfortable, and wanting to change position or change your circumstances: *As the lecture dragged on and on, the audience started to get restless.*

twitchy (*informal*) feeling anxious and nervous about something, and unable to stay still: *Grace was beginning to get a bit twitchy waiting for her exam results to arrive in the post.*

uptight (*informal*) very tense and unable

to relax: *I always get a bit uptight about going to the dentist.*

important *adjective*
considered to have a greater effect or more influence, or to need greater or more urgent attention than most things or people: *an important event in history.*

critical likely to have a decisive influence on the outcome of something, for example, on whether a plan succeeds or fails: *a critical development.*

crucial critical: *at the crucial moment.*

key on which or whom everything depends: *the key player in the team.*

main most important among a number of related things: *My main reason for coming to the Louvre is to see the Mona Lisa.*

major very important, standing out among other people or things in the same group: *one of the major 20th-century novelists.*

momentous being of great and lasting significance: *a momentous occasion.*

primary (*formal*) main, first in importance: *Our primary concern is the children's safety.*

significant having, or likely to have, a considerable effect: *There's been no significant change in the patient's condition.*

vital very important or necessary, so that you really cannot do without it: *vital information.*

improve *verb*

to become better, or to make something better: *If you practise your golf swing a lot, it will improve.*

advance make progress in knowledge or learning: *He began as a junior editor but he quickly advanced to publishing director.*

ameliorate (*formal*) to make circumstances better: *We have done everything in our power to ameliorate the circumstances.*

better yourself to reach a higher position in society or have a better quality of life: *Tracy is trying to better herself by going to college.*

cure to cause an illness or a problem to disappear: *Physiotherapy cured my backache.*

get better to improve, especially to recover your health after you have been ill: *I've been getting better since I started taking the new medicine the doctor gave me.*

enhance to add to the beauty or value of something: *Your sweater enhances the colour of your eyes.*

look up (*informal*) improve or become more promising: *Things are looking up now that I have a permanent job.*

make over (*informal*) to make major changes that are intended to improve the appearance of someone or something: *Susan looked ten years younger after she had been made over at the beauty salon.*

pick up (*informal*) to get better, for example in health or in sales: *Sales are picking up now after a slow start to the year.*

income *noun*

money that you receive from any source, for example from working or investments, and that you live on: *Families on a low income are entitled to state benefits.*

commission a sum of money that a salesperson earns for every sale that they make: *She has no salary, but works for a commission on all the goods she sells.*

earnings money that you receive in return for work: *He gives a percentage of his earnings to charity.*

pay the money that an employer gives you in return for the work you do: *I have had money taken off my pay because I was late one day.*

profits money that you make from a business, selling something, etc., after costs have been deducted from the whole amount that you receive: *Profits are down on this time last year.*

salary the money that you earn by working in a professional position or an office job, which is usually paid monthly: *Denis's salary as a bank manager is enough for the family to live on.*

takings money that is made on sales in a business such as a shop or a pub: *Our takings have gone up over the last few weeks.*

wages the money that you earn as an ordinary worker in, for example, a factory or shop, which is usually paid weekly: *I couldn't afford to buy a house on my shop assistant's wages.*

increase *verb*
to become, or to make something, bigger or greater in number: *Sales have increased since last month.*

add to to bring more of something of which you already have a certain amount: *You're only adding to my difficulties by trying to help.*

amplify to make something, especially sound, greater in intensity: *We will have to used microphones at the meeting to amplify the sound.*

augment (*formal*) to make something, but not usually a physical object, greater in size or quantity by adding to it: *I took an extra job at weekends to augment my salary.*

boost to make something greater and stronger: *Her success in the exams boosted her self-confidence.*

enlarge to make something bigger: *I am having a photograph enlarged so that I can frame it.*

expand become, or to make something, greater in size or scope, especially by moving outwards to occupy more space: *His waist has expanded by 4 centimetres.*

extend to make something, such as a house, larger or longer by adding something to it: *We are extending the house by adding on a conservatory.*

go through the roof (*informal*) (said usually about prices) to increase by a very large amount: *House prices have gone through the roof recently in this area.*

grow to increase in size, number, or intensity, especially to become bigger by a natural process: *Little Annie has grown five centimetres in the last six months.*

mount (up) to increase in amount or number: *The death toll from the earthquake in China continues to mount.*

multiply to increase in number: *Out-of-town shopping centres multiplied as car ownership increased.*

rise to increase in amount or number: *The price of petrol is likely to rise again.*

See also **rise.**

inexperienced *adjective*
having little or no knowledge or experience, especially of a particular activity or subject: *an inexperienced driver.*

amateurish of poor quality through skill or experience: *an amateurish performance.*

green (*informal*) inexperienced and

often naïve: *I was too young and too green back then to deal with living alone.*

inexpert having little skill in a particular activity: *an inexpert cook.*

new having no previous experience of a particular job or activity: *I am new to hang-gliding – this is my first time.*

unaccustomed not used to a particular activity: *unaccustomed to using a computer.*

unfamiliar knowing little or nothing about something or unaccustomed to it: *I was still unfamiliar with the surroundings of my new workplace.*

untrained having had no formal training in a particular job or activity: *an untrained singer.*

See also **ignorant.**

inferior *adjective*
of a low standard or low quality, or of a lower standard or quality than something else: *inferior goods.*

hopeless very bad at doing something, or very ineffective: *I'm absolutely hopeless at maths.*

inadequate of lower standard or quality than is required to do something properly: *an inadequate father.*

mediocre of middling to poor quality, definitely not good enough for you to feel positive about it: *All in all it was a pretty mediocre performance.*

rubbish (*informal*) of a very low standard or quality: *She's rubbish at spelling.*

second-rate having very little talent or skill: *He's just a second-rate pub singer.*

unsatisfactory not of the standard that someone wants or expects: *If you work is unsatisfactory, then you will have to do it again.*

useless unable to be used, because damaged, of very poor quality, irrelevant, etc., or (*informal*) very bad at doing something: *His head is full of useless information.*

See also **bad 4**.

informal *adjective*
done, or doing things, in a friendly and relaxed way, without strictly following the usual rules of politeness or procedure: *Call me by my first name; we're very informal here.*

casual not involving serious matters or feelings, or carried out in a very informal way: *a casual conversation.*

colloquial (used to describes words or language) used mainly in informal conversation, rather than in writing: *'Let the cat out of the bag' is a colloquial expression.*

easygoing not strict, taking a relaxed and good-natured view of what other people do: *an easygoing attitude.*

familiar friendly to an inappropriate degree: *Teachers should not be too familiar with their pupils.*

natural behaving in an ordinary, friendly way towards people, not trying to make yourself seem important or special: *Gita is a very natural young girl with no airs or graces.*

relaxed with no tension, comfortable and allowing people to feel at ease: *a relaxed atmosphere.*

unaffected natural in behaviour, or genuine and not pretended: *They greeted the news with unaffected delight.*

information *noun*
something, usually in the form of statements, numbers, etc., that enables you to know what something or someone is like or what is happening: *I'd like some information on holidays in Turkey.*

data information in the form of facts, numbers, or statistics: *The Human Resources Department keeps data on all employees.*

facts pieces of information that are proven to be true: *I have learned some interesting facts about whales.*

info (*informal*) information: *Did you get any info from Grace about her new boyfriend?*

intelligence secret information that is discovered by spies about an enemy country: *He was a government agent gathering intelligence in Germany during the war.*

knowledge facts and other informa- tion that you have learned, usually about a particular subject: *George's knowledge of local history is very impressive.*

material information that can be used as the subject of a written work: *He has collected lots of material for his next comedy series.*

news new information about something: *There is no further news on the missing schoolgirl.*

statistics information in the form of figures that show the relationship between two or more things: *Government statistics show a drop in unemployment.*

See also **news.**

innocent *adjective*

not guilty of having committed a crime or done wrong: *In the eyes of the law, a person is innocent until proven guilty.*

blameless not responsible for a wrong that has been done or a mistake that has been made: *Jamal is blameless in this situation.*

faultless having no mistakes or imperfections: *a faultless portrayal.*

guiltless (*formal*) innocent, not having done anything wrong: *Any one of us could have stopped her if we had wanted to, so none of us is guiltless in this case.*

in the clear (*informal*) not suspected or likely to be suspected of having done something wrong: *He was abroad at the time when the papers were stolen, so he's in the clear.*

irreproachable in which nobody can find anything to blame or any sign of wrongdoing: *an irreproachable record.*

not guilty found by a court of law not to have committed a crime with which you are charged: *He was found not guilty of murder.*

squeaky-clean (*informal*) very virtuous and innocent, sometimes unattractively so: *his squeaky-clean image.*

See also **naive.**

insolent *adjective*

aggressively insulting and disrespectful in your speech or behaviour: *an insolent scowl.*

brazen knowing that you are doing something that other people disapprove of and not caring what they think: *brazen hypocrisy.*

cheeky mildly disrespectful, sometimes in a charming way: *You cheeky little monkey!*

defiant boldly resisting authority: *a defiant attitude.*

disrespectful showing no respect or consideration for someone: *Don't be so disrespectful to your mother!*

impertinent disrespectful in your speech or behaviour: *an impertinent remark.*

impudent insulting and disrespectful in your speech or behaviour, especially towards someone who is older than you or socially superior: *an impudent child.*

presumptuous assuming that you can do something or behave in a particular way, when other people think that you are not really entitled to: *It was presumptuous of him to take it for granted he would be invited to the wedding.*

See also **rude.**

inspect *verb*

to look over something or someone and check that they are in a satisfactory state: *The Queen inspected the troops.*

case (*informal*) to examine a place with a view to committing a crime: *The burglars cased the joint with a view to breaking in.*

check out (*informal*) to look at someone or something, or to get information about them: *Check out the guy with the green hair!*

eye to look at someone or something in a way that suggests you are interested them or want them: *Jim was eyeing the cake, so I quickly offered him a slice.*

look over to inspect a person or their work, often quickly: *Let me look over your homework.*

oversee to supervise a group of people or their work: *As project leader, it is my job to oversee the group's work.*

review to look back over something that has been done in order to check it: *Let's review the progress we have made so far.*

take stock of to stop to consider what has been done so far before deciding how to progress: *When you reach the age of 40, it is common to take stock of your life.*

vet to inspect something or someone

carefully: *People who apply to work with children must be vetted by the authorities.*

See also **check**.

insult *verb*
to say hurtful or offensive things about someone: *He insulted her by calling her stupid.*

abuse to speak very harshly and offensively to someone: *The crowd abused the accused as he was hustled into court.*

call names (usually said about children) to describe someone in a hurtful or offensive way: *Children often call each other names in the playground.*

offend to make someone feel that you have no respect for them or the things they consider important: *I think I offended Ruth when I called her 'middle-aged'.*

put down criticize someone in a hurtful and disrespectful way: *She often puts her husband down in front of his friends.*

slag off (*informal*) criticize someone in a rude or offensive way: *They are always slagging off other bands in the papers.*

slight to be rude or unfriendly to someone or to pay them little attention: *I felt slighted when my name was omitted from the guest list.*

snub to be rude or unfriendly to someone you know or to ignore them completely: *When Tim met his ex-girlfriend at a party, he completely snubbed her.*

taunt to tease or mock someone with

hurtful or offensive comments: *The bullies cruelly taunted her about being fat.*

See also **rude.**

intense *adjective*
having a very powerful and concentrated quality: *intense pride.*

acute (used to describe uncomfortable

feelings) strongly and painfully felt: *acute embarrassment.*

consuming taking up all your attention and mental energy: *a consuming passion.*

deep sincerely felt and affecting you in a very powerful way: *deep shame.*

extreme of the very strongest kind: *extreme irritation.*

passionate very powerful and directed outwards towards someone or something that you are concerned with: *passionate love.*

profound deep: *profound sadness.*

strong powerful enough to affect your attitude or the way you behave: *strong feelings of jealousy.*

See also **strong.**

interesting *adjective*
which attracts or holds your attention:
an interesting documentary.

absorbing which holds your attention
for a long time: *an absorbing book.*

appealing which attracts you: *an
appealing idea.*

attractive very appealing and worthy of
consideration: *an attractive prospect.*

entertaining which holds your attention
and amuses you: *an entertaining film.*

exciting extremely interesting and
eventful: *an exciting trip to China.*

fascinating which attracts or interests
you very strongly and makes you want
to know more about it:
a fascinating conversation.

gripping exciting and dramatic:

*a gripping adventure
story.*

intriguing which attracts your attention
and is slightly mysterious: *I heard an
intriguing snippet of conversation.*

interfere *verb*
to involve yourself in other people's
affairs, and often try to change what they
are doing, in a way that is irritating to
them: *My mother keeps interfering in our
wedding arrangements.*

intervene to enter into a situation in
order to change it or take control of it:
*The teacher intervened just in time to
prevent the two boys coming to blows.*

meddle interfere: *My neighbour is always
meddling in other people's business.*

poke your nose in (*informal*) to pry or
interfere: *She can't resist poking her nose
in when we're discussing private business.*

pry to try to find out information about
other people's affairs: *Kindly stop prying
into my affairs!*

put/shove/stick your oar in (*informal*)
to offer advice or comment on other people's affairs when it is not wanted: *There's
no need for you to stick your oar in; we
can sort out our own problems, thanks.*

snoop (*informal*) to try to find out
information about
other people's
affairs, especially by
underhand means:
He snoops around
*the office when no one is around, looking
in people's drawers.*

See also **disturb**.

invade *verb*
to enter a country with military force, or
to go into a place where you are unwelcome: *The Anglo-Saxons invaded the
British Isles in the fifth century.*

attack to use force to try to harm or
capture someone or something: *The capital has been attacked from the air.*

descend on to arrive in a place in a
large numbers, in a way that is usually
unpleasant for the people who are there:
*Hordes of tourist descend on the town
from June onwards.*

march into to invade a country or area:
*The army marched into the region and
so the war began.*

occupy to station military forces in a
country or area to control it after you
have conquered it: *The Americans occupied Baghdad and most of northern Iraq.*

overrun to make a sudden military

assault on a country
and take possession of
it: *The country was
overrun by the
invaders.*

See also **attack**.

involve *verb*

to have something as an essential part
or element of doing it: *Being a parent
involves a lot of self-sacrifice.*

entail to have something as a part or
consequence: *What exactly does the job
entail?*

imply to have something as a necessary
or logical consequence: *The title 'Mrs'
implies that the person you are referring
to is a married woman.*

include to have something as a part or
element, usually as one or more of several parts or elements: *Modern-languages
degree course includes a year abroad.*

incorporate (*formal*) to include two or
more things within itself, or to make
something a part or element of something else: *The driving test incorporates
a practical exam and a theory exam.*

mean to have something as a consequence: *Going back to university will
mean a drop in the family income.*

necessitate (*formal*) to require:

 *Accepting this position
would necessitate relo-
cation to London.*

require to make it necessary to have or
do something: *Being a top-class athlete
requires dedication and sacrifice.*

take in to have two or more things as
parts or elements: *The cat family takes in
big cats like lions and tigers as well as
the domestic cat.*

job *noun*

the type of work that you do regularly
in order to earn money: *She has a job in
a bank.*

calling a type of work that you feel as
if you are compelled to do, usually one
that requires dedication and caring for
others: *Michael had a calling to the
priesthood.*

career the type of work that you do for
most of your life: *I would like to have a
career in journalism.*

employment the fact of having a job:
*After being out of work for 12 months, it
was good to be in employment again.*

occupation (*formal*) a job: *Mr Alan
Jones, thirty-nine years old, occupation
bank manager.*

position (*formal*) a post: *The position
of area manager has become vacant.*

post a job within an organization, which
has specified duties, especially a fairly
high-status job: *Alan applied for the
post of head teacher.*

profession a job, especially one that
requires a high level of education and
training, such as medicine, teaching, or
law: *He was an active member of the
medical profession.*

trade a skilled job that requires training:
*If you learn a trade, you'll make much
more money than you will as an ordinary
labourer.*

vocation a type of work that you
 feel as if you are
compelled to do,
usually one that
requires dedication
and caring for oth-
ers: *Nursing is generally regarded as a
vocation.*

work the job or responsibilities of your job that you do regularly to earn money: *I usually finish work at 5 pm.*

See also **duty**.

join *verb*
to bring two or more things into a position where they are touching one another and fixed together in some way: *Stand in a circle and join hands.*

attach to place something on something else so that it is touching it and remains in that position: *Attach the address label to your suitcase.*

bind to tie two or more things

 together firmly: *Bind the plant to the stick so that it grows straight.*

connect to join two or more things together directly, to join them indirectly by means of something else, such as a wire, that is attached to them and enables electric current or a similar force to pass from one to the other, or to be something that connects something to something else: *The amplifier is connected to the loudspeaker.*

fasten attach something, usually firmly, to something else: *Fasten the pedometer to your waistband, and it will measure the number of steps you take in a day.*

link to connect: *A walkway links the two buildings.*

unite to come together or bring people or things together: *The victims' families are united in their grief.*

joke *noun*
a funny story or a funny comment: *He told me a joke about a talking dog.*

gag (*informal*) a joke, especially one told by a comedian: *The entertainer sang a few songs and told a few gags.*

pun a remark that is meant to be funny because the words can have more than one meaning: *He made a pun based on the two meanings of 'bear'.*

quip a witty comment or retort: *She is always ready with a merry quip.*

wisecrack a sharp witty remark: *Sometimes his wisecracks can be quite cutting.*

witticism (*formal*) a witty comment: *an article on Oscar Wilde's witticisms.*

jump *verb*
to move into the air, with both feet off the ground, and back down again: *Jump over the puddle!*

bound to move energetically taking big long steps, or to make a big jump that usually covers a long distance rather goes high into the air: *The dog bounded in from the garden.*

hop to jump on one foot: *When I sprained my ankle, I had to hop to the phone.*

leap to take a big jump that either goes high in the air or covers a long distance: *A salmon leapt right up in the air from the river.*

skip to jump lightly raising first one foot and then the other, as children do: *The little girl skipped right up the path to the house.*

spring to make a big, sudden jump, often to attack something or someone: *The cheetah sprang from its hiding place onto its prey.*

vault to jump over something high, sometimes with the help of a pole for support: *The burglar vaulted over the fence and ran off.*

keep *verb*

to continue to have possession of something: *She has kept all the letters her husband ever sent her.*

hold to carry something in your hands and look after it: *Will you hold my handbag for me while I have a dance?*

preserve to maintain something in an unchanged condition: *We want to preserve this beautiful building for future generations.*

retain to keep something in your possession: *Retain your ticket in case an inspector boards the bus.*

save to keep something back for later use: *After cooking a chicken, I like to save the carcass to make soup.*

store to keep goods in a safe place for future use: *Store the wine in a cool place.*

withhold (*formal*) to refuse to give or grant something: *He was charged with withholding information pertaining to a crime.*

See also **save.**

kill *verb*

to end the life of a person or an animal: *My brother was killed in a motorcycle accident.*

assassinate to murder a well-known or important person: *President Kennedy was assassinated in 1963.*

bump off (*informal*) to murder someone: *The gang boss was bumped off by member of a rival gang.*

do in (*informal*) to murder someone: *She did her old man in with a carving knife.*

execute to put someone to death as a punishment for committing a very serious crime: *Ruth Ellis was the last woman to be executed by hanging in the UK.*

massacre to kill large numbers of people in a violent way: *Troops massacred the entire population of the village.*

murder to kill someone deliberately: *The woman was murdered by her jealous lover.*

put to sleep to end the life of an animal that is suffering, usually by giving it a lethal injection: *The vet put my cat down because it had cancer.*

slaughter to kill an animal for food, or to kill large numbers of people violently: *The pigs were transported to the abattoir to be slaughtered.*

kind

1 *adjective* helpful to others and considerate of their feelings: *It was kind of you to help me out.*

benevolent (*formal*) doing good deeds for those less fortunate than yourself: *a benevolent ruler.*

charitable inclined to take a kind and tolerant view of others: *She always takes a charitable view of people.*

compassionate sympathetic and understanding about others' pain or suffering: *She is a very compassionate woman, who helps out at the homeless shelter.*

considerate thinking of other people's feelings: *He is very considerate, always putting other people before himself.*

generous giving, or given, freely: *a generous gift.*

good pleasant, helpful, and honourable: *It was good of them to remember my birthday.*

helpful keen to do things to benefit others: *Thanks for your advice; that was most helpful.*

humane having or showing a desire to prevent suffering: *slaughtering animals for food by humane means so that they don't suffer.*

2 *noun* a number of people or things that have shared characteristics and are regarded as a group: *What kind of film would you like to see; a comedy or a thriller?*

breed a particular type of dog, cat, cow, etc., that has been bred to have particular physical characteristics: *The St Bernard is the largest breed of dog.*

category a name or description that can be applied to a particular kind of thing: *The films are listed in different categories: comedy, horror, adventure, and so on.*

sort a kind: *What sort of computer do you have?*

style a particular way of doing something: *the Mediterranean style of cooking.*

type a kind: *He is not the jealous type.*

variety a particular kind of something of which there are usually many kinds: *an apple of the Granny Smith variety.*

See also **group**.

knowledge *noun*
the information that you store in your memory and use to answer questions, solve problems, etc.: *I have no knowledge of his whereabouts.*

education the knowledge that you acquire at school, college, or university: *You need to have a good education if you want to have a good career.*

erudition (*formal*) learning: *He is a man of great erudition.*

know-how (*informal*) knowledge of practical or technical matters: *I don't have the know-how to install a washing machine.*

learning (*formal*) knowledge acquired through extensive study: *For all his learning, he was unable to answer this one simple question.*

scholarship knowledge acquired through extensive study: *She devoted her entire life to scholarship.*

wisdom knowledge acquired through experience of life and people and combined with good judgment: *The elders of the village are respected for their wisdom.*

See also **information**.

lack *noun*
the fact of being without something that is needed or desired: *Lack of privacy is one disadvantage of fame.*

absence the fact of not being present in a place or at an event or of not being available: *The absence of hard evidence made a conviction impossible.*

deficiency the fact of having less of something than you need: *An iron deficiency in the blood was causing me to feel fatigued.*

insufficiency (*formal*) the fact of having less of something than you need: *We were unable to go ahead with the purchase of the new computing equipment because of an insufficiency of funds.*

need the fact of wanting or having to have something in order to do something, or the state of not having enough of essential things such as money, food, or health care: *a charity that helps people in need in the poorest parts of the world.*

poverty the state of having little money and few possessions, or a deficiency of something: *If you don't want to live in poverty for the rest of your life, I suggest you start looking for a better-paid job.*

scarcity the fact of not being widely

available: *There is a scarcity of bananas at the moment.*

shortage the fact of having less of something, such as food or money, than you need: *a severe shortage of skilled workers.*

want the fact of being without something that is needed or desired, especially food or money: *The people of the village are dying for want of food.*

late *adjective*
arriving, or happening, after the arranged or expected time: *I was late for school this morning.*

behind having made less progress than you should have: *I'm a bit behind with my housework.*

belated arriving or happening later than the proper time: *belated birthday greetings.*

last-minute done or arranged at the last possible moment: *We are hoping to book a last-minute holiday.*

overdue having missed the proper date for some particular action: *Your library books are overdue.*

tardy (*formal*) arriving, or happening, after the correct or expected time: *Our dinner guests are a little tardy.*

unpunctual arriving or taking action after the correct or expected time: *They tend to be unpunctual in paying their bills.*

See also **dead**.

laugh *verb*
to make a sound in your throat because you are amused: *I could hear the children laughing merrily in the garden.*

cackle to laugh in a loud unattractive manner: *a group of women cackling.*

chortle to laugh quite loudly at something that amuses you: *'That's hilarious!' he chortled.*

chuckle to laugh quietly: *She sat, chuckling to herself, as she read her magazine.*

giggle to give a high-pitched childlike laugh: *The girls started giggling and couldn't stop.*

guffaw give a loud deep laugh: *The men were guffawing with laughter at the comedian.*

roar to give a loud deep hearty laugh: *The audience was roaring with laughter.*

snigger to give a quiet mocking laugh: *The rest of the class sniggered at Sam's mistake.*

titter give a high-pitched, embarrassed laugh: *Some of the children tittered nervously during the sex-education class.*

lazy *adjective*
disinclined to work or to do anything energetic: *She is too lazy to go to the gym.*

bone-idle (*informal*) extremely lazy: *He's bone-idle; his mother does everything for him.*

idle disinclined to work: *Get a move on, you idle layabout!*

inactive not doing anything, or not inclined to do much: *I have had an inactive day today.*

indolent (*formal*) disinclined to do anything energetic: *He was an incurably indolent and selfish teenager.*

lethargic having little or no energy: *I felt very lethargic after the flu.*

shiftless disinclined to work and having no motivation: *a shiftless scrounger.*

sluggish moving or progressing slowly and showing a lack of energy or drive: *The housing market is usually very sluggish in winter.*

leader *noun*
the person in charge of a group, an organization, or an activity: *the leader of the Conservative Party.*

boss (*informal*) your superior at work: *I asked the boss for a rise.*

captain the leader of a team, especially in a sport, or the person who is in charge of a ship or an aircraft: *The captain went up to receive the cup from the chairman of the Football Association.*

chief the person in charge of a group of people: *the chief of the tribe.*

head the person in charge of an organization: *the head of the company.*

manager the person in charge of a business firm or of a department: *the marketing manager.*

principal the person in charge of a school, especially in the USA: *Go to the principal's office!*

ringleader the person at the head of a group of criminals or wrongdoers: *Max was the ringleader of the bullies.*

supremo (*informal*) the person with most influence or power in a particular organization or field of activity: *the Italian football supremo.*

top dog (*informal*) the most important and influential person in an organization, usually the person in charge: *He's not happy being the top dog's deputy, he wants to be top dog himself.*

learn *verb*
gather or receive information or knowledge, usually in a particular subject, into your mind, or to find out how to practise a particular skill: *I am learning to drive.*

absorb take in information and store it in your brain: *Children absorb so much information in the first few years of their lives.*

assimilate (*formal*) to absorb information and be able to understand it thoroughly: *They can repeat what the teacher told them, but have they really assimilated what they've been taught?*

master to learn and understand a subject or a skill thoroughly: *I have mastered the art of playing the saxophone.*

memorize to learn something so that it is stored in your memory and you can repeat it exactly in its original form: *He only needs to see a number for a second to be able to memorize it.*

revise to go back over all you have learnt about a subject in order to prepare for an examination or test: *She's out playing tennis when she should be revising for her history exam.*
Only used in British English; the usual word in US English is *review*.

study learn about a subject, especially at school, college, or university: *Mohammed is studying aeronautics at university.*

swot (*informal*) to revise a subject for an examination: *Bryony is swotting for her Modern Studies exam.*

See also **knowledge; understand**.

lie *noun*

an untrue statement that a person makes to deceive someone: *He told her he was single, but that was a lie.*

falsehood (*formal*) an untrue statement: *Someone has been spreading falsehoods about me.*

fib (*informal*) a lie that is not very serious: *She told a tiny fib about her age.*

perjury the crime of telling a lie when under oath in a court of law: *The witness has been charged with perjury.*

porky (pie) (*informal*) a lie: *He's been found out telling porkies.*

tall story a story that someone tells that is difficult to believe, usually because it contains improbably adventurous or romantic events: *My grandfather used to tell us tall stories about his adventures in India.*

untruth (*formal*) an untrue statement: *The newspapers have been known to print untruths.*

white lie a lie that is told to spare someone's feelings: *When she told her friend she liked her new hairdo, that was just a little white lie.*

whopper (*informal*) a blatant lie: *He said he had a private jet; what a whopper!*

light *adjective*

not weighing much: *This bag is very light.*

buoyant light enough to float on air or in a liquid: *a buoyant vessel.*

flimsy light and thin, and easy to tear or damage: *a dress made of flimsy material.*

portable small and light enough to be carried about: *a portable television.*

slight small and light in build: *Jockeys must be of slight build.*

underweight weighing too little relative to your height: *underweight fashion models.*

weightless weighing nothing: *In space you are weightless because there is no gravity.*

list *noun*

a series of items such as words, names, or numbers arranged in order, usually written down one below the other: *a shopping list.*

catalogue a long list showing all the items that available in something, especially all the goods that you can buy from a firm: *a mail-order catalogue.*

checklist a list of things to attend to, which you tick off as you do them: *I made a checklist of things I need to pack.*

directory a list of details such as names, addresses, and telephone numbers: *a telephone directory.*

index an alphabetical list at the end of a book showing important items with relevant page numbers: *Look up 'Second World War' in the index.*

inventory a complete list of the items that are in a place such as a flat or house that you are renting, or of the items that a person or business owns, or of the good that a shop has to sell: *We made an inventory of the goods in stock.*

menu a list of options to choose from in a restaurant or on a computer screen: *the lunch menu.*

register an official record of some-

thing, for example of births, marriages, and deaths or of when children attend school: *The teacher takes the register every morning before classes begin.*

roll an official list of names and other details of people who are members of something or are entitled to vote: *the electoral roll.*

listen *verb*

to concentrate so that you hear what someone says, music, the radio, etc.: *I like to listen to CDs in the car.*

be all ears (*informal*) to listen very attentively: *'Are you paying attention?' 'Yes, go ahead – I'm all ears!'*

bug (*informal*) to place a secret listening device in a room so that you can listen in to private conversations: *The politician discovered that his room had been bugged.*

eavesdrop to listen secretly to a private

conversation between other people: *If you eavesdrop on other people's conversations, you may well hear something you don't like.*

hear to register a sound with your ears: *I heard a bang.*

overhear to hear by accident a private conversation between other people: *I overheard two girls criticizing my best friend.*

pay attention to give your full attention to what someone is saying: *Are you paying attention at the back of the class?*

tap (*informal*) to place a secret listening device in a telephone so that you can listen in to private telephone conversations: *The police had tapped the suspect's phone.*

long *adjective*

1 lasting for a considerable time: *a long holiday.*

extended lasting for a longer time than usual: *I'm taking an extended break from work.*

interminable lasting so long that it seems it will never end and becomes boring: *an interminable rant about the government.*

lengthy lasting for a long time, often

an inconveniently long time: *a lengthy wait at the bus stop.*

lingering which does not finish quickly but continues slowly for a long time: *a long lingering death.*

prolonged lasting longer than planned or expected: *a prolonged visit.*

protracted proceeding slowly and taking a long time, often an inconveniently long time: *protracted negotiations.*

sustained made to continue for a long

time: *a sustained silence.*

time-consuming which takes up a lot of your time: *Washing clothes by hand is very time-consuming.*

2 extending for a considerable distance, or for a specified distance: *It's a long way from here to London.*

extensive extending for a considerable distance and over a wide area: *a house with extensive grounds.*

in length extending for the specified distance: *three metres in length.*

lengthy (more often used to describe objects than distances) quite long: *You'll need a lengthy piece of rope to reach to the bottom of the well.*

look *verb*
to direct your eyes towards something or someone: *Look at this painting!*

gaze to look for a long time at someone or something, usually at something you find attractive or fascinating: *We gazed at the majesty of the mountains.*

glance to look quickly or briefly at

someone or something or in a particular direction: *I glanced back over my shoulder to make sure that no one was following me.*

glare to look angrily at someone: *John glared at me when I mentioned his wife.*

ogle to look at someone in a way that expresses sexual attraction: *She is fed up with being ogled by strange men.*

peep to have a quick look at someone or something: *She peeped at him through her fringe.*

scan to look at the whole of something, especially moving your eyes from side to side, either attentively or swiftly: *She was anxiously scanning the newspaper to see if her name was mentioned.*

stare to look for a long time at someone or something, usually at someone or something you find surprising or remarkable, and sometimes in a rude way: *He could not help staring at her.*

See also **see; watch**.

loud *adjective*
having a high level of sound: *a loud bang.*

blaring making an unpleasantly loud noise: *The television is blaring.*

booming making a loud deep sound: *a booming loudspeaker.*

deafening so loud as to cause temporary deafness: *a deafening racket.*

ear-piercing very loud and high-pitched: *an ear-piercing scream.*

noisy making an unpleasantly loud sound: *a noisy party.*

resonant loud and echoing: *the resonant sound of the church bells.*

shrill very loud and high-pitched: *the shrill screech of a bird.*

strident loud and harsh: *a strident voice.*

See also **bold.**

love *verb*
to feel strong affection for someone or something, or a great liking for doing something: *I love my parents very much.*

adore to feel deep love for someone or something: *She adores and looks up to her older sister.*

be crazy about (*informal*) to be deeply in love with someone: *He is crazy about his new girlfriend.*

be fond of feel affection for someone

or something: *They are very fond of their dog.*

be infatuated with feel very strongly attracted to and preoccupied with someone, but in a way that other people do not really approve of or think will last: *Her husband is infatuated with one of his work colleagues.*

care for to feel affection for someone: *A friend is someone you care for and whose company you enjoy.*

dote on to love someone excessively, to a degree that other people think is foolish: *They dote on their children to the point of spoiling them.*

have a crush on (*informal*) to feel a strong, but not necessarily lasting, attraction for someone, especially someone older than you: *Natalie has a crush on her art teacher.*

worship to love someone very much, to the point of idolizing them:
Gerry absolutely worships his wife; she can do no wrong in his eyes.

mad *adjective*
unable to understand reality and behave normally or sensibly, or showing a lack of understanding of reality and an inability to behave normally or sensibly: *He thought he was going mad.* It is not usual to describe people with a mental illness as *mad* when discussing their condition seriously.

barking (*informal*) (only used to
describe people)
completely mad:
*She's absolutely
barking, but harmless.*

barmy (*informal*) mad or very foolish: *He's driving me barmy with all his silly ideas!*

bonkers (*informal*) (usually used to describe people) mad: *Ollie is quite bonkers – you never know what he is going to do next.*

crazy very foolish or peculiar, or (*informal*) mad: *a crazy scheme.*

demented mad and likely to behave violently or be uncontrollable active: *We've been rushing round as if we were demented, trying to get everything ready in time.*

insane having a serious mental illness, or (*informal*) mad: *She went insane some years ago and has never fully recovered.*

mentally ill suffering from a psychological condition that makes you unable to behave normally: *His wife became mentally ill and was confined to a hospital.*

nuts (*informal*) very foolish or peculiar: *My friends are all nuts, but they're great fun.*

of unsound mind (*formal*) not well enough mentally to be considered legally responsible: *He killed his wife while he was of unsound mind.*

out of your mind (*informal*) mad: *Are you out of your mind? This plan could bankrupt the company.*

make *verb*
to form, build, or create something: *The little girl made a birthday card for her mother.*

assemble to build something, such as furniture or a model, by fitting the parts together: *I tried to assemble my new computer chair, but there was a screw missing.*

bring into existence create, produce, or originate something, such as a plan or system: *The National Health Service was brought into existence in the UK in 1948.*

build to create a building or other structure using strong materials: *We are having an extension built onto our house.*

construct to build something, such as a structure or a vehicle: *The Empire State Building is constructed from reinforced concrete and steel.*

fabricate (*formal*) to produce or create something from different materials, especially in a factory: *Dentures, crowns, and bridges are manufactured in a wide variety of materials.*

manufacture to produce or create goods in a factory, usually in large numbers: *I bought a beautiful chess set that was manufactured in Poland.*

produce to create or process something, sometimes in a factory: *The distillery produces the finest single-malt whisky.*

put together to build or create something from different parts or materials: *Ross put together a doll's house for his daughter.*

See also **build 1**.

man *noun*
an adult male human being: *a big strong man.*

bloke (*informal*) a man: *the bloke in the white T-shirt.*

boy a male child, or (*informal*) a man: *a night out with the boys.*

chap (*informal*) (sounds slightly old-fashioned and upper-class; usually used to describe a man in an informal but fairly respectful way) a man: *a decent chap.*

dude (*informal*) a man, especially a fashionably dressed one: *a cool dude.*

fellow (*informal*) a chap: *the little fellow.*

gentleman a man with good manners, or a polite way of referring to a man: *Mr Thomson is a real old-fashioned gentleman.*

guy (*informal*) a man: *He's a really nice guy.*

male (used in an impersonal way) a man or boy: *a hairdresser for both males and females.*

many *adjective*
a large number of: *many years ago.*

countless too many to be counted: *I have asked you countless times to tidy your room.*

innumerable (*formal*) too many to be counted: *on innumerable occasions.*

loads of (*informal*) a very large number or quantity of: *I've got loads of clothes that I will never wear again.*

lots of (*informal*) a large number or quantity of: *lots of presents.*

numerous (*formal*) a very large number of: *Numerous people have visited the exhibition.*

plenty a sufficiently large number or quantity of: *We have plenty of helpers for the jumble sale.*

several a fairly large number of: *I have several pairs of shoes to choose from.*

mean *adjective*
unwilling to spend money or to give to others: *He is too mean to buy a round of drinks.*

grasping excessively concerned with accumulating money and unwilling to spend it: *an unkind grasping man.*

miserly very unwilling to spend money: *She is too miserly to buy a poppy for Poppy Day.*

niggardly (*formal*) parsimonious in character, or very small in amount: *a niggardly amount.*

parsimonious (*formal*) unwilling to spend more money than is absolutely necessary: *a parsimonious old bachelor.*

penny-pinching (*informal*) always looking for ways to save money and unwilling to spend it: *their penny-pinching ways.*

stingy (*informal*) mean: *Don't be so stingy; we're collecting for a good cause!*

tight-fisted (*informal*) unwilling to spend money or to give to others: *He is too tight-fisted to buy Christmas presents.*

meet *verb*
be in the same place as someone, either by accident or by arrangement: *We arranged to meet in the station at four o'clock.*

bump into (*informal*) to meet someone unexpectedly: *I bumped into my aunt in town today.*

chance upon (*formal*) meet someone or find something unexpectedly: *On holiday we chanced upon some old college friends.*

come upon (*formal*) to chance upon: *Walking along the seashore, I came upon a crowd of children.*

encounter (*formal*) to meet someone,

usually unexpectedly: *Jane was shocked to encounter her ex-husband at the party.*

rendezvous to meet someone by arrangement at a particular time: *One evening he led a patrol to rendezvous with another group of officers.*

run into (*informal*) to meet someone unexpectedly: *I ran into my ex-boss at the conference.*

mercy *noun*
the act of not punishing or not harming someone who is in your power: *The guards showed no mercy to the prisoners.*

clemency (*formal*) the granting of a less severe punishment: *The judge rejected their plea for clemency.*

compassion sympathy and understanding: *She always treats people with kindness and compassion.*

forgiveness the act of excusing someone for some wrongdoing: *He begged his wife for forgiveness for his infidelity.*

humanity the quality of being kind and sympathetic to others: *The hostages were treated with humanity at all times.*

kindness the quality of being gentle and helpful to others: *Thank you very much for your kindness and hospitality.*

leniency treating someone less harshly

 than might have been expected: *The head teacher showed leniency towards the boy because he was not a persistent troublemaker.*

pity a feeling, or a show, of kindness towards someone who is suffering: *She took pity on the homeless man and gave him a hot meal.*

sympathy understanding for someone's feelings, especially the feelings of someone who is suffering: *Barry's employers have shown him a great deal of sympathy since his wife died.*

See also **forgive.**

mind *noun*
the part of a person that has the power to think, make judgments, imagine, and produce ideas: *He had one of the finest scientific minds of the 20th century.*

brain the organ of your body, located

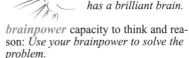 in your head, that controls your thoughts and bodily functions: *She has a brilliant brain.*

brainpower capacity to think and reason: *Use your brainpower to solve the problem.*

head your mind: *You think everyone is against you, but it's all in your head.*

imagination the ability to form mental images of things that you have never experienced: *I have never been to Japan, except in my imagination.*

intellect ability to think and reason: *people of superior intellect.*

intelligence ability to learn, to understand, and to use information and knowledge to solve problems, especially strong ability: *He has a keen intelligence.*

mentality a particular way of thinking: *I just don't understand the mentality of people who desecrate graves.*

subconscious the part of your mind

 that works in ways that you are not conscious of: *Somewhere in my subconscious I must have been harbouring a resentment that I was not even aware of.*

mistake *noun*
an instance of doing something wrong: *You have made three mistakes in your maths exercise.*

bloomer (*informal*) an embarrassing mistake: *I made a real bloomer – I called Eric's wife by the wrong name.*

blunder (*informal*) a stupid mistake: *Craig made a blunder which will cost the firm a lot of money.*

clanger (*informal*) a stupid or embar-

 rassing mistake: *What a clanger – Linda said the capital of Belgium was Amsterdam!*

error an instance of getting something wrong: *a typing error.*

faux pas (*formal*) an embarrassing social blunder: *I made a terrible faux pas – I asked Margaret how her husband was, and he died last month!*

gaffe (*formal*) an embarrassing mistake, especially a social blunder: *His first gaffe was to use the wrong cutlery at dinner.*

inaccuracy an instance of not reporting a fact correctly: *There are several inaccuracies in this report.*

omission an instance of missing out something that should have been included: *This list is incomplete – there are at least four omissions.*

mix *verb*

to put two or more substances together and work on them so that they form one substance or cannot easily be separated again: *Mix a few drops of water into the icing sugar to make a smooth paste.*

amalgamate to bring two things, such as organizations, together to form one: *The two unions have amalgamated.*

blend to mix ingredients or substances gradually together so that they form one substance: *Blend the fruits and yogurt to make a smoothie.*

combine to come together or bring things together to make one thing: *Combine flour, butter, and milk to make a white sauce.*

intersperse to include things at intervals or in separate places among another, larger, group of things: *The essay was interspersed with quotations from other writers.*

jumble to mix things up in a haphazard way: *Everyone's trainers ended up all jumbled in a pile.*

merge to join two things, such as businesses or pieces of text, together to make one whole thing: *I have merged the two lists into one alphabetical list.*

mingle to mix two or more things, such as feelings or smells, together, so that they are experienced at the same time: *I felt excitement mingled with fear.*

shuffle to mix up a pack of cards so that they end up in a different order: *Always shuffle the cards before you deal.*

mockery *noun* the act of teasing or

ridiculing someone by making hurtful or offensive comments about them or their actions: *He was just an object of mockery.*

contempt complete lack of respect, a feeling or behaviour that suggests that someone or something has no value: *The lord of the manor treated the servants with contempt.*

derision the act of showing that you think that something is ridiculous: *The suggestion was met with shouts of derision.*

disdain dislike and disrespect: *He continued to pursue her even though she treated him with complete disdain.*

jeering the shouting of mocking remarks: *There was much jeering and booing from the crowd.*

ribbing (*informal*) the act of teasing someone in a friendly jokey manner: *There is always a fair amount of ribbing among the guys in the rugby team.*

ridicule the act of deliberately making someone appear foolish by laughing at them or making hurtful comments: *She was subjected to much ridicule in the media.*

taunting the saying something to someone with the aim of hurting their feelings or making them try to attack you: *She suffered taunting by bullies about being fat.*

modern *adjective*

dating from or appropriate to the present time or the recent past: *modern literature.*

contemporary dating from, or being in the style of, the present time: *contemporary art.*

current taking place in or relating to the present time: *current events.*

new which has recently come into fashion or recently become available: *the new fitness craze.*

new-fangled new and unnecessarily complicated: *a new-fangled device.*

present-day relating to the present time: *present-day society.*

recent that has taken place in or relates to a time shortly before the present: *a recent development.*

state-of-the-art using the most up-to-date technology: *a state-of-the-art computer.*

up-to-date being the newest of its kind: *up-to-date technology.*

See also **fashionable; new.**

money *noun*
coins and banknotes that you use to pay for things: *I have no money in my purse.*

capital a large amount of money that you need to start up and run a business: *How can I raise capital to start a hairdressing business?*

cash money in the form of coins and banknotes, rather than cheques, credit cards, etc.: *I'm sorry but I haven't got any cash on me at the moment.*

change a small amount of money in the form of coins: *Do you have change for the bus fare?*

currency the type of money used in a particular country or area: *The dollar is the main unit of currency in the USA.*

dosh (*informal*) money: *He's got loads of dosh.*

dough (*informal*) money: *I've run out of dough.*

filthy lucre (*informal and humorous*) money, especially thought of as something sinful or acquired by doubtful means: *He's moved to Spain to count his filthy lucre.*

funds an amount of money saved 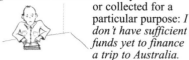 or collected for a particular purpose: *I don't have sufficient funds yet to finance a trip to Australia.*

legal tender a banknote or coin that you can legally use to pay a debt in a particular country: *I'm not sure that Scottish pound notes are accepted as legal tender in England.*

moving *adjective*
causing you to feel strong emotion, especially sadness: *a very moving speech.*

affecting causing you to feel strong emotion, especially sadness or pity: *an affecting piece of music.*

emotional portraying, and arousing, strong emotion, such as sadness or joy: *an emotional performance.*

heart-rending causing you to feel great sadness or pity: *a heart-rending story.*

heart-warming causing you to feel happiness or satisfaction that something good has happened: *It was a heart-warming moment in the film when the hero and heroine finally met up again.*

poignant causing you to feel strong emotion, especially sadness, regret, or longing: *poignant memories.*

stirring causing you to feel strong positive emotion, such as joy or patriotism: *a stirring national anthem.*

tear-jerking (*informal*) deliberately trying to move you to tears: *a tear-jerking film.*

touching causing you to feel an emotion such as love, gratitude, or sympathy: *Her gratitude was quite touching.*

upsetting causing you to feel distressed or offended: *It was upsetting to see the starving children in the news.*

See also **affect 2.**

mysterious *adjective*
strange and unexplained: *a mysterious illness.*

baffling very hard to understand or explain: *His attitude was baffling.*

enigmatic intriguing and hard to understand: *The hero of the film is an enigmatic figure.*

inexplicable unable to be explained: *for some inexplicable reason.*

inscrutable hard to understand or identify: *an inscrutable facial expression.*

mystifying extremely hard to understand or explain: *I find her hostility mystifying.*

puzzling hard to understand or explain: *a puzzling question.*

unexplained for which an explanation has not been found: *unexplained infertility.*

See also **strange.**

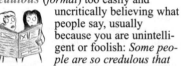

naive *adjective*
having or showing a very simple and trusting view of the ways in which people behave towards one another, usually because you are inexperienced: *In those days I was too naive to understand what was going on between them.*

artless not trying to be clever or sophisticated or to deceive people in any way, and so seeming either refreshingly direct or naive or unsophisticated: *In his artless way he seems to have got straight to the heart of the problem.*

credulous (*formal*) too easily and uncritically believing what people say, usually because you are unintelligent or foolish: *Some people are so credulous that they believe anything that is written in the newspapers.*

gullible very easy to deceive and too trusting: *You surely don't think I'm gullible enough to fall for that old trick.*

immature not behaving like an adult or having the understanding and judgment of an adult: *He's twenty-one, but very immature for his age.*

ingenuous (*formal*) saying simply what you think or behaving simply in the way you think is right, without realizing that other people are not always so straightforward: *She was too ingenuous herself to realize that although other people might be thinking the same things that she was, they were too polite to put their thoughts into words.*

innocent not knowing how things are done in the world, especially not knowing about the unpleasant or even wicked ways in which people sometimes treat one another: *When it comes to money matters, he's as innocent as a new-born babe.*

unsophisticated simple or crude, not clever or subtle in the way you deal with things: *Country people often seem very unsophisticated when compared with city dwellers.*

unworldly not knowing very much about how things are done in the real world or how people behave in society: *Scholars sometimes seem unworldly because they spend more time in thinking up theories than in putting their theories into practice.*

naked *adjective*

not wearing any clothes: *Do you think he's ever actually seen his wife naked?*

bare (used to describe parts of the body or objects, areas, etc.) without any covering: *Her arms and shoulders were bare.*

in the nude naked: *Do you feel embarrassed about appearing on stage in the nude?*

in your birthday suit (*informal*) naked: *The children were running around in their birthday suits.*

not decent (*informal*) not wearing enough clothes to feel comfortable about being seen by someone else, that is, usually, either naked or in your underwear: *You can't come in; I'm not decent.*

nude (usually used to describe peo-

ple represented or appearing in works of art such as paintings, films, or plays) naked: *a nude reclining figure.*

starkers (*informal and humorous*) naked: *They bet me £20 I wouldn't run down the street starkers.*

stark naked completely and usually dramatically naked: *There I was, stark naked, having just got out of the bath, when three armed policemen burst in.*

topless (usually used to describe women) with the top half of the body bare: *topless waitresses.*

undressed naked, in your underwear, or in the clothes you wear in bed: *I felt a bit embarrassed about having to open the front door while I was still undressed.*

name *noun*

a word that identifies someone or something: *It was not 'borrowing' – let's call it by its right name, it was 'stealing'.*

designation (*formal*) a word used to

describe something or someone, or the process of using a particular word to describe something or someone: *The status and designation of 'Academy' was granted to the school in 1961.*

epithet a descriptive word or expression that is frequently added to substituted for the name of a thing or person: *Homer almost always uses the epithet 'wine-dark' when he refers to the sea.*

label a word or expression commonly and often informally used to describe someone or something in addition to or in place of their real name: *It was so small but so powerful that it soon acquired the label 'The Mighty Midget'.*

nickname a name used to refer to a person informally or humorously, which is often a shortened or modified form of their real name or refers to a habit or characteristic that they have: *His nickname at school was 'Beans', because he loved to eat baked beans.*

tag a label or nickname, especially an unflattering one: *I know the National Theatre's production of* King John *was rather slow, but did it really deserve the tag 'King Yawn'?*

term a word or expression: *We don't call it a 'lawn-cutter'; the correct term is 'lawnmower'.*

title a word by which you address someone or refer to them and which shows their status (for example, *Mr, Mrs, Dr, Lord,*: *She's actually Lady Daphne Shufflebotham, but she rarely uses her title.*

necessary *adjective*
that you need to have or to do, often in order to be able to do something else: *It may be necessary for you to prove that you can speak English, if you want to apply for a job in the USA.*

compulsory that you must do, that you are given no choice about: *Attendance at school is compulsory for all children aged between 5 and 16 who are not being educated at home.*

essential extremely important, necessary, or relating to the basic nature of something: *Learning to cope with setbacks is an essential part of growing up.*

imperative (*formal*) necessary and very important: *It is imperative that we act now to prevent the spread of the infection.* Usually used after a verb.

indispensable that you cannot do without: *Harmonious agreement between the member states is an indispensable condition for the European Union to work well.*

obligatory compulsory: *The govern-*

ment is going to make it obligatory for anyone who wishes to continue driving after the age of 75 to retake the driving test.

required necessary, especially in order to comply with rules or instructions: Hamlet *is required reading for anyone taking the Shakespeare course.*

requisite (*formal*) required: *the requisite number of safety personnel.*

vital extremely important or necessary: *It is vital that this information should not fall into the wrong hands.*

See also **basic**.

new *adjective*
not used, owned, or known about before, or recently made, bought, discovered, etc.: *You look very smart in your new suit.*

fresh (used to describe fruits, vegetables, etc., or cooked things) recently picked or made and still in best condition; (used to describe ideas, actions, etc.) new, sometimes excitingly new, especially now replacing something that previously existed or was previously used and is no longer in best condition: *The old methods can no longer solve our problems, what we need now is a completely fresh approach.*

ground-breaking that does or investigates something that no one has done or investigated before, and makes new developments possible: *their ground-breaking work in microbiology.*

innovative showing an ability to

develop new ways of doing things: *In a time of rapid technological change, companies need to be innovative in the way they develop and market their products.*

novel new and rather unusual or surprising: *It's a novel way of earning a living, but at least she has no competition.*

original that nobody has thought of or done before, or that is not copied from anything or anyone else: *Your essay is rather short of original ideas.*

pioneering that is done before anyone else attempts to do the same thing: *Their successes would have been impossible without the pioneering work done by their predecessors in the field.*

See also **modern**.

news *noun*

information about events that have recently happened: *Now it's over to James for the rest of the day's news.*

announcement a written or spoken statement that gives a piece of information to the general public or a particular group of people for the first time: *The Prime Minister will be making an announcement of the date for the general election to Parliament shortly.*

article a piece of writing, usually on a serious subject, in a newspaper or magazine: *I read an article on the subject in today's* Times.

bulletin a news report on television or radio; an official statement giving information: *In newspapers and television news bulletins around the world, the talk is all about the bombings.*

headline a statement in large print at the top of a newspaper article or report telling you in a few words what the article or report is about, especially a statement on the front page announcing the main news of the day: *Under the headline GAS BUBBLE BURSTS, the* Daily Herald *reports on financial problems in the gas industry.*

message a usually short, written or spoken statement containing news or information, which is intended to be passed on to a particular person or group of people: *He left you a message to say that he wouldn't be able to come to the meeting this evening.*

report a written document or spoken statement that is quite long and provides detailed news, information, or discussion of a particular topic: *A report has just come in from our correspondent in Baghdad on the results of the general election in Iraq.*

story an event that the media believe is worth reporting, or an account of an event given in a newspaper or as an item in a news broadcast: *The story first appeared in the* York Evening News *and was then taken up by the national newspapers.*

tidings (*old-fashioned*) news: *When the king heard the glad tidings, he rejoiced.*

word news or information, especially reported orally by someone: *There's been no word yet on when the wedding will actually take place.*

See also **information.**

nice *adjective*

1 (used to describe things, events, etc.) arousing generally positive feelings in you, giving you enjoyment or pleasure, or that you like: *Did you have a nice time at the party?*

agreeable arousing generally positive but not particularly strong feelings, quite pleasant or appealing: *She found the sea air very agreeable.*

appealing causing you to wish to have it or do it, attractive: *The idea of not having to get up very early in the morning is very appealing.*

delightful arousing strongly positive feelings, very pleasant: *How delightful to see you again!*

enjoyable that you enjoyed or can enjoy: *Thank you for this evening: it's been most enjoyable.*

good arousing quite strong positive feelings, pleasant or enjoyable, or beneficial: *I hope you had a good holiday.*

lovely very pleasant or beautiful: *Wouldn't it be lovely if we never had to worry about money ever again!*

pleasant that gives you pleasure, or makes you feel comfortable and relaxed: *It brings back very pleasant memories of my youth.*

2 (used to describe people) kind and friendly: *Be nice to him, because he's not feeling very well.*

agreeable friendly and pleasant: *We invited some of our more agreeable neighbours in for a New Year's party.*

amiable friendly and pleasant to be

with, or which makes someone friendly and pleasant to be with: *Our new neighbour seems to be a very amiable sort of man.*

charming having a natural talent for making people like you or feel at ease with you: *I expected him to be rather formidable, but he's actually a very charming man.*

delightful having qualities such as friendliness and good nature that you appreciate very much: *They're a very nice couple, and their children are absolutely delightful.*

friendly showing that you like someone or that you want them to feel happy and at ease: *a friendly gesture.*

genial friendly and good-natured, especially making people feel relaxed and welcome: *our genial host.*

good-natured likely to treat people kindly and not likely to become angry or unfriendly: *She's too good-natured to take offence.*

likable that is easy to like, or that makes you like someone: *That is one of his less likable characteristics.*

obedient *adjective*
doing what someone tells you to do without questioning their instructions or arguing with them: *If all the children were as obedient as she is, the class would be much easier to manage.*

amenable likely or willing to accept something such as advice, persuasion, or a suggestion: *They might be more amenable if you offered to repay their expenses.*

compliant (*formal*) accepting orders or instructions, or fulfilling obligations, standards, etc., set by someone else: *Inspectors check whether restaurant owners maintain standards of cleanliness compliant with regulations under the Health and Safety Act.*

docile having a quiet, placid nature

and so unlikely to protest or disobey: *He's a very docile dog – he lets the children climb all over him.*

dutiful conscious of a duty to obey someone, especially your parents: *a dutiful daughter.*

law-abiding who does not break the law or cause trouble for the authorities: *The majority of the people in this area are ordinary law-abiding citizens.*

submissive obedient in a way that shows you are humble and acknowledge that others are superior to you or more powerful than you: *submissive to the will of the Lord.*

subservient excessively obedient and humble because you want to please people who are superior to you or more powerful than you: *A good servant knows how to be respectful without being subservient.*

obscure *adjective*

difficult to understand through being unclear or through involving knowledge that is not easily available or that not many people possess: *The meaning of this note is obscure.*

abstruse (formal) very difficult to understand usually because it involves knowledge that very few people possess or very complex ideas: *abstruse philosophical arguments.*

as clear as mud (informal) very difficult to understand, usually through not being clearly thought out or expressed: *Can you understand these instructions? They're as clear as mud to me.*

cryptic containing a secret or hidden meaning: *The text contains a few brief and cryptic references to the legend.*

esoteric (formal) very obscure and very specialized or secret, often able to be understood or known about only by people who have been given the secret by others who already know it: *Some of their beliefs are esoteric, and ordinary worshippers are kept in ignorance of them.*

impenetrable (formal) impossible to understand: *If it's impenetrable to someone who knows as much about the subject as Rose, how is the ordinary person supposed to understand it?*

recondite (formal) that few people

possess or know about: *recondite knowledge.*

unclear not easy to understand or be certain about, usually through containing an element of confusion: *It's unclear whether she intended this letter to be read before or after her death.*

observe *verb*

to show that you accept something such as a law or rule by doing what it tells you that you must do: *Drivers who fail to observe the speed limit can expect to be fined.*

abide by to accept and obey something such as a decision or a rule: *We agreed to abide by the referee's decision.*

adhere to (formal) to act in accordance with something: *We adhered strictly to the terms of the contract.*

conform to to be as something such as a rule or standard says it or you ought to be: *Does this machinery conform to European safety standards?*

follow to do what something tells you to do, especially when you are given a series of instructions: *I followed the recipe exactly, but the dish still didn't turn out right.*

keep to act in accordance with something, often a rule or an obligation that you have made for yourself: *He promised to be here by seven o'clock, but, of course, he seldom keeps his promises.*

obey to do what someone, or something such as a law, rule, or order, tells you that you must do: *Would you obey an order from a superior officer even if you knew the order was wrong?*

respect to show that you accept something such as the law or people's rights and do not wish to act in a way that breaks it or interferes with it: *I respect your right to say what you like on any subject, but that doesn't mean I have to agree with what you say.*

See also **say; watch.**

old *adjective*

having lived or been in existence for a long time, or for a specified period of time, usually a specified number of years: *I think you're old enough now to walk to school on your own.*

aged (*often humorous*) (usually used to describe people) old or very old: *She has to spend a lot of time looking after her aged parents.*
Usually used before a noun.

ancient (usually used to describe objects such as buildings or cities) very old, and usually attractive or interesting through being very old: *an ancient manuscript.*

antiquated (usually used to describe objects) very old-fashioned, completely out of date: *antiquated ideas.*

elderly (usually used to describe

 people and thought of as more polite than *old*) quite old or old: *Most of the residents of these flats are elderly people living on small incomes.*

middle-aged (usually used to describe people) no longer young, usually aged between 40 and 60: *I hate the music that my children listen to, so I must be getting middle-aged.*

old-fashioned not modern, of a kind commonly used in an earlier time, or (used to describe people) behaving or thinking in a way associated with an earlier time: *He still has an old-fashioned telephone with a dial.*

out-of-date/out of date not modern or fashionable any more, though often only recently having become so: *I only bought this computer three years ago, and it's already out of date.*

past its sell-by date (*informal and humorous*) out-of-date or old-fashioned: *That joke really is past its sell-by date now.*

past your/its prime no longer young or modern, past the period of being at your/its best: *She may be a little past her prime, but she's still a very good player.*

senile (usually used to describe people) old and suffering fro m mental and physical problems that reduce your ability to think, understand or remember things, or look after yourself: *I know who Madonna is, I'm not senile; yet!*

opinion *noun*

an idea or statement that expresses what a particular person or a particular group of people thinks or feels about a subject: *Nothing I've heard so far makes me want to change my opinion that this is a thoroughly bad idea.*

attitude the general way a particular person or group of people thinks and feels about something or someone, often shown in the way they behave towards them: *Your attitude to life changes as you get older.*

belief something that a person believes to be the case: *It's my belief that the victim knew his killer.*

conviction something that a person is convinced about, or a feeling of certainty about something: *Nothing seems to be able to shake her conviction that someone is following every time she goes out.*

feeling an impression or opinion, often one that is not entirely clear or that you are not entirely convinced about: *It's just a feeling; I don't have any evidence to support it.*

impression an idea that arises from the effect that someone or something has on you: *I got the impression that she knows rather more than she's willing to say.*

point of view a way of thinking about a subject that results from your particular nature, experiences, and opinions: *Try to* understand the point of view of the person who is arguing against you.

stance an opinion, or a point of view on a subject, especially one that is deliberately adopted and made public: *There's no sign that the government is likely to change its stance on the question of immigration.*

view an opinion: *We all know your views on religion.*

See also **advice; feeling.**

oppose *verb*

to disagree with something or someone, and to try to stop something happening or to stop someone doing what they wish or plan to do: *The union will oppose any attempt by the management to increase the working hours of the staff.*

be against not to be in favour of, or to disapprove of, something: *I've always been against capital punishment.*

confront to show your disagreement with, or opposition to, someone boldly, usually by meeting them face to face: *She decided she was going to confront her boss and ask him to explain his behaviour.*

defy to be bold and determined in refusing to obey someone or something or in challenging someone to do something: *They defied the Security Council and continued with their nuclear programme.*

object to be against something, usually because you feel it is wrong or not in your interest, and express your opposition to it: *Nobody objected when the Council originally announced its plan to demolish the building.*

resist to take action to defend yourself against someone who is attacking you, or to stop something being done to you: *The citizens of the country united to resist the invaders.*

stand up to refuse to be intimidated by someone who is threatening you: *Most bullies are actually cowards, and if you stand up to them, they'll leave you alone.*

take issue with to disagree with and argue against something or someone, usually in a polite way: *I'd like to take issue with you on that point.*

See also **conflict; disagree; fight; quarrel.**

order *noun*

a spoken or written statement that tells you that you must do something, usually made by someone who has authority over you: *The colonel gave orders for the regiment to prepare to launch an attack.*

command a spoken order given directly to someone especially by a military officer, or an instruction to a computer to perform a task: *On the command 'present arms', you will hold your weapon vertically in front of your body.*

commandment an order or instruction, especially a religious or moral instruction: *the Ten Commandments.*

decree an official command, especially one issued by the ruler of a country: *The decree authorizes the army to take control in an emergency.*

demand a request made in a forceful way: *If we give in to their demands, they'll ask for even higher wages.*

dictate what something such as reason or conscience tells you ought to do: *the dictates of conscience.*

directive an official instruction given by a non-military organization: *Head office has issued a directive on the recycling of waste.*

instruction a statement that tells you what you should do or how you should do something: *First read the instructions for setting up the computer.*

request an instance of asking someone to do something: *We've had a lot of requests from people for us to play this record.*

See also **organize; rule**.

ordinary *adjective*
not special, of the kind that people use or experience most often: *It started out as just an ordinary day.*

average considered as being representative of what most people, things, etc., are like or do, or being at the midpoint between two extremes: *How many cups of coffee do you think the average person drinks in a day?*

common often seen, done, or experienced: *It's common nowadays for young people to take a gap year between leaving school and going to university.*

conventional (used to describe a

method or object) that is usually used or has been used for a long time; (used to describe people) following the normal behaviour and opinions of most people: *Complementary medicine differs from conventional medicine.*
Only used before a noun.

everyday that is seen, used, done very frequently: *Artists often try to make people see everyday objects in a new light.*
Only used before a noun.

normal usual or average, especially reassuringly familiar or setting a standard by which you judge that things are different or wrong: *Temperatures during the day will be around normal for this time of the year.*

regular normal: *We're just regular people, nothing special.*
Used more in US English than British English.

routine very ordinary, not interesting or exciting: *Computers are good at handling routine tasks.*

standard ordinary, not having any special features, or being what everybody does or what rules say should be done: *It's standard procedure these days to ask for some form of identification before you allow anyone to enter the building.*

typical having the characteristics that most things or people of a certain kind possess, or exactly what you would expect of something or someone: *A typical day in the office begins within an informal meeting of all the staff to make plans, discuss problems, and set targets.*

usual of the kind that you are familiar with and expect to happen, most often do, etc.: *On that particular day I decided not to walk to work by my usual route.*

organize *verb*

1 to plan something and make the necessary preparations for it to be carried out: *We're organizing a trip to Stratford-on-Avon for members of the drama club.*

arrange to do what is necessary,

such as making plans and getting other people to agree to them, to make sure that something happens: *I've arranged for a taxi to pick you up from the hotel at seven o'clock.*

coordinate to make sure that plans or arrangements made by a number of different people work together and do not interfere with one another: *Your job is to coordinate the efforts of the various departments to improve productivity.*

deal with to take responsibility for organizing or doing something: *I'll deal with the financial side of things, and you concentrate on artistic matters.*

fix (up) (*informal*) arrange something: *I've fixed it so that we can pick up the tickets from the theatre box office.*

look after (*informal*) to deal with something: *Who's looking after transport for the delegates to and from the conference hall?*

make arrangements to arrange something: *We've made arrangements to meet outside the station at 6.30.*

see about (*informal*) to take responsibility for doing or getting something: *Could you see about some chairs for the people who arrived late?*

see to (*informal*) to deal with: *That's being seen to by the cleaning staff.*

2 to put things into a state where they are not confused or untidy and have a logical order: *Could you help me organize these files?*

arrange put something into a particular order, shape, or pattern: *We arranged the chairs in a circle.*

classify to decide what kind of thing

 something is and put it together with other things of the same kind: *This book is partly fact and partly science fiction, so it's rather difficult to classify.*

order to arrange things in a particular sequence or according to a particular system: *Probably the best plan is to order the entries alphabetically.*

put in order to make something tidy, or to order something: *We'll start by putting the room in order.*

sort to divide up a number of things into different groups according to what kind of things they are: *I've sorted your letters into three piles – 'deal with now', 'deal with tomorrow' and 'deal with next week'.*

sort out to organize things, especially to put things that are in a confused state into order: *It's going to take ages to sort out the mess left by my predecessor.*

own *verb*
to be in possession of something: *Do you own your home or is it rented?*

boast to possess or to have achieved something impressive: *The city boasts two cathedrals.*

enjoy to be fortunate enough to have something, especially something abstract: *My mother had always enjoyed good health until she reached her seventies.*

have to be the owner of something: *My parents have a holiday home in Spain.*

hold to be in possession of something, for example official documents: *Do you hold a current European passport?*

keep to continue to have possession of something, sometimes because it is of sentimental value to you: *Derek keeps the ticket stubs from all the football matches he goes to.*

maintain (*formal*) to have possession of or the use of something, such as a vehicle or a home: *The family maintains two cars.*

possess to be the owner of something: *Sarah possesses fifty pairs of shoes.*

retain to keep something in your possession: *Please retain your receipt in case you need to return your purchases.*

pain *noun*

an unpleasant feeling or state that hurts you, which may be physical, caused by an injury or an illness, or may be mental, caused by an event that makes you to feel sad: *Do you feel any pain when I press here?*

ache a pain in part of your body that continues steadily for a long time, but is usually not very severe: *It's not a stabbing pain, doctor, it's more of an ache.*

agony a state in which you feel very severe physical or mental pain: *I was in agony all night with toothache.*

cramp a state in which the muscles in part of your body suddenly and painfully tighten up, or a pain caused by this: *I woke up with (a) terrible cramp in my right leg.*

discomfort a general feeling of being uncomfortable or in pain, sometimes used as a euphemism for pain: *If you feel any discomfort, ask the nurse to give you a painkiller.*

itch a small irritating pain on the outside of your body, that usually makes you want to scratch your skin to relieve it: *My skin feels very dry, and I have a terrible itch.*

soreness pain that is usually felt when you have a wound or sensitive area on the outside of your body and something rubs against it: *I'll give you some ointment to relieve any soreness where you grazed your leg.*

stitch (*informal*) a pain, caused by cramp, that you suddenly feel in your side, often when you are running or taking exercise: *I've got a stitch, so I'll have to rest for a minute.*

suffering a state in which you experience severe physical or mental pain for a long

time: *I don't want you to keep him alive if it simply means prolonging his suffering.*

twinge a slight but often worrying pain

in part of the body: *I feel a twinge every time I bend my knee.*

See also **hurt.**

pale *adjective*

being a whiter or less intense variety of a particular colour, or showing a whiter colour in your skin than is normal, usually because you are ill or afraid: *You do look rather pale, perhaps you're sickening for something.*

ashen having a very pale or greyish

complexion, usually as a result of severe illness or a terrible shock or grief: *I don't think they should have let him out of hospital – he looked ashen when he got home.*

light (used to describe a colour) pale: *light blue.*

pastel (used to describe a colour) pale and soft in quality: *pastel pink.*

pallid pale or lacking a healthy colour: *a pallid complexion.*

pasty(-faced) pale and unhealthy-looking, especially in the face, usually not as a result of a particular illness, but of an unhealthy lifestyle and a lack of fresh air and exercise: *The pasty-faced ones are the ones who spend more time watching television or playing on their computers than they do running around outside.*

peaky (*informal*) slightly pale and ill: *She looks a bit peaky this morning; I don't think she slept very well.*

wan (*literary*) pale, usually from grief or illness: *He had the traditional wan and slightly forlorn look of an unhappy lover.*

white very pale, usually through fear or shock: *He went white when I told him the news.*

part

1 *noun* one of several smaller things that go together to make up a larger thing or into which a whole can be divided, or an item that has a particular function within a large machine such as an engine or a vehicle: *I've finished the first part of my essay.*

bit a piece, especially a small piece, often of something that has been broken or taken apart: *Be careful, I dropped a milk bottle and there are bits of glass all over the kitchen floor.*

chunk a sizable, three-dimensional piece of a solid material, usually with an irregular shape: *a chunk of metal.*

fragment a tiny piece left over after

something has been broken or destroyed: *The glass shattered into fragments.*

lump an irregularly shaped three-dimensional piece of a hard or soft material: *My bed was very uncomfortable because there were so many lumps in the mattress.*

piece a solid amount of something that is less than all of it and has usually been taken or broken off it: *Cut the cheese into bite-size pieces.*

section one of several parts into which something is deliberately divided: *The fuselage of the aircraft is made in sections, which are then welded together.*

slice a thin flat piece, often of food: *a slice of bread.*

2 *verb* (said about two or more people) to leave one another at the end of a relationship or at the end of a period of time together: *At least we parted on fairly friendly terms.*

divorce or get divorced (said about one person or a couple) to go through the legal process that ends a marriage: *They lived apart for several years before they finally got divorced.*

go your separate ways (said about

two or more people) to part and go off in different directions, or to end a business or personal relationship: *My partner and I decided that we no longer wanted the same things so it was better if we went our separate ways.*

part company (with) (*formal*) (said about one person or two or more people) to leave someone whom you have been accompanying, or to end a relationship: *We travelled together as far as Paris, and there we parted company.*

say goodbye (to) to leave someone, or to part, at the end of a period of time together: *When the time came to say goodbye, it was some comfort that we should be seeing one another again quite soon.*

separate (said about a couple) to stop living together and behaving as a couple, without necessarily getting divorced: *It's a rather odd situation – they say they've separated, but they're still both living in the same house.*

split up (with) (said about a couple) to separate or end their relationship: *She split up with Jim, and now she's got a new boyfriend.*

take your leave (of) (*formal*) to say goodbye: *Well, it has been very pleasant talking to you, but I must now take my leave.*

See also **separate.**

partner *noun*

someone who takes part in an activity with you and helps you carry it out, for example someone you dance with, someone who plays a game or sport with you against two other people, or someone with whom you have a formal agreement to share the responsibility and costs of running a business or doing a particular kind of work: *My business has grown substantially in the last few years, and I'm looking for a partner to help me run it.*

ally someone, either a person, an organization, or a country, who agrees to support and help you when you are fighting together against a common enemy or when you are trying to achieve a common aim: *When the American colonists were fighting for their independence, they found an ally in the French.*

associate someone whom you know and whom you do things together with, especially in business (sometimes used when you do not wish to specify your exact relationship with a particular person): *A business associate of mine recommended you to me.*

collaborator someone who works with you, for example, on a particular project: *He had a team of collaborators who did a lot of the research for the project.*

colleague someone who works with you in the same organization or is in the same profession as you: *I know her as a friend and colleague.*

mate someone who acts as an assistant to a skilled worker: *a plumber's mate.*

opposite number a person in the same job or position as you, but in a different organization: *The Secretary of State for Trade and Industry is having talks with her opposite number in the Polish government.*

See also **accompany.**

patient *adjective*

not getting angry or restless if you have to wait for something or someone, or if someone behaves in a way that causes you trouble or inconvenience: *If you wouldn't mind being patient for ten more minutes, I'll definitely see you then.*

calm quiet and not showing signs of worry or excitement: *He had the great ability to remain calm under pressure.*

composed able to control your feelings, not becoming nervous, angry, or upset: *As his confidence at public speaking increased, he became more composed.*

forbearing (*formal*) not getting angry when people annoy you or cause you trouble: *You're very forbearing – I would have lost my temper with them straight away.*

long-suffering experiencing trouble or inconvenience from someone over a long period of time and being forbearing about it: *Her long-suffering parents once again paid her fine.*

philosophical calmly accepting that you will not always get what you want and that you will experience difficulties in life: *He's trying being philosophical about it, but you can see he's bitterly disappointed.*

resigned accepting that something bad will happen to you and that you can do nothing to stop it happening: *He had heard that the company was closing down and was resigned to losing his job.*

stoical bearing pain or hardship without complaining: *She was so stoical in the way she bore her last long illness.*

tolerant forbearing, or accepting that other people are different or behave in different ways to you and not trying to change them: *a tolerant society.*

understanding willing to sympathize with our people and accept their explanations for why they do things: *He was very understanding when I explained why I was resigning.*

pay *verb*
to provide the money needed to buy something, or to give money to someone for something: *You pay for the food, and I'll pay for the drinks.*

cough up (*informal*) to pay, or to pay a certain amount of money, often unwillingly: *You lost the bet, so you'd better cough up.*

foot the bill to pay for something: *It's not fair if you damage my car and then expect me to foot the bill for the repairs.*

fork out (*informal*) pay for something,
 or pay a certain amount of money, often unwillingly: *I had to fork out £50 to get the TV repaired.*

invest use or spend money in a way that you hope will bring you profit or benefit in the future, for example, by buying shares in a company: *I invested £10,000 in a small company making electronic equipment.*

meet the cost of (*formal*) to pay for something: *We shall have to put a certain amount of money aside to meet the cost of maintaining the new equipment after it has been installed.*

pay back repay someone or something: *If you lend me £10 now, I'll pay you back on Monday – I promise.*

repay to give someone an amount of money that they lent you previously, or to give back an amount of money that you borrowed from someone: *We can't ask the bank for another loan, until we've finished repaying the loan we took out last year.*

settle (up) to pay someone what you owe them: *If you don't mind paying for me now, I'll settle up with you later.*

peace *noun*
a quiet, restful state without noise or disturbing activity or in which you do not feel anxious or troubled: *Look, I've been busy dealing with people all afternoon and I just want five minutes peace.*

calm a quiet state in which movement or activity is gentle, especially a state in which there are no waves on the sea or there is no wind blowing: *the calm before the storm.*

hush a state where there is little or no sound, especially after noise ceases: *There was an expectant hush as the president stood up to speak.*

serenity a peaceful and happy state:
 She was feeding her baby with a look of complete serenity on her face.

silence absence of sound, often a state in which no one is speaking: *The crowd stood in silence for two minutes, remembering the dead.*

stillness absence of sound and, often, movement: *The stillness was broken only by the occasional cry of a bird.*

tranquillity a peaceful state usually in a place, scene, or period of time: *the tranquillity of the lakeside scene.*

See also **calm.**

persuade *verb*
to make someone do something, especially by talking to them and giving them good reasons why they should do it: *I tried to persuade him to give up smoking and go on a diet.*

bring round (*informal*) to make someone change their opinion or do something by explaining to them good reasons why they should do it: *You know you will never bring him round to your way of thinking unless he is going to benefit it from himself.*

convert to make someone change their present belief, opinion, or attitude, especially their religious belief, and adopt a new one: *They tried to convert him to Christianity.*

convince to make someone sure about something by using strong arguments in favour of it: *What can I do to convince you this plan will work?*

incite to use language, especially emotional language, to make a group of people do something bad or violent: *Agitators incited the crowd to tear down the barriers and attack the police.*

induce to make someone do something: *Nothing would induce me to go swimming in that icy water.*

influence to use the power that you have over someone, for example, because you are older than they are or because they admire you, to try to make them do, think, believe, etc., something: *You mustn't be influenced by what the newspapers say.*

prevail (up)on (*formal*) to succeed in persuading someone to do something: *Eventually I prevailed upon them to withdraw their objections to the plan.*

sway (mostly used in the passive) to influence someone who is undecided about something to change their opinion: *He was easily swayed by the strong opinions of others.*

talk into to persuade someone to do something by talking to them, often when they are at first unwilling to do it or when they regret doing it afterwards: *You shouldn't have let him talk you into buying the car if you couldn't really afford it.*

win over to succeed in persuading someone to agree with you or do what you want: *I think it was her charm rather than the force of arguments that eventually won him over.*

See also **convincing; urge.**

picture *noun*

a representation of the appearance of an object, person, scene, etc., made on a flat surface with pencil, paint, etc., or a photograph: *I'll draw you a picture to show you what the house will look like when we've added the extension.*

cartoon a comic or satirical drawing, often on a topical subject: *A cartoon in today's newspaper depicts the prime minister as a toothless lion.*

diagram a simplified drawing, often using symbols, that shows not how something looks, but how its parts are related to or connect with one another: *a diagram of the wiring in a car engine.*

drawing a picture made up of lines in pencil, ink, etc.: *a drawing of a bull by Picasso.*

illustration a picture, or drawing in a book: *The book contains over 300 full-colour illustrations.*

image a reproduction of the appearance of someone or something, either physically created or in the mind, including a picture appearing in a mirror or on a TV or computer screen: *I have a very clear image in my mind of how he looked when I last saw him 20 years ago.*

painting a picture made by putting paint on a surface: *The* Mona Lisa *is probably the most famous painting in the world.*

photograph an image of something captured by a camera and then printed: *Are you sure you don't recognize the man in this photograph?*

plan a drawing that shows the layout of something that already exists, for example, the rooms in a building or the streets in a town, or that serves as a guide to someone who is building or laying out something: *According to the original plans for the house, this corridor led to a small staircase.*

portrait a picture of a particular person: *a portrait of the Queen.*

sketch a drawing, painting, or diagram made quickly and roughly, often as preparation for a properly finished work or to help you remember something: *I made a sketch of where the vehicles were after the accident.*

place *noun*

an identifiable point or area on the earth's surface, or a particular building, village, town, etc.: *the place where I was born.*

area a particular portion of horizontal space on the earth's surface, or within a room, building, town, etc.: *Which area of town do you live in?*

location (usually used when discussing business or technical matters) the position of something or someone or a site where something can be built or done: *The business is moving to a new location on the outskirts of town.*

position the place where something or someone is: *From our position on the roof of the building, we could see the procession winding its way through the streets below.*

scene a place where something is happening or happened: *the scene of the crime.*

setting an area or the surroundings in which something happens: *The lakes and mountains make the perfect setting for a relaxing holiday.*

site the place where something happened in the past, or a place where something can be done, especially where a building can be built: *We're looking for a suitable site for a new office building.*

situation the position of something, especially a building, in relation to the other things around it: *The hotel has a pleasant situation overlooking the beach.*

spot a place, especially a small place and one that it is pleasant to be in: *I've found the perfect spot for our picnic.*

surroundings the landscape, buildings, or objects that are around a particular place, building, etc.: *It's a pretty house, but it's in rather unpleasant surroundings.*

whereabouts the position of someone or something that you are looking for: *If you know the whereabouts of this man, you should inform the police immediately.*

plan

1 *noun* an idea or a statement of what you intend to do, how you intend to solve a problem, etc., made before you actually do it: *I have a plan that I think might work.*

agenda a list or plan of things that you intend to do, especially that you intend to discuss during a meeting: *The next item on the agenda is the Club's annual dance.*

intention something that you decide that you are going to do: *It was never my intention to do all the work myself.*

method a planned way of doing something: *This photocopier uses a new method of producing high-quality copies.*

plot a secret plan to do something

dramatically bad, such as to kill someone or overthrow a government: *a plot to blow up the king and the parliament.*

project a plan for doing something that will involve work or effort on your part over a period of time: *My project for this year is to redecorate all the bedrooms in the house.*

proposal a plan or suggestion, especially one that is formal or written down, for others to decide on: *The commission is considering a proposal to help tackle global warming.*

scheme a plan, usually one involving dishonesty or trickery, or (in British English) an official organized plan for a particular activity such as training people or saving money for a pension: *She wanted you to think George was in love with her – that was part of her little scheme to get him away from you.*

strategy (usually used when talking about business or military matters) a plan setting out your goals and how you intend to achieve those goals over a fairly long period of time: *Opening up new markets in developing countries is part of the company's strategy for the next 5 years.*

2 *verb* have a plan or the intention to do something, to make plans, or to make a plan for a particular thing, event: *We were just planning our holiday for next year.*

aim to have something as your goal, to want and intend to do something: *We're aiming to finish the work by the end of next week.*

contemplate (*formal*) to have a plan to do something in the future, or to think about doing something in the future: *Before we contemplate expanding our business in Europe, we ought to try to increase our share of the UK market.*

envisage to have an idea or a plan of what you will do in the future: *Do you envisage making many changes when you take over as party leader?*
In US English the verb *envision* is often used in this sense.

intend to have decided that you will do something: *I intend to wait a while before I finally make up my mind.*

mean to intend to so something, especially (and often used in the negative) to have the deliberate intention of doing something bad: *I didn't mean to hurt you.*

plot to make a plot: *They were plotting to overthrow the government.*

propose (*formal*) to intend or plan to do something: *And how exactly do you propose to finance this project?*

scheme to make plans involving dishonesty or trickery or with bad motives: *He was scheming to get himself promoted ahead of me.*

See also **idea; picture**.

please *verb* to give pleasure to someone, or to win someone's approval: *He'd do anything to please her, but she just doesn't find him attractive.*

cheer up to make someone who has been feeling sad feel happier: *I tried to cheer him up by taking him out to the pub.*

delight to make someone feel happy or excited: *The clowns delighted the crowd with their antics.*

gratify (*formal*) (often used in the passive) to make someone feel happy or satisfied or proud: *I was very gratified to find that people still remember me after all these years.*

humour to do what someone wants, even though you do not particularly want to do it, in order to make them happy or to prevent them becoming angry or sad: *Humour him or you'll make his bad mood even worse.*

oblige (*formal*) to please someone and make them feel grateful to you: *Would you oblige me by fetching my walking stick? It's in the cupboard under the stairs.*

polite *adjective*

speaking to and behaving towards other people in a way that shows that you respect them or that conforms to the standards of behaviour that people expect in society: *Remember to be polite and always say 'please' and 'thank you'.*

civil using polite language and not being rude or hurtful to someone, but often in situations where you actually feel angry with them or contemptuous of them: *She annoys me so much I have great difficulty in remaining civil to her.*

courteous (*formal*) polite, especially

in doing or saying things that show respect for other people: *They may not expect you to reply to their letter, but it would be courteous to reply to it, nonetheless.*

deferential showing great or exaggerated respect for someone, suggesting that you are unimportant compared with them: *He's an important man and deserves respect, but he won't like it if you're too deferential to him.*

formal observing all the rules that society makes for addressing or behaving towards other people in public: *Don't be so formal; you can call me Sue, not Dr McKenzie.*

respectful showing respect: *He made a respectful bow and left the room.*

well-behaved behaving in a way that conforms to the standards that people expect in society: *a very well-behaved young man.*

well-bred brought up by your family to be polite and well-mannered: *A well-bred young gentleman would not leave a young lady to find her own way home.*

well-mannered having good manners, behaving in the way that society expects you to behave: *It's a pleasure to sit down for a meal with such well-mannered children.*

poor *adjective*

in a state where you do not have very much money or very many possessions: *We're too poor to send our children to private schools.*

bankrupt (used to describe a person or a company, business, etc.) officially recognized as not having enough money to pay your debts or to continue doing business as normal: *When the bank refused to extend the loan, the firm went bankrupt.*

broke (*informal*) not having any money or enough money, usually temporarily: *I'm always broke at the end of the month.*

destitute having virtually no money

or possessions and unable to afford the basic things you need to live: *She had no money of her own, so, when her husband died, she was left destitute.*

hard up (*informal*) fairly poor, not having very much money: *Could you lend me £20? I'm a bit hard up at the moment.*
Usually used after a verb.

impoverished (usually used to describe areas, countries, groups, etc., rather than individuals) not having much money or many resources: *The government offered special incentives to firms to set up businesses in impoverished areas.*

needy not having the things that most people have, and therefore needing money or help: *She organized a collection for the needy families in the village.*

penniless very poor or destitute: *I'm not a penniless student any more – I've got a job!*

poverty-stricken (usually used to describe areas or groups rather than individuals) very impoverished: *When the harvest failed again, the poverty-stricken villagers had no choice but to seek work in the towns.*

See also **bad 4.**

popular *adjective*
liked or wanted by many people: *a popular entertainer.*

favourite that a particular person or group likes most: *What's your favourite colour?*

in demand wanted by many people, often in order to act in a particular capacity: *He's very much in demand as an after-dinner speaker.*

in favour being liked by a particular person or particular group: *It seemed that her career was going nowhere, but now, suddenly, she's back in favour with the general public.*

sought-after that many people want

 to buy or own: *Ming vases are quite rare, so they're very sought-after by collectors.*

widespread happening or found in many different places or among many different people: *There's a widespread belief that it's now too late to do anything about global warming.*

praise *verb*
to say things that show that you admire someone or something that they have done: *You complain about him when he does things wrong, but you never praise him when he does things well.*

applaud to show that you like what someone has done by clapping your hands, or to praise someone or something: *The audience stood up and applauded at the end of the act.*

commend (*formal*) to praise someone, especially officially, for showing a good quality such as courage or honesty: *The police commended her for the courage she showed during the attempted robbery.*

compliment to say something nice to someone to show them that you have noticed something about them or something that they did and you like it: *It's not often that someone compliments me on my cooking.*

congratulate to say something (especially *congratulations*) to praise someone who has achieved something: *Let me be the first to congratulate you on your success.*

flatter to praise someone or say

 nice things about them when they do not really deserve it, often in order to make them like you or to get something from them: *He tried to flatter her by saying she looked just like Catherine Zeta Jones.*

pay tribute to to praise someone or something, or express your gratitude to someone, in public and often at a formal occasion: *I'd just like to pay tribute to the men and women of the emergency services who saved so many lives during the recent disaster.*

praise to the skies (*informal*) to praise someone or something very enthusiastically: *The critics praised it to the skies and called it the film of the decade.*

recognize (often used in the passive) to show by saying or doing something, such as giving someone an award, that you know that someone is talented or has done something good: *Her contribution to this vital discovery has never been properly recognized by her fellow scientists.*

pretence *noun*

acting as if you were someone other than the person you really are or as if you were doing something other than what you are really doing, or an instance of doing this: *He's not really a war hero, it's all pretence.*

charade an action or event that has no real purpose or meaning: *Everyone knows that the president has all the real power, and that what goes on in parliament is just a charade.*

cover something, for example a false identity and life history or a legal business, that is intended to prevent people from finding out who someone really is or what they are really doing: *Your cover is that you're a businessman attending a trade fair in London.*

disguise something that changes your appearance, for example a false beard or a different kind of clothes from the ones you usually wear, and is intended to stop people from recognizing you: *He tried to slip past the police in disguise.*

façade a pretence that is intended to hide your real nature, situation, or feelings: *Behind the confident façade, she's actually a very frightened woman.*

front an activity, especially a legal business, that hides the fact that someone is doing something illegal: *The gang set up a betting shop as a front for their money-laundering operation.*

show pretence, especially in order to make people believe that you are doing something that you are not really doing: *They made a show of ending their quarrel, but everyone knows they still hate one another.*

veneer an outward appearance of some good quality that is intended to hide the bad qualities underneath: *a thin veneer of respectability.*

prevent *verb*

to cause something not to happen or not to be done, or to cause someone not to do something: *There must be some way we can prevent the water from leaking out of the tank.*

avert to prevent something that seems likely to happen, especially a bad thing such as an accident or crisis, from actually happening: *The driver's quick thinking averted a nasty accident.*

avoid to succeed in not doing or undergoing something or in preventing something from happening, usually something that is harmful: *I want to avoid giving offence to any of our foreign visitors.*

forestall take action in advance to try to prevent something from happening or someone from doing something: *The government quickly moved troops into the area to forestall a possible invasion.*

keep from to prevent someone or something from doing something: *How can we keep the newspapers from getting hold of the story?*

nip in the bud to stop something early before it can develop, especially before it can develop into a serious problem: *By keeping the group under surveillance, we should be able to nip any trouble in the bud.*

preclude (*formal*) make it impossible for something to happen or for someone to do something: *Does the fact that he has a criminal record preclude him from being a candidate in the election?*

rule out to make it impossible for something to happen or for someone to do something: *The bad weather ruled out any attempt to break the record.*

stop to prevent or preclude: *If they insist on going, there's nothing we can do to stop them.*

See also **hinder.**

problem *noun*

something that causes worry or anxiety, something that needs to be solved or put right in order to enable you to do something effectively, or something that prevents a machine from functioning properly: *He never discusses his personal problems with anyone in the office.*

difficulty something that makes it hard to do or achieve something, or a state in which you have problems of various kinds: *You may have difficulty in understanding some of the technical language in this document.*

disadvantage something that makes a thing less good, useful, etc., than it might otherwise have been: *Since the advantages outweigh the disadvantages, I suggest we should go ahead with the plan.*

drawback a disadvantage or a problem that makes something less good than it might have been: *The proposal looks great; the only drawback is the cost.*

hassle (*informal*) problems or diffi

culties, especially caused by people being unpleasant: *My boss is giving me a lot of hassle because I'm behind with my work.*

hitch (*informal*) something that goes wrong and prevents something from happening as it should: *We're unable to bring you that report from Beirut because of a slight technical hitch.*

plight a state in which you are in danger, suffer hardship, or have a serious problem: *The plight of the refugees has been ignored by the government.*

predicament a situation that is difficult to deal with: *I'm in a bit of a predicament here; I can't decide which candidate to choose, because they are equally well qualified.*

setback a problem that hinders progress or puts you into a worse state than you were in before: *We suffered a serious setback when there was a fire in the office and many important documents were destroyed.*

snag (*informal*) a small problem that makes it difficult to do something: *We hit a snag when we tried to feed the data into the computer.*

trouble something that causes worry or anxiety, or a state in which you have difficulty in doing something or in dealing with something or someone: *I having trouble getting my car to start on cold mornings.*

promise *verb*

to tell someone that you will definitely do something, that something is definitely the case, or that you will definitely give them something: *I promised I'd meet her at the station at six o'clock.*

assure to tell someone that something is definitely the case: *He assured me that there was no cause for alarm.*

give your word to promise something solemnly, suggesting that you will lose your reputation as an honest person if you do not keep the promise: *I'll repay every penny: I give you my word.*

guarantee to state that someone can quite definitely rely on something happening: *I guarantee that if you start reading this book you won't be able to put it down until you've finished it.*

pledge to promise solemnly to give something or to do something: *They pledged their support for the cause.*

swear to promise something solemnly, especially calling on God to witness what you are saying: *Do you swear to tell the truth, the whole truth, and nothing but the truth?*

undertake (*formal*) to accept the responsibility for doing something, often by signing a contract to do it, or to promise to do something: *The lessee undertakes to maintain the property in good condition for the duration of the lease.*

vow to promise solemnly or swear to do something: *They vowed to avenge their murdered brother.*

proud *adjective*
feeling very pleased and satisfied, especially about something that you have achieved yourself or that someone connected with you has achieved: *I'm so proud of you for having the courage to stand up to those bullies.*

arrogant feeling that, or behaving as if, you are much better and more important than anyone else and have the right to give them orders: *He's far too arrogant to think that he needs advice, but he's always quite happy to give it.*

boastful saying things that show that you think that other people should admire and envy things that you do or own: *I don't like the boastful way she talks about her new house.*

cocky (*informal*) (used especially to describe young people) excessively confident that your own ability and knowledge is very great and superior to other people's: *Don't get too cocky and think that, because you did well in 1 exam, you don't have to work hard for the others.*

conceited having an excessively high opinion of your own abilities and importance: *His parents always praise everything she does to the skies, and as a result she's become very conceited.*

haughty behaving in a way that suggests you think yourself to be superior to other people, especially socially superior to them, and that you do not really want to have anything to do with them: *He always had a haughty look in his eyes.*

pompous self-important and tending to act or, especially, speak in a grand way that other people find inappropriate and rather ridiculous: *Excessive use of the pronoun* one *in the sense of 'you' can sound pompous.*

self-important believing yourself to be, and acting as if you were, a very important person, often because of a job or position that you have: *The mayor was a fussy, self-important little man.*

snobbish valuing people because of their position or reputation, especially their social position, rather than for their personal qualities, so tending to show little respect for ordinary or lower-class people: *They have a very snobbish attitude towards people who come from the 'wrong' part of town.*

vain conceited, especially with regard to your personal appearance: *The fact that I want to look nice when I go out doesn't make me vain.*

prove *verb*
to provide evidence that makes it clear beyond doubt that something is the case: *The film from the security camera proves she was in the area at the time the crime was committed.*

authenticate to prove or certify that something is genuine: *The picture has been authenticated by an expert from the National Gallery.*

bear out to provide evidence to support something that someone has said: *This bears out what I said yesterday about him being unreliable.*

certify to state definitely that, or to be evidence of the fact that, something is true or correct: *You have to certify on the back of the photograph that it is a true likeness of the person applying for a passport.*

confirm to state something once again in order to make sure that the information someone has is correct, or to corroborate something: *Could you please confirm your name and address?*

corroborate (*formal*) to provide additional evidence to show that what someone has said is true or correct: *She has not yet been able to find anyone who will corroborate her story.*

demonstrate (*formal*) to show something: *I can demonstrate the water-repellent properties of this material by means of simple experiment.*

establish to find out about and provide evidence for something: *We're still trying to establish the time of the victim's death.*

show to make something clear or prove it to someone: *This just goes to show that you shouldn't believe everything you read in the newspaper.*

verify to confirm or state something in order to make sure that the information someone has is correct: *You can check the original documents to verify the accuracy of the information.*

pull *verb*
to be in front of something or someone and touching them and use effort to move them either towards you or along behind you: *Grab hold of my hand, and I'll pull you up.*

drag to pull someone or something roughly or forcefully, especially so that they move along in contact with the ground: *His foot was caught in the stirrup, and he was dragged along behind the horse.*

draw to pull something along or out of something, especially with a steady and even effort: *a coach drawn by six white horses.*

haul to pull something (usually something large or heavy) strongly, steadily,

and with effort: *Six of us harnessed ourselves to the sledge to haul it over the ice.*

heave to pull or push something with a concentrated burst of effort: *When the captain gave the signal, they all heaved the cart up the hill.*

tow to use a powered vehicle to pull another unpowered vehicle along: *The car broke down and had to be towed to the nearest garage.*

tug to give something a quick, sharp pull: *I felt someone tugging at my sleeve.*

yank (*informal*) to pull something roughly or carelessly: *He yanked the door open and rushed out.*

punish *verb*
to do something that hurts or disadvantages someone who has committed a crime or done something wrong: *She's being punished for a crime she didn't commit.*

bring to justice (*formal*) to make someone who has committed a crime face trial and punishment by a court: *We shall not rest until the perpetrators of this heinous act have been brought to justice.*

convict (said about a court or jury) to state that someone is guilty of a crime that they have been charged with: *If convicted, if she faces a heavy fine or possibly a prison sentence.*

discipline (usually used in the passive) to punish someone and keep order in something such as organization or armed force: *He was disciplined for behaving inappropriately at work.*

fine to punish someone by making them pay a sum of money to the authorities: *I was fined for speeding.*

lock up (*informal*) to send someone to prison: *She got away with a fine when I think she ought to have been locked up.*

make pay to take revenge on someone or to punish them, usually not for something that the state regards as a crime: *She decided that she was going to make him pay for the insult.*

penalize to impose a penalty on someone, usually in a sport or contest, often by giving an advantage to their opponent: *You can be penalized for arguing with the referee.*

sentence (said about a judge or court) to state what a person's punishment will be after they have been convicted of a crime: *He's been sentenced to life imprisonment.*

purpose *noun*
the use to which something can be put, or something that you wish to achieve by doing something: *The purpose of this meeting is to discuss arrangements for the firm's Christmas party.*

aim what someone wishes to achieve or something is intended to achieve: *a statement setting out the aims of the organization.*

function the use for which something is made: *A screwdriver won't make holes in wood; that's not its function.*

goal an aim: *One of my goals in life is to become a millionaire before I'm forty.*

intention something that you decide you are going to do, or the purpose or aim of something: *I have no intention of resigning.*

object an aim: *The object of the exercise to find out what sort of advertising is most likely to bring in new customers.*

objective a place or point that you are trying to reach, for example, when you are on a journey or when you are working on something, or an aim, especially one that is part of a bigger process: *My first objective was to persuade my colleagues that my plan would benefit them as much as it would benefit me.*

point the purpose of an action or of something you say: *There's no point in applying if there are no vacancies.*

push *verb*
to be behind something or someone and touching them and use effort to move them either away from you or along in front of you, or to be above something and use effort to move it downwards: *She pushed him out of the way.*

drive to be behind something or someone, but not touching them, and use force or urging to make them move away from you or along in front of you, or to push something in or down with great force: *The wind was driving the rain into our faces.*

nudge to push someone or something gently, especially to push someone gently in the side with your elbow: *She nudged me and whispered, 'Don't look now, but isn't that David Beckham sitting three rows in front of us?'*

poke to push something narrow such as your finger or a stick into an opening in something, or to prod something or someone: *Be careful waving that stick about, you nearly poked me in the eye.*

press to push something downwards or inwards by applying weight or pressure on top of it: *I pressed the button to ring the bell.*

prod to use something narrow such as your finger or a stick to push against something: *He prodded me in the ribs with his bony finger.*

propel to cause something to move,

especially rapidly, often by pushing it from behind: *He gave me a push that propelled me into the room.*

shove to push or put something or someone somewhere roughly or carelessly: *Just shove a few things into a suitcase, we're only going for two days.*

squeeze to push on something from two or more sides at once, as when you hold something in your hand and close your fingers around it: *You have to squeeze the bottle to get the sauce out.*

puzzle *verb*
to make it difficult for someone to find an answer, explanation, or solution for something even though they are thinking hard about it: *What puzzles me is why she waited such a long time before she called an ambulance.*

baffle to leave someone completely

unable to understand, explain, or solve something: *The police admit that they are baffled by this apparently motiveless crime.*

bewilder to make someone feel confused and helpless: *The speed at which technology is advances bewilders many people.*

confuse to make someone unable to understand clearly what is happening or what is being said or to distinguish clearly between different things: *You're confusing me – is it the brown wire or the blue wire that goes on this terminal?*

disconcert (often used in the passive) to surprise someone and make it difficult for them to react to what has happened in a controlled way: *I was rather disconcerted when she announced that she was leaving right away.*

faze (*informal*) (often used in the passive) to disconcert someone: *He had to face some very hostile questioning, but showed no sign of being fazed by it.*

mystify (often used in the passive) to baffle someone: *The whole town is mystified by the sudden disappearance of one of its most prominent citizens.*

perplex (often used in the passive) to make someone feel anxious or worried because they cannot understand, explain, or solve something: *The problem that perplexes me most is how we're going to survive financially when Jane has to give up her job.*

quarrel *verb*

to have an angry disagreement with someone or with each other, usually with someone that you know or have been friends with before and usually without actually exchanging blows: *They quarrelled with their neighbours over a tree in their neighbours' garden, which they said was blocking the light to their back window.*

argue to disagree with someone about something and try to change their view, sometimes angrily: *There's no point in arguing, I've already made up my mind.*

bicker to argue or quarrel about

small matters without getting very angry or violent: *I'd be surprised if their relationship lasts, because they're always bickering with each other.*

fall out (with) to cease being friends with someone, or to quarrel with someone who was a friend: *They fell out because Roger thought Peter was having an affair with his wife, and, as far as I know, they've never spoken to one another since.*

fight (*informal*) to quarrel, sometimes exchanging blows as well as angry words: *We don't fight very often and when we do, it's usually about money.*

have a row (with) (*informal*) to quarrel: *George had a row with his boss and he's afraid he may lose his job over it.*

squabble to quarrel noisily over a trivial matter: *The children are always squabbling over who should sleep in the top bunk.*

See also **argument**; **conflict**; **fight**; **oppose**.

question *verb*

to express the opinion that something may not be true or trustworthy: *I wouldn't question Kay's judgment – she has excellent taste.*

call into question to question something, or to make something appear doubtful or untrustworthy, especially a person's honesty, integrity, or similar qualities: *When my honesty has been called into question, surely I have the right to defend myself.*

challenge to state definitely that you believe something to be incorrect: *In this article she challenges the widely held belief that the answer to our energy crisis is to build more nuclear power stations.*

dispute to express disagreement with something: *Nobody now disputes that global temperatures have risen in the last 50 years.*

distrust or *mistrust* to feel that something or someone may not be genuine or good: *I distrust their motives for wanting to buy the company.*

doubt to feel unsure whether something is true, right, or real: *I don't doubt that he has talent, but has he got enough talent to make a living as a writer?*

have reservations about to feel that you cannot accept that something is completely true or right or that someone is completely trustworthy: *I think that most of her arguments are very sound, though I have reservations about the conclusions she draws from them.*

query to question the accuracy of

something, such as a spelling or a price: *We queried our telephone bill, as it was unusually high.*

See also **ask**.

quick *adjective*
taking comparatively little time to do, or doing something in a very short time: *I had a quick wash and then went down to dinner.*

brisk done at a fairly vigorous pace:

a brisk walk.

fast going, or able to move, at a high speed: *a fast car.*

hasty acting or done quickly or too quickly because you have little time or because you realize that something is urgent: *Don't be so hasty. Take a little while to think before you make your final decision.*

hurried done hastily because you have little time, and sometimes carelessly: *I wrote a hurried note explaining why I had to leave.*

prompt done without delay: *Thank you for your prompt reply to my letter.*

rapid at a fast speed or rate: *in an era of rapid social change.*

speedy happening or dome very quickly or without delay: *We wish you a speedy recovery.*

swift (usually used to describe movement) fast or quick: *I wanted to be sure I could make a swift exit at the first sign of trouble.*

See also **fast.**

quiet *adjective*
not producing or characterized by much noise, or not loud: *Be quiet when I'm talking to you!*

faint very quiet, quite difficult to hear: *a faint rustling noise.*

hushed quieter than usual, especial-

ly deliberately made quieter than usual: *People waited in the church, talking in hushed voices.*

inaudible unable to be heard: *There was so much noise in the hall that parts of the speech were almost inaudible.*

muffled not heard as clearly or not sounding as loud and sharp as usual, because there is something between you and the source of the sound: *a muffled explosion.*

silent producing or characterized by no sound at all, or not speaking: *Everyone in the room fell silent.*

soft not loud and usually having a gentle quality: *a soft voice.*

See also **calm**.

quite *adverb*
(can be used for either a positive or a negative assessment of something) to a certain degree or extent, not very: *This soup is actually quite good.* Not used with comparatives.

a bit (*informal*) to a small degree or by a small amount: *I feel a bit tired this evening.*

a little to a small degree or by a small amount: *If you wouldn't mind standing a little further back.*

fairly (usually used for neutral or positive assessments) not completely or very, but to some degree: *I'm fairly certain that's what he meant, even if he didn't actually say it.* Not used with comparatives.

moderately (usually used for neutral or positive assessments) not completely or very, but to some degree: *a moderately priced CD player.* Not used with comparatives.

rather (usually used for neutral or positive assessments) to some extent: *It's rather unusual to see daffodils in flower this early in the year.*

reasonably (usually used for neutral or positive assessments) not completely or very, but to a usually satisfactory degree: *We're reasonably happy with the way things turned out.*
Not used with comparatives.

slightly by a small extent or amount: *It's only slightly more expensive than the other one.*

somewhat (*formal*) to some extent: *I* *was somewhat surprised to see him at a political meeting.*

See also **very**.

R

rain *noun*
drops of water falling from the clouds: *Rain is forecast for this afternoon.*

downpour a heavy fall of rain: *I got caught in a downpour as I was coming home from the shops.*

drizzle a light, but steady fall of rain: *After some light drizzle, the day should turn dry.*

rainfall (usually used in technical discussions of weather conditions) the amount of rain that falls: *The rainfall for this month has been about average.*

shower a fall of rain that lasts for a comparatively short time: *It's only a shower; it'll be over in a few minutes.*

storm a period when there is heavy rain accompanied by strong winds and sometimes thunder: *Those black clouds mean there's going to be a storm.*

thunderstorm a storm with thunder and lightning: *You shouldn't shelter under a tree in a thunderstorm.*

refuse *verb*

1 to say that you will not do something or that you do not want something: *When I asked her to come with me to the police station, she refused.*

decline (*formal*) to refuse to do something, or not to take or accept something, usually politely: *I regretfully had to decline their invitation to their daughter's wedding.*

deny to say that something is not the case or that you have not done something that someone else says you have done: *He denies that he was in the building at the time the incident took place.*

pass up (*informal*) not to accept or take something, usually something beneficial or enjoyable, when it is offered to you: *I had to pass up the chance of going to the theatre with them.*

reject to say that you do not want something or someone, often suggesting that they are not good enough for you: *My novel has so far been rejected by every single publisher I have sent it to.*

say no (to) to refuse something: *I wouldn't say no to a cup of tea.*

spurn to reject something or some-
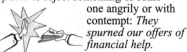
one angrily or with contempt: *They spurned our offers of financial help.*

2 to say that you will not give someone something that they want or ask for: *The authorities refused permission for the company to build on land next to the river.*

deny not to give, grant, or allow someone something: *He felt that he'd been denied the chance to tell his side of the story.*

turn down not to accept something such as a request, application, or suggestion, or not to accept someone who wants to join something: *I applied to join the police force, but they turned me down.*

withhold (*formal*) not to allow some-

one to have something, often temporarily: *The mortgage company are withholding part of the loan until we've had the roof repaired.*

regret *noun*

a feeling of sadness about something that has happened, often a bad action, mistake, etc., that you yourself have committed, coupled with a wish that it had not happened: *I want to express my regret for any inconvenience you may have suffered.*

contrition (*formal*) a feeling of guilt and remorse: *I would be more inclined to forgive him if he showed any sign of contrition.*

grief deep sadness, especially because someone has died: *We share the grief of those who have lost loved ones in this conflict.*

penance something unpleasant you

do to show that you realize you have sinned or done wrong and wish to punish yourself in order to make up for it: *As a penance, he vol-
unteered to clean the toilets for a week.*

penitence (*formal*) repentance: *In order to show penitence, you must first make a full confession of what you have done wrong.*

remorse a feeling of deep and painful sadness because you know that you have committed a bad action: *During all his time in prison, he never expressed any remorse for his crime.*

repentance realization that you have committed a crime or sin, sorrow for it, and a wish to behave better in future: *Do you think her repentance is sincere?*

sorrow a feeling of deep sadness, regret, or disappointment, or something that causes someone to feel sad: *Times of joy are almost inevitably followed by times of sorrow.*

release *verb*
to allow someone or something that is
held, captured, etc., to be free or move
freely again: *The animals are nearly
ready to be released into the wild.*

deliver (*literary*) to save or rescue
someone from something bad: *'Deliver
us from evil' is a line in the Lord's
Prayer.*

discharge to officially allow a person

to leave a hospital or
the army, air force,
etc.: *The patient was
discharged from hos-
pital.*

emancipate (*formal*) to free someone
from slavery or a similar condition: *An
Act of Parliament was passed emancipat-
ing all the slaves in British territories.*

free to release a person or animal that is
in captivity, to release something that is
held, tied, or stuck, or to remove a
restriction or burden from someone: *I
managed to free my right arm and then
tried to untie the ropes that were bind-
ing my legs.*

let go to stop holding or gripping something, or to release someone or something: *Let go of my arm; you're hurting
me.*

liberate to release someone who is a
prisoner or slave, or to enable a country
or area that has been under the control
of an enemy to govern itself again: *This
was one of the first villages to be liber-
ated when Allied forces landed in
France.*

set free to release a person or animal
that is in captivity: *The hostages begged
their captors to set them free.*

unleash (usually used figuratively) to
allow something violent that has previously been restrained to operate with
full force: *The government's attempt to
impose new taxes unleashed a storm of
protest.*

relentless *adjective*
not stopping and not decreasing the
amount of effort that is put into doing
something or the amount of pressure put
on other people to make them do something: *the relentless quest for perfection.*

inexorable (*formal*) that cannot be prevented from happening or from doing
something: *an inexorable fate.*

insistent demanding that something
should be done, and not allowing someone else to ignore the demand: *She was
most insistent that I should call you
straight away.*

persistent continuing to do something or
ask for something, even if people refuse
or if you do not succeed at first: *I wasn't
going to go out with him, but he was so
persistent that eventually I gave in.*

pitiless showing no pity for people or
their weaknesses: *pitiless cruelty.*

remorseless continuing without stopping regardless of people's wishes or
feelings: *remorseless questioning.*

unrelenting not stopping or decreasing:

*The work continued at
the same unrelenting
pace.*

reliable *adjective*
able to be trusted to do what they say they
will do or what you want them to do: *I'm
sorry to hear that John let you down; I
don't know what could have happened as
he's usually so reliable.*

conscientious working hard and being
careful and thorough
so as to make sure
that everything you
have to do is done
well: *She's very con-
scientious and always
checks and rechecks her work for mistakes in spelling or grammar.*

dependable able to be trusted to do what they say they will do or what you want them to do: *I need someone who is dependable to be my assistant.*

honest morally good and trustworthy, especially not likely to steal or to tell lies: *He's too honest to try to cover up any mistakes that he made.*

mature showing the qualities expected of an adult, such as good judgment, responsibility, and a serious attitude to life: *I expect him to be mature enough to understand there are no simple solutions to problems of this kind.*

responsible showing an ability or a willingness to carry out tasks or deal with situations sensibly without needing to be supervised by someone else: *Unless you show that you can behave in a responsible way, they'll never make you captain of the team.*

thorough not leaving out any necessary part of something that has to be done, but dealing fully with every aspect of it: *They were very thorough and read every single document relating to the case.*

trustworthy able to be trusted, not likely either to deceive or cheat you, reveal information that is supposed to be secret or confidential, or fail to do anything that they are supposed to do: *She often has access to confidential information and has always shown herself to be completely trustworthy.*

See also **devoted; faithful.**

religious *adjective*
to do with the knowledge or worship of God, or showing belief in God or interest in the spiritual side of life: *We don't go to church, but that doesn't mean we're not religious.*

devout sincerely believing in God and taking your religious duties seriously: *Devout Muslims make a pilgrimage to Mecca at least once in their lives.*

ecclesiastical connected with the Church or churches: *ecclesiastical architecture.*

holy of or like God, set apart for the service of God; spiritually pure; devout: *Believers are called to lead a holy life.*

pious showing great devotion to God and respect for religious doctrine in the way you behave: *Not all medieval monks were pious; some of them were very worldly and ambitious.*

reverent showing respect for God or

sacred things: *a reverent silence.*

sacred considered to be special and to deserve particular care and respect, especially because of being connected with God or religion: *sacred relics.*

spiritual not relating to the body or earthly life, but to the soul, religion, or divine beings: *a spiritual experience.*

remain *verb*
to continue to be in the same place or in the same condition: *We have remained friends ever since our schooldays.*

continue to keep happening or existing: *The controversy surrounding the Minister's business interests continues.*

endure to continue to exist, or con-

tinue to be successful, for a long time, without becoming less: *Their friendship endured for over twenty years.*

go on to continue to exist or happen: *His affair with his secretary is still going on.*

last to continue to exist for a long time: *The ill will between the two families has lasted since 1975.*

persist to continue to exist, especially for a long time: *If the pain persists, you should see a doctor.*

stay to continue to be in the same place, position, or condition: *This song stayed at Number One for three weeks.*

survive to continue to exist or continue to flourish in spite of difficulties: *Somehow our local butcher's has survived while many small shops have closed since the large supermarkets moved into the area.*

remember *verb*
to retain knowledge, information, experience, etc., that you had in the past and be able to bring it back from your memory, or not to forget to do something: *I can remember things that happened fifty years ago better than I can remember things that happened last week.*

call to mind to bring something back to your memory: *He called to mind how he had seen his mother dying.*

hark back to think or speak about something that happened in the past, often in a way that other people find irritating or strange: *She keeps harking back to the 1960s.*

look back to remember and think about the events of a particular period in the past: *Looking back over your long and distinguished career, what do you consider to be your greatest achievement?*

recall to be able to bring something back from your memory: *I can't quite recall her exact words, but she was very scathing about her brother.*

recognize to be able to identify someone or something that you have seen or known in the past when you see them again: *Would you recognize the man who attacked you if you saw him again?*

recollect (*formal*) to recall something, or not to forget something: *Recollect that, fifty years ago, television was still a relatively new medium.*

remind to cause someone to remember something, especially to say or do something that helps someone to remember what they intended to do: *Remind me to write a note to Jean thanking her for her present.*

reminisce talk pleasantly about things that happened in the past, especially with another person who shared the experience: *They were reminiscing about their days in the army.*

think of (*informal*) to recall something: *I can't think of his name, but I know it begins with B.*

replace *verb*
to act or function instead of something or someone else: *Gary Neville has to miss this game through injury, so Wes Brown replaces him at right back.*
See also **replace with** below.

deputize for to do the job of someone else, usually a more senior person, temporarily: *I'm deputizing for the managing director while he's on holiday.*

fill in for (*informal*) to act as a temporary replacement for someone, or deputize for them: *I can't go to the meeting next week, so would you mind filling in for me?*

replace with to remove or omit something or someone and use something or someone to do the same job: *When the ink cartridge is empty, you simply replace it with a new one.*

stand in for (*informal*) to act as a temporary replacement for someone, or deputize for them: *My job is to stand in for the star if she can't perform for any reason.*

substitute for to use something or someone instead of something or someone else: *Your can substitute 20 grams of breadcrumbs for 20 grams of flour in this recipe to produce a lighter dough.*

succeed to be the person who holds a particular position after someone else: *Paul succeeded his brother Hugh as managing director of the company.*

supersede to replace something that

is now obsolete: *The word-processor has superseded the old-fashioned typewriter.*

supplant (*formal*) to replace someone or something that is not ready to be replaced: *She hatched an elaborate plot to supplant her rival as the king's favourite mistress.*

respect *noun*
a feeling that something or someone is good or valuable and ought to be treated with care and paid attention to: *You should treat the religious beliefs of other people with proper respect.*

admiration a feeling that something or someone deserves praise: *I'm full of admiration for the way you handled the situation.*

consideration respect for the feelings of other people, usually coupled with kind or lenient treatment: *Show some consideration for her, as she's not been well.*

esteem (*formal*) your judgment (usually favourable) of the goodness or value of another person: *She stands very high in my esteem.*

estimation (*formal*) your judgment (good or bad) of the moral qualities of another person: *He has gone down in my estimation since he treated his wife so badly.*

regard a feeling of respect and admiration for someone or something: *My regard for her talents and her personal qualities is as high now as it ever was.*

reverence a sense of great respect for God, a great person, or something

important: *We need to rediscover a reverence for the environment.*

veneration very deep respect, of the

kind you might show to a saint, a sacred object, or a really great person: *He has a profound veneration for his ancestors.*

See also **admire**.

responsible *adjective*
having the job of dealing with or looking after something and able to be blamed if that job is not done properly: *The captain is responsible for the safety of the ship and its passengers.*

accountable responsible or answerable: *I can't be held accountable for decisions that were taken by other people.*

answerable having to explain and

justify your actions to a particular person who has the power to punish you in some way: *You'll be answerable to me if anything goes wrong.*

at fault (*formal*) having acted wrongly: *The committee concluded that the director had been at fault in authorizing the project without proper consultation.*

guilty proved to have committed a crime or done something wrong, or feeling sorry and worried because you know you have done something wrong: *I was guilty of poor judgment, not of any crime.*

in charge (of) being the person who controls a particular operation or particular group of people: *She left her deputy in charge while she was abroad on business.*

liable legally obliged to pay a particular sum of money, for example, as tax or compensation: *liable for income tax.*

to blame having caused something that did harm or was wrong: *Nobody was really to blame for the accident.*

See also **reliable**; **sensible**.

restrain *verb*
not to allow something, someone, or yourself to become too violent or forceful or to express themselves openly, or to prevent someone, for example a prisoner, from behaving violently by holding them, handcuffing them, etc.: *I couldn't restrain myself any longer and burst out laughing.*

control not to allow something, someone, or yourself to act freely, especially to limit or restrain something or someone: *Government efforts to control immigration have so far failed.*

curb to keep something under strict control and, usually, to reduce it: *He should try to curb his enthusiasm and act more rationally.*

hold back to restrain something such as tears or laughter, or to stop something from progressing or developing as fast as it would like: *Business is being held back by government restrictions.*

inhibit to prevent an event or process from developing: *Does the Internet encourage or inhibit learning?*

keep under control to control: *If you can't keep your children under control, you'll have to take them out.*

limit not to allow something to exceed a particular amount or extent, or not to allow someone complete freedom: *You'd be wise to limit the amount of time you spend on each question in the exam.*

restrict to limit something, especially to allow less of something than something

or someone needs or wants: *The amount that each candidate in the election can spend on publicity will be restricted to $20,000.*

suppress to take action to make sure that something cannot operate, show itself, or express itself at all: *All opposition to the regime was suppressed.*

result *noun*
what is produced by a cause or by an action, or the final score in a contest that shows who won, etc.: *The only result of your actions has been to make an already difficult situation worse.*

aftermath the period after a dramatic or important event in which the effects of it are felt or assessed: *In the aftermath of the disaster, many important safety issues had to be reconsidered.*

consequence what something causes, an event that is the result of a previous event: *The inevitable consequence of poor hygiene is that diseases spread more rapidly.*

effect something produced by a cause, often a state or reaction: *I don't know what effect the book had on other readers, but it depressed me terribly.*

outcome what a process leads to, or the result of a contest: *Whatever the outcome of these negotiations, neither side is likely to get everything it wants.*

reaction what someone does as a result of something that happened to them or of what someone else says or does: *My first reaction was one of surprise.*

repercussions results taking place over a period of time that are usually harmful or unfavourable to someone: *The ban on smoking in public places is bound to have serious repercussions for the tobacco industry.*

sequel what happened after and as a result of a particular event, or a book, film, etc., showing what happened after the events depicted in a previous book, film, etc.: *She's writing a sequel to* Pride and Prejudice.

upshot an event that is result of a previous event or process: *The upshot was that we decided to share the costs of the trip.*

reveal *verb*
to make visible or known, deliberately or accidentally, something that has previously been invisible or unknown: *The curtains opened to reveal the battlements of the castle at Elsinore.*

bring to light to find and reveal something that was previously hidden or secret: *The manuscript lay undiscovered in the archives for centuries and has only recently been brought to light.*

display to make something visible, for example, on a screen, especially to put something in a place where it can be easily seen by a lot of people: *a notice displayed in a shop window.*

exhibit to display a work of art or something valuable or interesting in a place where the public can see it: *Her paintings are being exhibited at an art gallery in London.*

expose to remove the covering from something, especially something that would normally be kept covered, so that it becomes visible; to find and reveal something that was previously hidden or secret: *The wallpaper has come off, exposing the bare plaster.*

lay bare to remove the covering from something, especially something that would normally be kept covered, so that it becomes visible; to find and reveal something that was previously hidden or secret: *The information laid bare the enemy's true intentions.*

show to allow or enable someone to see something: *You haven't shown us your wedding photos yet.*

uncover to remove the covering from something, especially something that is meant to be shown at least occasionally: *Don't uncover the sandwiches until we're ready to eat them.*

unveil to show something such as a statue or a plaque publicly for the first time at a special ceremony in which a cover is removed from it, or to display or announce something such as a new car or a set of plans for the first time: *A plaque commemorating the royal visit was unveiled by Her Majesty the Queen.*

See also **betray 2**.

revenge *noun*
a punishment that is given to someone for having harmed you, defeated you, etc., especially a punishment that you give them personally: *She had her revenge the following year, when she knocked the same opponent out in the first round of the competition.*

redress (*formal*) the putting right of a wrong that has been done to you: *In a civilized society people seek redress through the courts; they do not revenge their injuries personally.*

reprisal an action carried out, especially by an army, to punish someone who has attacked or harmed them: *Troops were ordered not to take reprisals against the civilian population.*

retaliation the act of attacking or harming someone who has previously attacked or harmed you: *The terrorists say they took the hostages in retaliation for the attack on the base.*

retribution some form of compensation for the fact that a crime has been committed against you, such as the punishment of the person who committed the crime: *Society is surely entitled to demand retribution when a person deliberately breaks the law.*

vendetta a long-lasting situation between two or more people or groups in which one harms the other, the other retaliates, the first retaliates for that attack, etc.: *The unfortunate lovers are caught up in the vendetta between their two families.*

vengeance (usually used in describing dramatic feelings and situations) revenge: *He vows he will exact vengeance on those who had him falsely imprisoned.*

reward

1 *noun* something, especially a sum of money, that you receive in return for some achievement or for a good deed: *The police are offering a substantial reward for any information leading to the arrest of the murderer.*

award something that you are presented with to honour some achievement: *Archie won an award for the best-kept garden in the village.*

benefit a regular payment made by the government to a person who needs financial help because of unemployment, illness, etc.: *The family has been living on benefits since the father lost his job.*

bonus a single, or sometimes an annual, payment made by an employer to an employee who has done especially good work, or as a share in the profits: *On top of the salary, the job offers a profit-sharing bonus.*

premium a sum of money paid in addition to the usual payment for something, for example in addition to a salary or a price: *Solo travellers often have to pay a premium for a single room.*

prize something, such as a sum of money or a trophy, that you are given to honour some achievement, or in return

for winning a competition or sporting event: *The prize for winning this competition is a holiday for four in Florida.*

prize money a sum of money that you win in a competition or a sporting event: *Contestants in this quiz show can win up to one million pounds in prize money.*

profit money that you gain, for example from a business deal, when the amount that you receive is more than you have spent: *Because property prices have increased enormously since we bought our house, we made a huge profit when we sold it.*

2 *verb* to give someone a sum of money or a gift in return for some achievement or for a good deed: *The girl was rewarded for her honesty by the person who had lost the wallet that she found and handed over to the police.*

honour pay tribute to someone who is held in high esteem: *The veteran actor was honoured by the British Academy with a lifetime achievement award.*

pay to give money to someone in return for work or for something else that they have done for you: *The old lady pays her neighbour's son to look after her garden.*

recompense (*formal*) to give some-

thing, especially money, to someone in return for their efforts or to compensate for injury, loss, or inconvenience: *The airline apologized for the long delay and assured us that we would be recompensed.*

remunerate (*formal*) to pay someone money in return for work: *Anyone who is prepared to work over the weekend will be well remunerated for their efforts.*

tip to give a small sum of money to someone such as a waiter or hairdresser, to show that you appreciate what they have done for you: *I was happy to tip the waitress handsomely, since the service had been excellent.*

rich *adjective*

having a lot of money and possessions: *They must be rich if they can afford two houses and three cars.*

affluent rich, or in which most people are comparatively rich: *the affluent society.*

better off having more money and possessions than before, or comparatively rich: *We're definitely better off now than we were three years ago.*

loaded (*informal*) very rich: *Of course she has nice things – her parents are loaded.*

prosperous doing well in life or business and having or earning lots of money: *a prosperous company.*

rolling in it or *rolling in money* (*informal*) very rich: *If they own a private jet, they must be absolutely rolling in it.*

wealthy rich: *a wealthy country.*

well off fairly rich, or having many advantages, compared to other people: *You no longer have to be well off to own a car.*

well-to-do (*old-fashioned*) (only used to describe people) having more money than most ordinary people: *She comes from a well-to-do family.*

See also **wealth.**

ridiculous *adjective*

contrary to common sense and ordinary behaviour in a way that might make people laugh scornfully, or very foolish or funny: *You look absolutely ridiculous in that hat.*

absurd contrary to reason and common sense, ridiculous and odd: *It's absurd to suggest that she might have been involved in the plot.*

farcical absurd and often making the people involved look very foolish: *We ended up in a farcical situation where everybody knew the secret but nobody knew that anyone else knew it.*

laughable not to be taken seriously because ridiculous: *The idea that people will actually benefit from having to pay higher taxes is simply laughable.* Most often used after a verb.

ludicrous absurd: *He came up with the absolutely ludicrous idea of extracting energy from moonbeams.*

nonsensical that does not make sense, that is nonsense: *a nonsensical suggestion.*

rise *verb*

move or lead upwards, to become higher, or to be tall or high: *The sun rises tomorrow morning at 6.00 am, precisely.*

ascend (*formal*) to go upwards: *a pillar of smoke ascending a few hundred metres into the air.*

climb (said especially about an aircraft) to fly upwards to a greater height: *The aircraft took off and then climbed steeply to 2000 metres.*

loom (up) to be tall or high and look rather threatening: *As we turned the corner, the mountain loomed into view.*

soar to fly or rise up high into the air: *The eagle soars above the mountain tops.*

swell (up) to become bigger and higher as its surface expands because of the material collecting inside: *My ankle has swollen because an insect bit me.*

tower to be very tall, especially to be much taller than something standing next to it or things standing around: *He towers over his wife, who's rather short and dumpy.*

See also **climb; increase**.

road *noun*

a way with a specially hardened surface that vehicles can travel along: *They're digging up the road again outside our house.*

avenue a street, usually a fairly wide street in a smart area of town: *We strolled down the avenue.*

bypass a road built to carry traffic around a town or village: *The bypass was built to reduce the amount of traffic passing through the town centre.*

high street the most important street in a town (but not usually in a very big city), often where most of the shops, businesses, and public buildings are: *There's a bank in the high street, next door to the library.*

Only used in British English. The equivalent in US English is *main street*.

footpath a way, which may or not be paved, intended for people who are walking, especially in the country: *Follow the footpath through the next field until you come to a stile.*

lane a narrow road, especially in the country, or a specially marked section of a road for traffic moving in a particular direction: *Take the right-hand lane as you come up to the traffic lights.*

motorway a specially built road for high-speed traffic that usually does not run through towns and village and has a limited number of places where you drive onto it or off it: *It only takes an hour to get to London on the motorway.*

Only used in British English. The equivalent in US English is *superhighway*.

pavement an area at the side of a road or street, reserved for pedestrians: *Cyclists aren't supposed to ride along the pavement.*
Only used in British English. The equivalent in US English is *sidewalk*.

ring road a circular road that runs all the way around a town or city: *I can get to my mother's house quicker by going round the ring road than by going through the centre of town.*

street a road in a town, usually with buildings on each side of it: *They live just across the street from us.*

track a way for vehicles or walkers that does not have a paved surface: *The house was at the end of a rough track that was not really meant for motor vehicles.*

rough *adjective*

1 not smooth, having a surface that has small things sticking out of it: *His cheek felt rough because he had not shaved.*

bristly having short stiff hairs on it or in it: *a bristly beard.*

bumpy having an uneven surface with quite large rises and falls: *a bumpy road.*

coarse having a surface or texture with quite large lumps or bumps in it: *coarse sandpaper.*

gnarled having an uneven surface with irregular lumps and twists in it: *the gnarled trunk of an old tree.*

lumpy having many small solid pieces in it instead of a smooth texture: *lumpy porridge.*

rugged not smooth or even, but having a strong look: *rugged rocks.*

uneven not level and smooth: *The lawn is too uneven for us to play bowls on it.*

2 quickly made and not intended to be complete or completely accurate: *I'll just give you a rough idea of what's involved.*

approximate not completely accurate,

but close to the exact number, time, etc.: *These figures are only approximate.*

estimated calculated in advance before you know the exact figures, amounts, etc.: *Our estimated time of arrival is 15.30.*

general relating to the main or basic features of something, but not including details: *I think she's got the general idea of what's wanted.*

hazy not knowing something exactly or accurately and therefore vague: *I'm a bit hazy about the details of this job.*

sketchy not complete, lacking in detail: *Their account is rather sketchy and fails to mention some of the most important events that took place during this period.*

vague not precise or completely clear, or not knowing or expressing something precisely or very clearly: *I have a vague memory of him saying something of the sort.*

rude *adjective*
showing a lack of respect for someone, impolite, or (often used to describe words or language) indecent: *It's rude to interrupt when somebody's talking.*

abusive forcefully expressing the idea that someone is bad, ugly, worthless, etc., especially when that person is present: *abusive language.*

crude offensive; referring to sex or parts of the body in an unpleasant way: *crude jokes.*

derogatory (*formal*) expressing the idea that someone is bad, ugly, worthless, etc.: *a derogatory remark.*

discourteous (*formal*) impolite: *It would be discourteous of us not to go after we have accepted the invitation.*

ill-mannered very impolite or badly behaved: *When children are so ill-mannered, it's usually the parents who are to blame.*

impolite not conforming to the usual standards in society for how you should behave towards other people: *I hope you don't think it impolite of me to ask, but how old are you?*

indecent referring or relating to things, especially sex or bodily functions, that people usually do not mention for fear of offending others: *People shouldn't talk about their sex lives in public; it's indecent.*

insulting making someone feel that you think they are bad, ugly, worthless, etc.: *It's so insulting to be treated like an absolute ignoramus.*

offensive causing people to feel

angry and upset through showing no respect for their feelings, beliefs, etc.: *Are you deliberately trying to be offensive?*

pejorative (*formal*) (used to describe words or language) expressing the opinion that someone or something is bad: *I was not using the word in its pejorative sense.*

See also **insolent; insult**.

rule *noun*
a statement that tells people how they must behave in a particular situation, for example, when playing a game or sport: *It's against the rules to hit the ball twice.*

condition something that you have to do in order for something else to happen or for you to have something: *It's a condition of his appointment that he should successfully pass a medical examination.*

decree a statement saying that something must happen made by a ruler or by a judge or court: *The king issued a decree banning the sale of alcohol anywhere in his kingdom.*

guidelines instructions or advice on how to do something: *Clear guidelines have now been issued to all staff on how to claim expenses.*

law a rule made by the state that all citizens have to obey: *a new law allowing pubs to stay open twenty-four hours a day.*

(the) law what the state commands or forbids, or all the laws considered together, or all the laws relating to a particular subject: *You can't drive a motor vehicle without a licence, that's the law.*

regulation an official rule, made by a government or other authority, dealing with a particular activity or a matter such as health and safety: *It says in the building regulations that you have to fit an extractor fan in a toilet that does not have a window.*

statute a written law made by a lawmaking body such as a parliament: *a statute from the reign of Edward III.*

See also **order**.

run *verb* to move on legs at a fast pace: *I had to run to catch the bus.*

bolt to run very fast, especially in fear: *Running for his life, he bolted down the road.*

charge rush towards an enemy to attack them, or to move fast and determinedly in a particular direction regardless of anything or anyone who might be in your way: *He charged down the corridor shouting at people to get out of his way.*

dart to move very quickly and suddenly: *A small animal darted across the path in front of us.*

dash (*informal*) to run very fast, usually because you are in a hurry, or to leave hurriedly: *He quickly gathered up his things and dashed out of the room.*

gallop (usually said about a horse or rider, but sometimes also about a person running) to run very fast: *The horse galloped across the field towards us.*

jog to run at an easy pace, especially for exercise: *I jogged around the track a couple of times to warm up for the race.*

race to run or move very fast, or (said about a machine, engine, etc.) to function at a much faster rate than normal: *My heart was racing, and every hair on my body seemed to be standing up on end.*

rush to move very fast, often because you are in a hurry: *She rushed into my office waving a message that had just come through on the fax.*

sprint to run very fast, especially over a short distance: *She came around the final bend and sprinted for the finishing line.*

tear (*informal*) to move very fast and often carelessly or dangerously: *He leapt onto his motorbike and tore off down the road.*

trot (usually said about a horse or rider, but sometimes also about person on foot) to run at a fairly easy pace with regular short steps: *The children from the local riding school came trotting down the lane.*

See also **control; hurry; work 3**.

sad *adjective*
feeling or showing emotional distress or pain: *a sad song.*

dejected (usually only used to describe people) in a sad state of mind, usually only for a short period of time: *He looked a bit dejected, so I tried to cheer him up.*

depressed feeling sad over a longer period of time, or suffering from a mental condition that makes you feel hopeless and unable to react normally to people and events: *I get depressed just thinking about the amount of work I still have to do.*

disappointed sad because something that you hoped would happen or that you expected to happen has not happened: *She was very disappointed when she wasn't picked for the hockey team.*

dismal unpleasant and causing people to feel sad and hopeless: *The weather has been pretty dismal for the last few days.*

downcast (usually only used to describe people) dejected, especially because of disappointment about something: *There's no need to be downcast, because you didn't win. You tried your best.*

melancholy feeling, showing, or causing a usually mild degree of sadness, which is sometimes not entirely unpleasant: *The garden in winter is a melancholy place.*

miserable feeling very sad, or unpleasant, and causing great sadness: *He feels utterly miserable at being let down by his best friend.*

mournful expressing or showing grief in a very obvious way: *I expected the funeral to be a mournful occasion, but it was actually quite jolly.*

unhappy in a sad state of mind, usually over a long period, or causing pain and distress: *an unhappy love affair.*

upset (usually only used to describe people) feeling sad and sometimes angry because of something that has happened: *Naturally, I'm upset that they didn't even bother to phone me.*

wistful feeling or showing mild sadness mixed with longing for something: *The boy looked at the toys in the shop window with a wistful expression.*

See also **dismay.**

safe *adjective*
not harmed or injured or in further danger: *They were in the hotel when the bomb went off, but they're all safe, thank heaven.*

alive and well not hurt, ill, or in trouble (used especially when no news has been heard from someone for a long time): *He sent an e-mail to say he was alive and well, but his mobile phone had been stolen.*

all right (*informal*) not hurt, ill, or in trouble: *I'm all right, but Martha's leg was broken.*

in one piece (used to describe people and things) not harmed or damaged: *I dropped my best china teapot, but, luckily, it's still in one piece.*

intact (used mainly to describe things) not broken or damaged: *Make sure the goods are properly wrapped, so that they arrive intact.*

out of danger not likely to be harmed or to die, especially not likely to die as a result of a medical condition: *The doctor said her condition improved during the night, and she's now out of danger.*

unscathed not harmed or injured, especially after being involved in an accident or disaster: *If you seen the state of the car, you'd say it was a miracle they got away unscathed.*

sarcastic *adjective*

using words that mean the opposite of what they literally say in order to ridicule or humiliate someone: *Before you say anything sarcastic, let me just remind you that it's my first attempt at painting anyone's portrait.*

caustic openly and often cruelly critical of people or their behaviour: *She refused to speak to reporters after the caustic comments some of them made about her acting.*

derisive showing open mockery and contempt, for example, because what someone says is obviously ridiculous or hypocritical: *His promise to do better next time was greeted with derisive laughter.*

ironic(al) using words that mean the opposite of what they literally say for humorous effect: *When I said I'd never been happier than when I was in prison, I was being ironic.*

mocking showing, usually openly and in an unkind way, that you think that someone or something is ridiculous: *a mocking laugh.*

sardonic showing, usually in a quiet, superior way, that you think that someone or something is ridiculous: *He listened to the policeman's clumsy attempts to question the suspect with a sardonic smile.*

scornful showing openly that you reject or despise someone or something: *'I wouldn't marry you, if you were the last man on earth', was her scornful reply.*

snide (*informal*) trying, usually in an indirect and sneering way, to make someone appear ridiculous: *Instead of making snide comments about the new recruits, why don't you help them?*

save *verb*

to prevent someone or something from being harmed, destroyed, or lost when they are in trouble or threatened by something: *a campaign to save the tiger.*

deliver (*literary*) to free someone from something, especially a moral danger or evil: *We pray to be delivered from the consequences of our past sins.*

preserve to keep something that is

considered to be valuable, often something historic such as an old building or an ancient custom, when it is in danger of being lost or destroyed: *The original façade was preserved, but the rest of the building was demolished.*

recover to find or get back something that has been lost: *The flight recorder has been recovered from the wreck of the aircraft.*

redeem to save someone or something from being considered very bad, by being good: *She only redeemed herself by working extra hard for the rest of the day.*

rescue to save someone or something, especially after an accident or disaster: *The fishermen were rescued by helicopter after their boat sank.*

salvage to recover material that can be reused from the scene of an accident or disaster: *After the floodwaters went down, people were allowed back into their houses to try to salvage their personal belongings.*

See also **save.**

say *verb*

use particular words or express particular ideas when speaking or writing: *I couldn't understand a word he was saying.*

comment to say something in relation to a particular subject: *Prime Minister, there have been reports in the press that you may be thinking of resigning. Would you care to comment?*

declare to say something in a formal or official way or in a way that suggests that you think that what you are saying is important: *I declare this meeting closed.*

mention to speak the name of a particular person, thing, or subject, or to say something about them, when discussing something: *He did discuss the question of payment, but he didn't mention any particular sum.*

observe (*formal*) to express an opinion or state a fact: *I merely observed that it was cold for the time of year.*

point out to make people aware of something by saying something about it: *I just wished to point out that the proposed changes will affect the tenants as much as the landlords.*

refer to to make someone or something the subject of something you are saying either by mentioning them directly or by showing indirectly that you are thinking of them: *She didn't mention him by name, but there was no doubt about whom she was referring to.*

remark to say something that conveys a particular piece of information or expresses a particular opinion, often in a fairly casual way: *I just happened to remark that she was looking rather pale and she took it as a deadly insult.*

state to say something in a definite way for other people to take note of: *I wish to state my objections to the proposal.*

See also **speak; tell.**

scatter *verb*

throw things, or to make people or things move, in different directions so that they are not grouped together but cover a wide area with spaces in between them: *Scatter the seed over the flowerbed.*

break up to divide a mass or group into separate parts or units: *They broke up the business and sold off the most profitable parts.*

dispel to drive away something, especially something unpleasant such as negative feelings: *What she said dispelled all my doubts about whether the plan would work.*

disperse to make something go away, especially a crowd of people or a mass of something such as fog or gas, by taking action to break it up: *Police used tear gas to disperse the crowd.*

dissipate to use up a resource, e.g., money, wastefully on a number of different things until there is none left: *By the age of thirty, his entire fortune had been dissipated.*

separate to move things or people

so that they are apart from one another: *We separated the books into two piles.*

spread to move something so that it covers something else in a layer: *Spread the compost over the flowerbed.*

search *verb*

1 examine a place, often in a systematic way, in order to try to find something: *Police searched the house, looking for stolen goods.*

comb to search an area very carefully and systematically: *Police combed the woods for any trace of the missing child.*

go through to examine a place or, especially, a collection of things or something made up of separate parts, in order to try to find something: *I went through the whole document again, but I still couldn't find the paragraph you mentioned.*

look around to examine a place, usually in a casual way: *I looked around the garden, but I couldn't find your ball.*

rummage to search a usually small place in an unsystematic and untidy way: *I rummaged around in the cupboard and found an old shirt I thought I'd thrown away.*

scour to search an area in a very active and thorough way: *We scoured the second-hand bookshops looking for a copy of* Great Expectations.

2 (search for)

to make a usually serious and systematic attempt to find someone or something, which may be either a physical object or something abstract: *We're still searching for the answer to this question.*

forage to search an area intensively looking for something, especially food to eat: *The children were well trained in the art of foraging for food in the forest.*

hunt to search for someone or something in a very active and serious way: *Police are hunting the killer of 6-year-old Jimmy Briggs.*

look for to try to find something or someone, often in a fairly casual way: *I'm looking for the tin-opener – have you seen it?*

seek to look for or ask for something abstract, or (*literary*) to search for a person or thing: *They sought guidance from an expert in legal matters.*

sift to examine something such as documents, evidence, or memories closely and thoroughly to try to find something

significant: *The officials sifted though the archives to find the missing photograph.*

secret *adjective*
deliberately not made known to other people: *a secret plan.*

confidential (said about information) to be kept private, not public: *The report was marked 'Strictly confidential' and was to be seen only by the top executives.*

covert carried out secretly, usually because it would be dangerous or cause trouble if people knew what was happening: *covert military operations.*

discreet done in a way that does not attract attention to what you are doing: *to make discreet enquiries.*

furtive showing a wish that other people should not see or know about what you are doing: *a furtive glance.*

private concerning only one person or a particular group of people, not the general public: *It's a private matter between me and my wife.*

stealthy acting, moving, or done very quietly and slowly in the hope that no one will notice what is happening: *He began to hear stealthy footsteps from down the corridor.*

surreptitious (*formal*) (usually used about a bad action) done in a stealthy way: *the surreptitious removal of documents from the safe.*

undercover using disguise and deception to avoid danger and obtain information: *an undercover police office.*

underground (usually used to describe activities hostile to a government) done or operating in secret: *an underground resistance movement.*

see *verb*
to perceive someone or something with your eyes: *You can sometimes see the French coast from the cliffs of Dover.*

catch sight of see someone or something that has previously been invisible to you, often suddenly or unexpectedly: *I caught sight of him again as left the wood and began climbing the path up the hill.*

discern (*formal*) to see something in difficult conditions by looking carefully: *Peering through the fog, I was barely able to discern the taillights of the car ahead.*

glimpse or *catch a glimpse of*
to see someone or something very briefly, or not clearly or completely: *I caught a glimpse of her through the shop window as she hurried by.*

make out to be able to recognize or
 understand something that is difficult to see clearly: *I can make out a few words, but most of the text is completely illegible.*

notice to see something or someone and register in your mind that you have seen them: *Now you mention it, I did notice a man of that description standing outside the house yesterday afternoon.*

perceive (*formal*) to become aware of something through one of the senses or with the mind: *Such small objects in the night sky are difficult to perceive even with the aid of a telescope.*

sight to see someone or something that you have been looking out for: *We finally sighted land after thirty days at sea.*

spot to see someone or something that you have been looking for or that may be hidden or not very noticeable: *Did you spot the deliberate mistake?*

witness be present when an action or an event, especially an important one, takes place, or to see someone doing something: *We were in London on that day and witnessed the unveiling of the statue.*

See also **look; watch.**

selfish *adjective*
unpleasantly concerned with your own needs and wishes and ignoring those of other people, especially in everyday matters: *Don't be selfish, let your sister have a turn.*

egoistic believing in or acting on the principle that your main concern should be to get what you want or need: *You expect artists to be egoistic; it comes with being dedicated to their art above everything else.*

egotistic(al) vain about your own abilities and achievements and tending to talk about them a lot (a more condemnatory word than *egoistic*): *It's very difficult to have a proper conversation with someone who's so thoroughly egotistical and boasts about all they've done the whole time.*

inconsiderate rather selfish in not paying proper attention to other people's needs or wishes: *Young people can be very inconsiderate of the difficulties faced by the old.*

self-absorbed focusing your attention on your own thoughts and feelings: *If you hadn't been so self-absorbed, you might have noticed how unhappy your brother has been these last few weeks.*

self-centred always concerned only
 with yourself and your own interests: *Living alone for all these years has made him rather self-centred.*

self-seeking trying to gain money or advantages for yourself at the expense of other people: *She denied that her actions had been self-seeking, and pointed out that she had given nearly half the money she had raised to charity.*

thoughtless not paying proper attention to other people's needs or wishes: *It was very thoughtless of him to forget to send you a birthday card.*

sell *verb*
to give someone something in exchange for payment: *I'm sorry, we sold the last copy yesterday.*

carry (said usually about for example a shop) to stock: *There's very little demand for typewriter ribbons nowadays, so we don't carry them.*

deal in to run a business that sells a particular kind of goods: *He deals in second-hand books.*

hawk to sell things by knocking on

people's doors and asking them to buy: *I sold a few copies of my novel by hawking them around local bookshops.*

peddle to sell goods while travelling from place to place: *Gypsy women traditionally used to peddle clothes' pegs and sprigs of lucky white heather.*

retail (said about a business) to sell goods to the people who will own and use them: *The shop is licensed to retail wines and spirits.*

sell off (said about a business) to sell something that you no longer want, usually at a lower price that usual: *We're selling off our winter goods to make way for new spring lines.*

stock (said usually about for example a shop) to have a particular kind of goods available on the premises ready to be sold: *We actually stock six different brands of trainers.*

send *verb*
to arrange for a person or thing to go or be transported to a place: *She sent a message to say that she was too ill to come to the meeting.*

consign (*formal*) (used especially in the context of business) to send goods to someone: *a shipment of raw materials consigned to a factory in Belgium.*

direct to send something, usually by post, to a particular person or address: *Letters of complaint should be directed to the Customer Services Department at our head office.*

dispatch (mainly used in the context

of business) to send something such as goods from the place where they are made or stored: *Goods are usually dispatched within 24 hours of receipt of order.*

forward to send something received at one address onward to another address: *The people who bought our house agreed to forward any mail to our new address.*

mail to send something such as a letter or parcel using an official postal service: *I think I mailed the letter to your old address by mistake.*
Used in US English and, though less commonly, in British English.

post to mail something: *I posted it yesterday, so you should get it tomorrow.*
Only used in British English.

remit to send money to someone, especially to send money earned abroad to your home country: *He remits most of his wages to his wife and children in India.*

sensible *adjective*
showing good judgment and an understanding of how to deal with people and situations effectively: *That's very sensible advice, and I think you should take it.*

down to earth (usually used to describe people) realistic and practical, and not using fancy language or advocating f ancy ideas: *The doctor's very down to earth, he won't try and blind you with science.*

level-headed (usually used to describe people) behaving or reacting calmly and showing good judgment: *I thought she was too level-headed to get involved in such a crazy scheme.*

practical good at or good for dealing with situations that occur in real life: *What we need is a practical solution to the problem.*

prudent wise and careful, especially

with money: *It would be a prudent use of your money to invest it more widely.*

rational using reason rather than emotion when dealing with an issue or problem: *a rational approach to the question.*

realistic showing an understanding of what is possible in real life: *Be realistic, we'd never be able to raise £50,000.*

reasonable based on reason or showing an ability to use reason and good judgment, especially in not expecting too much of other people: *Our demands are perfectly reasonable, and we know that the management can afford to pay what we are asking.*

responsible able to carry out tasks and deal with situations in a sensible manner: *Is she responsible enough to be left in charge of three small children?*

sound (usually used to describe ideas, arguments, etc.) based on clear thinking and good judgment and difficult to argue against: *These are three sound reasons for not going ahead with the plan.*

wise showing good judgment, often based on long experience: *I think you were wise not to insist on having your own way in this matter.*

See also **careful.**

sentimental *adjective*

showing or producing tender or romantic feelings, often too easily: *a sentimental love song.*

emotional showing strong feeling, especially of the kind associated with sadness: *He gets very emotional when he has to say goodbye to people.*

mawkish exaggeratedly or unpleasantly sentimental, very obviously intended to produce a great deal of tender feeling: *The description of the heroine's death was positively mawkish.*

nostalgic showing a great affection or longing for the past: *a nostalgic look back to the Paris of the 1950s.*

soft-hearted (used to describe people) easily made to sympathize with or feel pity for other people: *You're too soft-hearted, I never give money to beggars.*

soppy (*informal*) that makes you cry

or makes you feel very tender and romantic: *a soppy love story.*

tender showing gentleness and care or affection for other people: *This is one of the few tender moments in what is basically a very violent film.*

touching causing you to feel an emotion such as gratitude or sympathy: *It's very touching that the dog is so obviously devoted to the children.*

separate

1 *adjective* not joined to or included with something else, or not shared with someone else: *They were sitting at separate tables.*

detached not attached to something else, especially not built beside another house and sharing a dividing wall with it: *The house we are buying is detached and surrounded by a lovely garden.*

different not the same as, or not of the same type as, something or someone else: *The view from the back of the house is different.*

distinct clearly divided from, or

clearly not the same as, something else: *The book is divided into two distinct sections.*

independent separate from and not under the control of something or someone else: *Formerly part of Czechoslovakia, Slovakia became an independent republic in 1993.*

individual consisting of one single and separate item, or for only one person or thing: *Each student receives individual tuition.*

isolated existing or happening as single and separate instances of something that are not connected with one another: *There have been isolated cases of bird flu, but there is no sign of an epidemic.*

particular not general but special, referring or relating to one thing or person or a distinct group: *I have a particular reason for not wanting to travel on that date.*

unconnected having no link or relationship with something else or with each other: *Although the two crimes have some similar features, the police believe they are unconnected.*

unrelated unconnected, or not belonging to the same family as someone else: *We have the same surname, it's true, but we're unrelated.*

2 *verb* to put something or someone in a position where they are not attached to or not with something or someone else, or to become separate: *We separate the more able from the less able pupils and teach them in different classes.*

come apart to break or divide into separate pieces: *If you hold both ends and twist gently, the pen should come apart quite easily.*

detach to remove something or part of something from a thing that it is joined

to: *Detach the yellow strip before putting the ink cartridge into the printer.*

disconnect to make something no longer physically attached or joined to something else: *Disconnect the appliance from the electricity supply before attempting to repair it.*

dismantle to take something made from a number of different parts, such as an engine, and remove all of its parts one by one: *Surely you don't have to dismantle the whole engine just to repair an oil leak!*

divide to cut or separate something

into a number of parts: *It's rather difficult to divide a cake into seven equal parts.*

fall apart to break or divide into separate pieces in a way that you did not intend or that causes damage to something: *I did not break the chair – it just fell apart when I sat on it.*

sever to cut something or cut it off, or to end something such as a link or connection between two or more things: *His right arm was severed in an industrial accident.*

take apart to dismantle something, usually something that is constructed in a fairly simple away: *If the shelves in the bookcase you made aren't level, you'd better take the whole thing apart and start again.*

See also **alone; part 2.**

serious *adjective*
not showing amusement, or not intending or intended to cause amusement: *Please be serious for a moment and tell me what you really think.*

grave showing that something very sad or with very important bad consequences has happened: *The doctor came back into the room, and his expression was grave.*

grim showing a mixture of seriousness and a fierce, determined, or threatening quality: *The captain told us with a grim smile that there were no reinforcements; our orders were to fight to the last man.*

pensive thinking deeply about something: *He looked pensive, so I asked him what was on his mind.*

preoccupied thinking and worrying about something very important or threatening, or showing that you are doing this: *She had obviously been too preoccupied to hear what I was saying to her.*

sober not excited or affected by emotion; serious and realistic: *I asked him for a sober assessment of our chances of escape.*

solemn very serious, quiet, and dignified: *His face wore a solemn expression more suitable for a funeral than a wedding.*

sombre suggesting that sad or worrying things are happening: *The atmosphere at the meeting was rather sombre, since everybody had already heard the bad news.*

stern showing that you expect people to be serious and will not be pleased if they try to be funny: *Our teacher could be very stern, if she thought we were trying to play tricks on her.*

thoughtful thinking rather than reacting to what is happening, or showing that you are thinking: *He's very thoughtful today, do you think there's something wrong?*

See also **important.**

shake *verb*

to move quickly from side to side or up and down while remaining basically in the same position, or to make something do this: *Shake the tablecloth before you fold it up and put it away.*

jiggle to shake something small in a light or casual way: *He has an irritating habit of jiggling the keys on his keyring while he's talking to you.*

quake (*often humorous*) to tremble violently, usually through fear: *The sound of his footsteps on the stairs would make us quake and hide under the blankets.*

quiver to shake with many fast small movements, sometimes through fear or alarm: *The arrow stuck, quivering, in the very centre of the target.*

shiver (usually said about a person) to quiver, especially with cold: *Don't stand shivering on the doorstep, come in!*

shudder to shake once violently or with a few violent movements, sometimes through horror: *The though of how close we came to being killed makes me shudder even now.*

sway make large and often fairly slow side to side or up and down movements: *The branches were swaying the wind.*

tremble (usually said about a person) to quiver, especially with fear or emotion: *Her hand was trembling so badly that she nearly spilt her coffee when she tried to drink it.*

vibrate (said about things) to shake with many fast, small movements: *The strings of a violin or piano vibrate to produce sound.*

share *noun*

a part or amount of something that is given to one person or group when something is divided up equally or systematically between two or more people or groups: *What are you going to do with your share of the money?*

allocation (*formal*) an amount of something, especially money, provided from a central fund to a particular person or group or for a particular purpose: *We've already spent most of our allocation from the budget for this year.*

cut (*informal*) an amount that someone takes as their share of something, especially a sum of money, that is being divided up informally or illegally: *By the time everyone else has taken a cut, there'll be very little left for us.*

portion a part or amount of something such as food or money that is being divided up: *You shouldn't have given them such large portions, now we're running out of stew.*

quota an amount that someone is officially given or allowed to take: *If fishermen exceed their quotas, they have to throw the surplus fish back into the sea.*

ration an amount of something that is scarce, for example food or petrol, that a person is allowed to have: *Our weekly ration is just 500 grams of bread, 100 grams of fat, and 200 grams of meat.*

shock *verb*
to make someone suddenly and unexpectedly feel a strong and distressing emotion: *The scenes of violence were intended to shock viewers.*

appal (mostly used in the passive) to fill someone with a strong negative feeling such as horror or disgust: *All right-thinking people are appalled by such horrendous crimes.*

horrify (mostly used in the passive) to fill someone with horror or with a strong negative feeling: *I was horrified to think that I might have been indirectly responsible for the accident.*

offend to make someone feel angry or disgusted because things they value highly, such as religious beliefs or moral principles, are being attacked: *You didn't stop to think that you might offend people by using bad language.*

outrage (mostly used in the passive) to fill someone with anger, especially because they think a wrong or injustice has been done: *The decision to demolish the historic building outraged conservationists.*

scandalize (mostly used in the passive) to shock someone by doing something

that they think is immoral or improper: *In those days the neighbours would have been scandalized by people living together before they were married.*

unsettle to make someone feel mildly distressed or worried, or to make them lose their self-confidence: *Something seems to have unsettled him: he can't concentrate on his work.*

upset to cause a fairly strong and distressing feeling in someone: *It really upset your mother that you decided not to come home for Christmas.*

See also **dismay; surprise.**

shorten *verb*
make something less long: *Can you shorten the legs of these jeans for me, please?*

abbreviate to make a word less long by missing out the less important letters: *Trinitrotoluene is usually abbreviated to TNT.*

abridge to make a piece of writing such as book less long by leaving out some less important passages: *He refused to allow anyone to abridge his novel, arguing that every single word of the text was important.*

condense to express something using fewer words, which usually involves not only leaving things out but also rewriting certain things: *She wants me to condense a 2000-word essay into an article containing just 500 words.*

curtail (*formal*) to make something that would normally go on longer finish in a shorter time: *We shall have to curtail our discussions, as the minister has a further meeting at four o'clock.*

cut to make something, especially a piece of writing or a performance, less long by removing or omitting parts of it, or to remove or omit part of something in order to make the whole thing shorter: *The play last five hours, so, of course, directors usually cut it.*

dock to shorten or remove the tail of an animal: *The sheep look different because their tails have been docked.*

prune to shorten the branches or

 stems of a plant, or to cut a text: *The roses will need to be pruned before next spring.*

trim to make something, especially hair or a plant, a little shorter by cutting off a small amount: *He trimmed his beard.*

See also **cut; decrease**.

shout *verb*
to speak or say something more loudly than usual because you want people to hear you: *There's no need to shout; I can hear you perfectly well.*

bawl to shout very loudly and in an angry, rude, or frightening way: *Jim's idea of maintaining discipline is to go and bawl at the kids if they're naughty.*

bay (usually said about a large group of people) to make very loud, angry, and threatening noises like wild animals: *By the end of the match the crowd were baying for the referee's blood.*

bellow to shout in a loud deep voice,

 often angrily or in pain: *'Get out of my way', he bellowed.*

call (out) to try to attract someone's attention or tell them something by shouting in their direction: *Call me if the phone rings while I'm in the garden.*

cry (out) to speak in a loud voice suddenly, usually because you feel pain or a strong emotion: *'Why are you tormenting me like this?' she cried out.*

raise your voice to start to speak more loudly than usual, especially as a sign that you are getting angry: *He's one of*

those rare people who can keep order in a classroom without ever having to raise his voice.

roar to shout in a very loud voice that may be fierce or threatening or may show enthusiasm or pleasure: *The crowd roared their approval of the judge's choice.*

scream make a very loud high-pitched sound that usually suggests fear or pain, or to shout something in a loud high-pitched voice: *People were screaming for help from the upper floors of the burning building.*

shriek make a very loud high-pitched sound (even shriller and more disturbing to hear than a scream) that usually suggests panic, or to shout something in that kind of voice: *'There's a spider running up my leg!' she shrieked.*

yell to shout very loudly and usually in an uncontrolled way: *Stop yelling and I'll give you what you want.*

See also **cry**.

shrewd *adjective*
having or showing practical intelligence based on experience of life and people's behaviour: *She's shrewd enough to know when it's best not to interfere.*

calculated (used to describe actions) done after thinking carefully about the advantages and disadvantages: *Taking over a nearly bankrupt company was a calculated risk.*

calculating (used to describe people disapprovingly) thinking carefully about the advantages and disadvantages for yourself of any action: *a cold calculating villain.*

crafty (mainly used approvingly) shrewd and knowing how to get an advantage over other people, usually by acting quietly and carefully, and sometimes by using tricks or deception: *He's a crafty old devil, so he's probably not telling us everything he knows.*

cunning (used approvingly and dis

approvingly) crafty, usually ingenious, and often involving an element of secrecy or deception: *I've worked out a cunning plan to avoid paying any tax on the deal.*

knowing showing that you know something that other people do not and that you therefore have an advantage over them: *a knowing smile.*

perceptive (used approvingly) showing an ability to notice what is happening or what people are feeling or thinking: *His book is a study full of perceptive insights.*

sharp very observant and aware of what is going on and able to think quickly: *She's very sharp, so she's bound to have noticed the mistake.*

sly (mainly used disapprovingly) done or doing things in a crafty, secretive, or underhand way: *You notice how, while praising Geoffrey, she slipped in a sly reference to her own contribution to his success.*

wily (used approvingly, usually to describe people) shrewd and careful, knowing a lot about tricks and deception and sometimes using them: *He's far too wily to be taken in by a simple trick like that.*

See also **clever**.

shy *adjective*

nervous about meeting and talking to people or appearing in public: *I asked him to play his violin, but he's too shy.*

bashful (used mainly to describe young people) shy, modest, lacking in self-confidence, and usually likely to blush or become confused: *Don't be bashful; tell us a little more about yourself.*

coy shy or unwilling to be frank, but usually in a way that does not seem entirely genuine, as if you were trying to attract attention by appearing to avoid it or as if you had something to hide: *He's rather coy about revealing exactly how much he earns.*

diffident modest and usually rather shy: *She's not an easy person to interview because she's so diffident.*

inhibited unable to express your feelings or desires or to enjoy yourself fully because of psychological restraints: *I'm far too inhibited to take my clothes off in public.*

modest not boasting about your own abilities or achievements, but tending to suggest that they are not very great: *You're too modest; it was a really excellent performance.*

reserved unwilling to be frank and open when talking to people and rather quiet and shy in manner: *He's usually so reserved, but today he really opened up to me.*

reticent hesitant and cautious about revealing information or expressing opinions: *They're understandably rather reticent when it comes to discussing their plans for the future.*

retiring preferring to live a quiet life avoiding much contact with the public or the media, or with other people in general: *They were very pleasant when you met them, but because they were a rather retiring couple, you didn't meet them very often.*

self-conscious shy and awkward because you think too much about what other people might be thinking about you: *He was so self-conscious about his appearance that he seldom went out.*

self-effacing preferring not to talk about yourself or to take credit for your achievements: *He made light of his achievements in his usual self-effacing way.*

timid showing a great lack of confidence in social situations and often unable to act through nervousness and shyness: *He was too timid even to ask her what her name was.*

withdrawn very unwilling to be with or communicate with people, so that they think you may be ill: *He's become very withdrawn since his wife died.*

sign *noun*
something that represents or expresses something else, such as that something exists, that something is happening, or what someone is thinking or feeling: *When the baby seems irritable, it's usually a sign that he's getting tired.*

demonstration an action or event that shows what someone or something can do: *a demonstration of the awesome power of the sea.*

evidence signs or pieces of information that show that something has happened or is the case, for example that someone has committed a crime: *There's no evidence that connects her with the murder.*

 gesture a deliberate movement of part of the body that conveys a wish, command, or what someone is thinking or feeling: *He held up his hand as a gesture to us to be silent.*

indication something, often a small thing, that shows that something has happened, is happening, or will happen: *Is there any indication that she's likely to change her mind?*

mark something, usually an action, that is intended to show a feeling or attitude: *We removed out hats and stood in silence as a mark of respect for the dead.*

signal an action, gesture, word, etc., that is meant to communicate a message to someone or make them do something: *Don't move until I give the signal.*

symbol something that represents something else, especially an object or a design that stands for something abstract: *The dove is a symbol of peace.*

symptom a sign of something bad, especially of an illness: *A sore throat and a runny nose are the usual symptoms of a cold.*

token something, often a small object, that is given to someone as a sign of your feelings or attitude towards someone: *Please accept this gift as a token of our gratitude for all you have done for us.*

silly *adjective*
not sensible or wise, but usually not causing great harm or damage: *It was silly of me to come out without an umbrella.*

foolish not sensible or wise (usually in a more serious context and implying stronger condemnation than *silly*): *I made a very foolish mistake when I trusted him with my money.*

imprudent not thinking enough about the possible bad consequences of your actions insofar as they affect yourself: *Isn't it rather imprudent to invest so much money in a product for which there is no obvious market?*

irresponsible not showing enough concern for the possible bad consequences of your actions insofar as they affect other people: *It would be downright irresponsible to teach your daughter to sail before you've taught her how to swim.*

misguided acting on wrong principles or assumptions: *a misguided attempt to save the company some money.*

rash acting hastily, without thinking properly about what you are doing: *I made a rash promise to finish the work by tomorrow.*

reckless completely disregarding the possible bad consequences of your actions for yourself and other people: *reckless driving.*

senseless done without a good reason and producing no good results: *a senseless waste of resources.*

unwise not showing good judgment: *It would be unwise to invest all your money in a single venture.*

See also **stupid**.

simple *adjective*

not made, written, or decorated in an elaborate way: *Try to write in simple sentences.*

classic simple and elegant in style, not trying to follow the fashion of any particular time: *a classic tweed jacket.*

everyday not intended for special occasions or to impress people: *This dress is perfectly good for everyday wear.*

homely of a kind that you have at home: *a restaurant that specializes in plain homely food.*

no-nonsense avoiding complicated techniques or fashionable theories: *a no-nonsense approach to the teaching of grammar.*

plain without decoration: *a plain white tablecloth.*

unpretentious not trying to impress people by being elaborate, clever, or fashionable: *an unpretentious lifestyle.*

unsophisticated (usually used disapprovingly) lacking highly developed skills or techniques: *Using a megaphone is a rather unsophisticated method of communicating with the workforce.*

See also **easy; ordinary**.

sincere *adjective*

meaning what you say when you say it, or expressing real feelings or opinions: *Was he being sincere when he said I deserved the promotion more than he did?*

fervent expressing real and strong emotion: *fervent prayers for his recovery.*

frank openly expressing what you think or feel: *We had a frank discussion about the problems we are having in our relationship.*

genuine real or that someone really feels: *I think she felt genuine remorse for what she had done.*

heart-felt deeply and strongly felt: *We should like to offer you our heart-felt sympathy for your loss.*

honest truthful, especially about what you think or feel: *To be absolutely honest with you, I never expected the plan to succeed.*

straightforward not trying to hide what you think or feel but expressing it directly and truthfully: *I don't think you're being entirely straightforward with me.*

truthful telling the truth: *a truthful answer.*

unaffected speaking or behaving naturally and not trying simply to impress other people: *It's rare to find a politician who seems so unaffected when speaking to ordinary people.*

unfeigned (literary) genuine: *Party members greeted the new policy with unfeigned enthusiasm.*

wholehearted (usually used to describe positive emotions) really and strongly felt: *I'm willing to offer you my wholehearted support.*

See also **frank.**

size *noun*
(used in relation to physical objects and abstract things) how big or small something is, especially a commercial product, or bigness as such: *The sweaters come in all sizes from small to extra large.*

area (used in relation to physical objects) the amount of horizontal space covered by something: *How do you work out the area of a circle?*

bulk (used in relation to physical objects and bodies) bigness combined with heaviness and, usually, awkwardness: *He heaved his vast bulk out of the chair.*

dimensions (used in relation to

physical objects and abstract things) size, especially the height, length, and breadth of something: *I need to know the dimensions of the room to work out how much wallpaper will be needed.*

extent (used in relation to physical objects and abstract things) how far something reaches or how much of something there is: *The insurance company sent a representative to assess the extent of the damage.*

magnitude (*formal*) (used mainly in relation to abstract things or to the brightness of stars) bigness: *We are not really equipped to deal with a problem of this magnitude.*

proportions (used in relation to physical objects and abstract things) size, especially the height, length, and breadth of something big: *a figure of larger proportions than I had ever seen before.*

range the number of different types of something that exist or are available: *Students can choose from a range of essay topics.*

scale (used mainly in relation to abstract things) extent or size, especially in relation to other examples of the same thing: *We had not fully realized the scale of the task that we were faced with.*

scope the range or number of subjects that something such as an enquiry or investigation is able or allowed to deal with: *The government broadened the scope of the enquiry to include the effects of the disaster as well as its causes.*

sleep *verb*
to rest in an unconscious state: *We don't have a spare bed, so I hope you won't mind sleeping on the sofa.*

be asleep to be sleeping: *All the guests were still asleep when the fire started.*

doze to be in a light sleep for a short time: *I woke up at five o'clock and then dozed until the alarm went off at six.*

drop off (*informal*) to fall asleep: *I went to bed feeling very tired, but it took me a long time to drop off.*

fall asleep to go into a sleeping state: *I fell asleep as soon as my head hit the pillow.*

have or *take a nap* to have a short sleep: *I sometimes take a nap in the afternoon, if I'm going out in the evening.*

have forty winks (*informal*) to have a short sleep: *He's upstairs having forty winks.*

nod off (*informal*) to fall asleep,

especially when you are trying to, or are supposed to, stay awake: *Several people nodded off during the sermon.*

rest to be inactive, and either conscious or unconscious, so that your body can recover its vitality: *I was resting on the bed, but not asleep.*

snooze (*informal*) to doze: *No snoozing after the alarm clock goes off!*

slow *adjective*
going, or only able to move, at a low speed: *Progress so far has been slow.*

gradual proceeding slowly and in steps or stages or by adding or subtracting small amounts: *a gradual increase in production.*

leisurely moving in a relaxed way without attempting to hurry: *a leisurely walk along the side of the lake.*

measured kept reasonably slow so that something can be done carefully: *Don't rush your speech; a measured delivery will ensure that everyone hears and understands clearly what you are saying.*

ponderous moving or proceeding slowly and giving an impression of heaviness or awkwardness: *ponderous footsteps.*

sluggish moving very slowly and showing a lack of energy or drive: *The twig barely moved on the surface of the sluggish stream.*

unhurried deliberately not going fast: *Despite the crisis, she continued to deal with business at the same unhurried pace.*

small *adjective*
not big; of limited size: *a small portion of vegetables.*

compact conveniently small, espe- cially not taking up much space or taking up less space than a full-size version of the same thing: *The tool can be dismantled and fits inside a compact carrying case.*

little small, often small and pretty, or small in a way that arouses protective feelings: *What a dear little puppy!*

mini (usually used to describe commercial products) miniature: *a mini car.* Usually only used before a noun.

miniature made or bred to be a much smaller version of a large object or animal: *a miniature dachshund.* Usually only used before a noun.

minute very small indeed: *The particles are so minute, they can only be seen with the aid of a microscope.*

petite (usually used to describe women) short and slim: *This dress would only fit someone who was really petite.*

pocket small enough to fit inside the pocket of a jacket, etc.: *a pocket dictionary.*

short not tall or long: *a short skirt.*

slight small and not usually very significant; (when used to describe people) with a slim, light body: *I think you've made a slight mistake.*

tiny very small (but larger than *minute*): *Just a tiny drop of gin and a lot of tonic, please.*

smell *noun*
a quality or flavour given off by something and detected through the nose: *The house was full of the smell of fried onions.*

aroma a pleasant smell: *What is that beautiful aroma coming from the kitchen?*

bouquet the smell given off by wine: *a white wine with a very delicate bouquet.*

fragrance a pleasant smell, especially a particular smell given to a commercial product: *lavatory cleaner with pine fragrance.*

odour a pleasant or unpleasant smell (*odour* is a slightly more refined word than *smell*): *body odour.*

pong (*informal and humorous*) an unpleasant smell: *What's that terrible pong? I know, it's your socks!*

reek a strong and unpleasant smell: *the reek of cigarette smoke.*

scent the smell naturally given off by a plant or an animal: *The flowers are very colourful, but they have a wonderful scent.*

stench a very strong and disgusting smell: *The body had remained undiscovered for several days, and the stench was almost unbearable.*

stink (*informal*) a strong and unpleasant smell: *We sprayed the room with air freshener to try to get rid of the stink.*

whiff a slight smell of something pleasant or unpleasant: *I thought I smelt a whiff of gas.*

smile *verb*
to curve your mouth to express amusement or pleasure: *He's the only person on the photograph who's not smiling.*

beam to smile broadly in a way that expresses great and genuine happiness: *When I said how pretty she looked, she absolutely beamed.*

grin to smile broadly and show your teeth in a way that may express real pleasure or amusement, may be artificial, or may express some unpleasant emotion: *He must have been pleased, he was grinning from ear to ear.*

leer to smile in an unpleasant way that usually expresses sexually desire for someone: *I don't like the way he keeps leering at my sister.*

simper to smile in an affected or exaggerated way, often while saying something: *'Oh, how very kind of you to say so', she simpered.*

smirk smile in a way that suggests you feel superior to someone or are enjoying the fact that they are in trouble: *Stop smirking and help her clear up the mess.*

speak *verb*
to use your voice to communicate something to someone in words: *I spoke to him about it yesterday.*

address to direct something you are saying to a particular person or group: *I wasn't addressing you, I was speaking to my friend Mr Roberts here.*

express to communicate something such as an idea or a feeling through words or by some other means: *I should just like to express my appreciation to everyone who has helped us to organize this event.*

pronounce to speak or make a sound in a particular way: *The letters -ough can be pronounced in several different ways in English.*

say to use particular words or express particular ideas when speaking or writing: *What did he say when you spoke to him yesterday?*

state to say something in a definite way for other people to take note of: *I wish to state my objections to the proposal.*

talk to speak, especially to exchange words and ideas with another person: *We can't talk here; let's go into my office.*

tell to communicate something to someone in words: *I told him all about what happened.*

utter to produce a sound with your voice, or to say something: *She uttered a terrible cry and sank unconscious to the floor.*

voice (*formal*) to express something in speech: *He has been known to voice opinions that some people might consider subversive.*

whisper to speak, or say something, in a very quiet voice: *Just whisper it in my ear, if you don't want anyone to hear it.*

See also **say; tell.**

special *adjective*
different from what is normal or ordinary, usually in being better, more enjoyable, or involving particular ceremonies: *a special occasion.*

distinctive having a particular,

noticeable or recognizable quality that makes it different from others: *She has a very distinctive laugh.*

especial (*formal*) greater than usual: *Take especial care to spell her name correctly.*

exceptional of a kind that is not experienced very often: *He has a quite exceptional talent.*

extraordinary very unusual, generally through being either very good or very strange: *That was an extraordinary thing to say at someone's wedding.*

memorable easy to remember, usually through being very good, enjoyable, etc.: *Your kindness to us made our holiday especially memorable.*

notable definitely good enough to be worth recording or remembering: *a notable achievement.*

noteworthy good or unusual enough to be worth recording or remembering (often used with a negative): *Nobody said anything that was particularly noteworthy.*

See also **favourite; important; unusual.**

speech *noun*
a text that is spoken aloud to a group of people at an occasion such as a meeting or a wedding: *The prime minister is making an important speech today to the European Parliament.*

address a formal speech on an important occasion: *In his televised address to the nation, the king urged people to remain calm and to go about their normal business as far as possible.*

lecture a speech made to convey

information and teach people, especially students, about a subject: *I missed the professor's lecture on Shakespeare, so can I borrow your notes?*

presentation a lecture, often accompanied by visual material such as slides or charts, given in a business context: *Can you do a presentation on the new computer system to a group of Chinese businessmen?*

sermon a lecture on a religious or moral subject, usually given by a member of the clergy: *He took some words from St Paul's Second Epistle to Timothy as the text for his sermon.*

talk an informal speech or lecture: *Mr Brown has kindly offered to give us a short talk on the subject of common garden pests.*

speed *noun*
how fast or slowly something or someone is moving or something is done, or quickness: *a speed of 20 kilometres per hour.*

acceleration the fact of changing

from a slower to a faster speed, or the ability to change from a slower to a faster speed: *This car has wonderful acceleration.*

momentum the energy possessed by something that is moving that enables it to keep moving even when the force that first made it move is no longer operating: *The sledge gained enough momentum running downhill to carry it a long way up the slope on the other side of the valley.*

pace speed, especially of something moving on legs: *He surely won't be able to keep this pace up for four more laps.*

rapidity quickness, usually in doing something rather than in moving: *the great rapidity of technological change.*

rate speed, especially the speed at which something happens or is done: *The factory must increase its rate of production to become profitable again.*

tempo speed, especially how fast a piece of music is to be played: *A more relaxed tempo would suit this piece better.*

velocity speed, especially in scientific or technical contexts: *The rocket must attain a velocity sufficient to enable to overcome the pull of Earth's gravity.*

See also **hurry; quick.**

steal *verb*
take something of value from someone without their consent: *Someone broke into our house and stole my computer.*

burgle to break into a building in order to steal: *The house was burgled while the owners were on holiday.*

embezzle to steal money that has been entrusted to you by a person or an organization: *While working as a computer operator in a bank, he managed to embezzle £20,000.*

loot to steal goods in large quantities from shops and businesses during a riot, a war, or some other kind of emergency: *There wasn't a single shop in the main street that hadn't been looted.*

make off with to escape taking with you something you have stolen: *The gang raided a warehouse and made off with £100,000 worth of cigarettes.*

nick (*informal*) to steal something, usually something small: *I put my watch down on the table for a second, and somebody nicked it!*

pilfer to steal small things of little value, e.g., from where you work: *Staff were caught pilfering paper clips.*

pinch (*informal, rather old-fashioned*)

to steal something, usually something of little value: *I used to pinch things sometimes, when I was a kid.*

rip off (*informal*) cheat or rob someone, or to steal something: *If you pay $20 for something that usually costs $10, of course you feel you've been ripped off.*

rob to deprive someone or an organization of something of value: *We were robbed of all our foreign currency before we'd even got out of the airport.*
As a general rule, you rob *someone* and you steal *something.*

shoplift take goods from a shop without paying for them: *People who shoplift often don't need the things they steal.*

take to remove something without the owner's consent, to steal: *The house was broken into, but nothing of real value was taken.*

stop *verb*
1 to come to a standstill after moving, or to make something come to a standstill: *The car slowed down and then stopped.*

come to rest (usually said about an object that is moving, but is not powered or being driven) to stop moving forwards: *The boulder rolled all the way down the slope and came to rest at the bottom.*

draw up (said about a vehicle) to approach slowly and stop next to a particular place: *A shining limousine drew up outside the entrance to the hotel.*

halt (*formal*) to stop, or to stop

 something: *The sentry ordered us to halt and show our papers, before allowing us to proceed.*

park to stop a vehicle and leave it standing in a place: *The only problem with driving into central London is that it's difficult to find anywhere to park.*

pull up (said about a vehicle or its driver) to stop in a particular place: *I had to pull up at the side of the road because one of the children was feeling sick.*

2 not to do something any more after doing it for a period of time: *I've stopped smoking at last, after 30 years.*

break off to stop, usually suddenly,

 in the middle of doing or saying something: *She broke off in the middle of our conversation to go and answer the door.*

call it a day (*informal*) to stop working or engaging in an activity finally, using after a long period: *You've been hard at it since eight o'clock this morning, and I think it's time to call it a day.*

cease (*formal*) to come to an end or stop: *The noise of drilling ceased as suddenly as it had begun.*

cut out (*informal*) to stop doing something annoying, or using or consuming something that might be harmful: *I had to cut out butter and cheese in order to lose weight.*

discontinue (*formal*) to decide not to go on doing or making something: *The programme was discontinued because it proved unpopular with viewers.*

leave off (*informal*) to stop doing something, often temporarily: *The rain left off just long enough for me to slip out to the shops.*

quit (*informal*) to stop doing something, often something annoying: *Will you please quit hassling me!* More commonly used in US English than in British English.

See also **abandon; finish; prevent.**

story *noun*

a description in words of an imaginary or real event or series of events: *Will you tell us a story, before we go to sleep?*

account a description in words of what happened at a particular place or time or to a particular person, which is usually but not always factual: *Your account of the incident differs in several respects from the accounts given by other witnesses.*

anecdote a short and usually amusing account of something that happened: *He has a fund of anecdotes from his days in the army.*

narrative (*formal*) an account of a series of events, or the plot of a novel: *a narrative of events that took place in the year 1865.*

novel a literary work that is usually quite long and tells a story in prose: *She has finished her novel and is now trying to find a publisher for it.*

parable a short story that is intended to teach a moral or religious lesson, especially one told by Jesus and recorded in the Bible: *the parable of the Good Samaritan.*

plot the series of events in which the characters in a work such as a novel, play, or film are involved, as opposed to the characters themselves, the settings of the events, etc.: *There is no plot, the characters just sit around and talk to one another.*

saga a long story, or series of stories, describing many characters and events of a long period of time: *It is a saga covering three generations of a farming family in the Highlands of Scotland.*

short story a literary work that is much shorter than a novel and usually deals with one event or one character: *He has had several short stories published in magazines.*

tale a story, usually a short, unpretentious, or folksy one, often one written for children: *If these walls could speak, they'd have some interesting tales to tell.*

yarn (*informal*) a story or account,

 usually one that is told aloud and often one that is not very credible: *He spun me some yarn about helping to catch a lion that had escaped from the zoo.*

strange *adjective*
not as you would usually expect, or not of a kind that you know about or easily recognize, and so causing you to feel surprise, wonder, or sometimes fear: *He says he heard strange noises in the night.*

bizarre startlingly strange, very unlike what is normal and often grotesque: *Her behaviour was so bizarre that I began to think she might need psychiatric help.*

curious unusual enough to arouse your interest or make you think: *It's curious that he's never mentioned her before.*

odd curious or strange, sometimes amusingly strange: *Does it make me look odd if I wear a red jacket and a yellow waistcoat?*

outlandish strange and ridiculous, often through being exaggerated in some way: *He made some outlandish claim about being related to the royal family.*

peculiar strange or curious: *There*
 was a peculiar smell coming from the kitchen.

queer strange in a way that is often worrying or unpleasant: *I had a queer feeling that someone was watching me.* Be careful about using *queer* to describe people, as it is also sometimes used informally to mean *homosexual*.

surreal very strange and of the kind that you might see in a dream or nightmare: *surreal images.*

weird very strange, usually in a rather frightening way and often in a way that suggests the supernatural: *Don't you think it's weird that he went for a walk in the woods one day and just disappeared.*

See also **eccentric; ugly; unusual**.

strict *adjective*
making sure that people do exactly as they are supposed to do, or that something is exactly as it is supposed to be: *Our teacher's very strict and insists that homework is always handed in on time.*

authoritarian using the power that you have, often harshly, to make sure that nobody disobeys you: *an authoritarian regime.*

firm making sure, but not in unkind
 way, that people do what they are supposed to do or that you get what you want: *The boss is firm but fair in the way he deals with the employees.*

inflexible very strict, not allowing any changes, excuses, exceptions, etc.: *It should be an inflexible rule that any player who receives two red cards should be banned from playing for the rest of the season.*

rigorous very strict and thorough, or carried out in a strict and thorough way: *rigorous discipline.*

stern showing strictness and disapproval towards anything that is done wrong: *My father looked very stern, and I wondered what exactly I had done wrong.*

stringent (usually used to describe checks or tests) very rigorous: *Stringent tests must be carried out to make sure that the product is absolutely safe.*

uncompromising unwilling to let rules, standards, or principles be modified or relaxed: *an uncompromising attitude towards offenders.*

strong *adjective*
able to exert a lot of physical force, for example to move or lift things, or able to resist weight, pressure, etc., without breaking or collapsing: *We need three strong men to help us move the grand piano.*

beefy (*informal*) (used to describe people) big, heavy, and strong-looking: *Get a couple of beefy blokes to stand at the door and only let people in if they have proper invitations.*

brawny (used to describe people) with strong muscles: *He doesn't look brawny enough to be a blacksmith.*

forceful exerting physical, intellectual, or moral, force: *I gave it a rather more forceful shove, and it moved a little.*

mighty exerting a lot of power and force, or very big and strong: *He struck it three mighty blows with his hammer.*

powerful having physical, intellectual, or political power, exerting a lot of force: *a powerful energy.*

resilient able to return to its original shape after being bent, stretched, etc., or able to recover after suffering distress, misfortune, etc.: *She'll get over the loss, she's pretty resilient.*

robust strongly made so as to be able

to resist weight, pressure, etc. or rough treatment: *The boxes need to be robust enough to withstand being dropped out of a helicopter.*

sturdy strong and usually quite small or short and thick, or robust: *sturdy little legs.*

See also **intense.**

stubborn *adjective*
showing an unwillingness to change your opinion or your course of action even when people try to persuade you to or when it seems reasonable to do so: *He can be very stubborn when he doesn't get his own way.*

difficult (*informal*) unco-operative and unhelpful: *She's not really against the plan, she's just being difficult.*

dogged showing an admirable determination to achieve something even if it takes a long time and many attempts: *Their dogged persistence eventually paid off.*

intransigent (*formal*) completely unwilling to change your mind about something: *Senior party members remained intransigent in their opposition to any change in the constitution.*

obstinate stubborn and usually

unreasonable: *Her obstinate refusal to accept a compromise made it impossible for us to reach an agreement.*

persistent not stopping what you are doing, or doing the same thing over and over again, in order to achieve something, often in a way that is annoying: *She was so persistent that in the end he had to agree to see her.*

unco-operative unwilling to help other people do or get what they want: *The dispute could have been settled much sooner, if the unions hadn't been so unco-operative.*

stupid *adjective*

having or showing a lack of intelligence or common sense, often in a way that causes trouble for yourself or other people: *How could you be so stupid as to leave your passport at home?*

dim (*informal*) (used mainly about people) unintelligent: *He's a perfectly nice chap, just a bit dim.*

dumb (*informal*) stupid: *That was a*

really dumb thing to do. More commonly used in US English than in British English.

idiotic (usually used to describe actions or attitudes rather than people themselves, often humorously) very stupid or silly: *He's come up with some idiotic scheme to make money by selling vegetables on eBay.*

ignorant lacking knowledge, either generally or about a particular subject: *If you weren't so ignorant, you'd know that* Macbeth *was written by Shakespeare.*

mindless (usually used to describe actions or states) showing a complete lack of thought or purpose: *mindless violence.*

thick (*informal*) (used mainly about people and usually in an unkind way) unintelligent: *He's too thick to get into university.*
More commonly used in British English than in US English.

unintelligent having or showing a lack of the brain power needed to understand things, solve problems, etc.: *You have to be pretty unintelligent not to be able to add up 3 + 3.*

See also **ridiculous; silly.**

subject *noun*

a thing or matter that someone talks or writes about, or that a student studies at school or university: *I'm giving a short talk on the subject of organic farming.*

argument a series of linked ideas or

statements that express someone's point of view on a subject: *You can delete that paragraph, because it's irrelevant to your main argument.*

issue a particular matter that people discuss, or argue or think about: *Reform of the education system is going to be one of the main issues in the election campaign.*

matter something that someone talks about, writes about, or has to deal with: *May I discuss a personal matter with you?*

point a particular idea that someone is trying to communicate, or an idea that forms part of an argument: *He seems to talk endlessly around the subject without ever getting to the point.*

question an issue, or a topic in the form of a grammatical question: *We were discussing the question of women's rights.*

subject matter the information or material that is communicated in a book, a lecture, etc.: *Do you think this is suitable subject matter for an article in the local newspaper?*

theme a main subject that is dealt with in a long work or in a series of separate discussions, etc., and unifies the whole: *I have chosen Repentance as the theme for a series of sermons I shall be giving during Lent.*

thesis an argument, especially a long argument on an academic subject written to qualify for a doctor's degree at a university: *I wrote my thesis on Napoleon's contribution to the French legal system.*

topic a thing or matter that someone talks or writes about, usually smaller in scope than a subject or covering a particular aspect of a subject: *We finished discussing the state of the club's finances and moved on to another topic.*

suggest *verb*

1 to offer an idea, usually an idea for a particular course of action, for other people to accept or reject: *I suggest that you go home and think about it before you make a final decision.*

advise to offer someone an idea for what they should do that you think is a good one and will help them: *I would advise you not to go the police until you have more evidence.*

propose to suggest a definite course of action, often in the course of a formal meeting where a proposal would usually be followed by a vote: *I propose that the meeting be postponed until next month.*

put forward to offer something such as an idea or a plan for other people to consider: *I'd like to come back to the suggestion put forward by Andrew at last week's meeting.*

recommend to advise someone in a

positive way to do something, usually showing quite strongly that you think it is a good idea: *The doctor recommended that I should take more exercise.*

submit *(formal)* (mainly used in legal contexts) to suggest something: *I submit that the defendant was in no way to blame for the accident.*

2 to communicate something without stating it directly or making it completely clear what the situation is: *The evidence suggests that the victim knew her attacker.*

hint to provide a small piece of information that suggests to someone what the situation is or what you intend to do: *He hinted that there were more revelations to come.*

imply communicate an idea indirectly,

by using words that can be understood as having an extra meaning in addition to their obvious one: *He said that he could not comment now, which probably implies that he will comment later.*

indicate to communicate an idea or information either directly or indirectly: *Did he indicate when the elections were likely to take place?*

insinuate to suggest a negative idea about someone in an underhand way: *You seem to be insinuating that I was somehow responsible her death.*

intimate *(formal)* to hint or imply: *She intimated that she would be willing to sell her story if the price was right.*

See also **advice; idea.**

support *verb*
show your approval of an idea, plan, etc., and help to realize it, or to give help and encouragement to enable someone to achieve something or to cope with a difficult situation: *The Conservative Party supports free enterprise.*

back to support someone or something by showing your approval or, sometimes, by giving them money: *If you decide to go ahead with the plan, we'll back you all the way.*

be in favour of to approve of a plan, proposal, idea, etc.: *I'm in favour of giving parents the right to choose which school they send their children to.*

champion to be an active and leading supporter of a cause: *She championed the feminist cause long before it became fashionable to do so.*

encourage to show your approval of a course of action and advise, or try to persuade, someone to adopt it: *We should be encouraging people to save money for their retirement.*

foster to make it possible or easier for

something to develop: *We hope this visit will foster good relations between our two countries.*

promote to take action to bring something to people's attention and encourage them to do it, buy it, etc.: *They're promoting a scheme for employees to buy shares in the company they work for.*

See also **defend; help**.

sure   *adjective*
believing quite strongly that you know something or have done something or remember correctly what happened: *Are you sure this is the right way to Richard's house?*

certain believing very strongly that you know something, etc.: *I can be absolutely certain about the time, because I looked at my watch just after I heard the gun go off.*

confident able to rely on your own or

someone else's ability to do something, or on something happening: *You can be confident that the economic situation will improve next year.*

convinced very sure, often as a result of thinking about something for some time: *The more I examined the case, the more convinced I became that the police had arrested the wrong man.*

definite accurate and precise, or clear and unmistakable, in what you say: *Can you be a bit more definite about the time that the incident took place.*

positive completely certain: *I'm positive he said ten o'clock, not ten thirty.*

See also **confident.**

surprise   *verb*
to shock someone slightly by doing or saying something unexpected: *Well, you do surprise me, I thought the two of you were very happy together.*

amaze (often used in the passive) to fill someone with wonder: *a discovery that amazed the scientific world.*

astonish (usually used in the passive) to surprise or amaze someone greatly: *I'm absolutely astonished, I never thought you'd be able to finish the work so quickly.*

astound (usually used in the passive) to surprise or amaze someone very greatly: *We were astounded by the sheer size of the project.*

stagger (usually used in the passive) to shock or surprise someone greatly: *He was staggered by the enormity of the task ahead of him.*

startle to shock and frighten someone by suddenly doing something: *I'm sorry, I didn't mean to startle you, the door was open so I came in.*

stun (*informal*) (usually used in the

passive) to surprise someone in a pleasant or unpleasant way, so that they find it difficult to react: *I was stunned when they told me I'd got an Oscar nomination.*

take aback (usually used in the passive) to surprise someone, usually in an unpleasant way, so that they find it difficult to react: *I was taken aback by the rudeness of her reply.*

See also **dismay.**

taste

1 *noun* the impression made by a food when you put it into your mouth, for example whether it is sweet, sour, bitter, etc., or whether you find it pleasant or unpleasant: *I don't like the taste of goat's milk cheese.*

flavour a distinct, pleasant and usually fairly strong taste: *We need to add something to the soup to give it more flavour.*

savour (*literary*) a distinctive, pleasing, and usually non-sweet flavour: *The salad, so delicious the evening before, had lost its savour by the following lunchtime.*

smack a particular taste that you can distinguish in the general flavour of something: *Do I detect a smack of anchovies?*

tang a strong and sharp or acid

taste: *the refreshing tang of lemon juice.*

2 *verb* (said about people) to put something, or a small amount of something, into your mouth in order to experience its taste, or (said about food) to produce a particular taste: *Would you taste the soup to see if it needs more salt?*

sample (often used in polite invitations or requests) to try a particular kind of food or drink, or to try several kinds of food or drink to see which one you prefer: *I'd love to sample some of your fish stew.*

savour to consume something slowly

taking time to enjoy its flavour: *The beef was cooked to perfection, and I savoured every mouthful.*

try taste something, or a small amount of something, to see if you like it: *How do you know you don't like squid if you've never tried it?*

teach *verb*
to pass on knowledge or skill to another person, or to groups of people especially in a school, university, etc.: *She teaches French to students on the Business Studies course.*

coach to help someone, usually one person or a small group, prepare a subject for an exam or test, or to teach someone a special skill: *We hired someone to coach Lucy for her maths A level.*

drill to teach something by making

people repeat it several times: *The teacher drilled the students in preparation for their exams.*

educate to pass on knowledge in a variety of subjects and the general skills needed in life to someone: *She was educated at Grimethorpe High School for Girls and the University of Southampton.*

instruct (*formal*) to pass on knowledge or skill in a particular subject: *Sergeant Jenkins instructs the new recruits in the care and handling of their weapons.*

lecture to teach students, usually in a university, by giving long talks on a subject: *He lectures in history at Ohio State University.*

train to pass on a particular skill, or the skills and knowledge needed for a particular task, job, or profession, to someone: *Before you introduce the new machines, you need to train a sufficient number of employees to use them.*

tutor to coach someone, or to teach one student or a small group of students at a university or school: *She tutors us in economic geography.*

tell *verb*

give people information about something by speaking or writing to them about it, or to speak or write something such as news or a story so that other people can hear it or hear about it: *You should have told us that you're a vegetarian.*

communicate (*formal*) pass on information to someone by speaking to them or by contacting them by telephone, radio, letter, etc.: *The pilot communicated his position to the control tower.*

fill in (*informal*) to tell someone about something, usually about something that they were unable to hear about before for some reason: *I'll just fill you in on what's been happening while you were away.*

inform (*formal*) to give someone a particular piece of information: *I am writing to inform you that your application has been successful.*

let know to give someone a particular piece of information: *Let us know when you're arriving, and we'll meet you at the station.*

notify (*formal*) to inform someone officially about something, or to give a piece of information to someone in authority: *You must notify the tax authorities immediately if you leave your present employment.*

recount (*formal*) to tell a story or describe an event: *The Gospels recount the story of the life of Jesus Christ.*

relate (*formal*) to recount something: *The opening chapter relates how a little boy meets an escaped convict in a churchyard.*

report to give people information about something, especially through the media or in the form of a lengthy written document: *Our correspondent in Pakistan reports on efforts to bring aid to the survivors of the earthquake.*

See also **say; speak.**

tempt *verb*

to arouse the desire to have or do something in someone, or (when used in the passive) to feel inclined to so something: *Can I tempt you to try some of this delicious raspberry meringue?*

cajole to use persuasive or flattering language to persuade someone to do something that they are at first unwilling to do: *He's very charming, but don't let him cajole you into buying something that you don't really need.*

coax to use gentle persuasive methods to gradually persuade someone to do something that they are at first unwilling to do: *The baby was very afraid of the sea, and we had to coax him even to go near enough just to get his feet wet.*

entice to use something attractive as a method of getting someone to do what you want them to: *An attractive window display will often entice passing customers into the shop.*

inveigle (*formal*) to use trickery or underhand methods to persuade someone to do something: *She inveigled him into parting with most of his hard-earned wages.*

lure to offer something attractive as bait in order to get someone to go somewhere where something bad may happen to them, for example, into a trap, or to do what you want: *They used to the promise of very high returns to lure investors into buying shares that eventually proved to be worthless.*

sweet-talk (*informal*) to use persuasive, flattering, or tempting language to persuade someone to do something: *She sweet-talked her father into lending her the money.*

See also **persuade**.

thief *noun*

someone who steals something from someone: *A thief stole my wallet.*

burglar someone who enters someone else's house or any building in order to steal things from it: *Burglars broke in and stole all our hi-fi equipment.*

confidence trickster someone who gains another person's trust, for example, with a promise to help them make money, and then steals any money or property that person gives them: *A group of confidence tricksters set up a phony pension fund.*

con-man/con-artist (*informal*) a confidence trickster: *He was so obviously a con-artist that I can't believe they fell for his scheme.*

mugger (*informal*) someone who

threatens or attacks people in the street and robs them: *I'd only just left the hotel, when a mugger pulled a knife on me and demanded my cash and credit cards.*

pickpocket a person who stealthily removes cash, wallets, purses, etc., from people's clothes, usually in crowded places: *Beware of pickpockets when travelling on the underground.*

robber a person who robs someone or a place: *a gang of bank robbers.*

shoplifter someone who steals goods from a shop: *'We prosecute shoplifters.'*

swindler someone who uses dishonest methods or trickery to get money from people, but does not physically rob them: *These 'get-rich-quick' schemes are usually run by swindlers.*

thin *adjective*

not thick, narrow, or having a body with little flesh on it: *a piece of thin wire.*

anorexic suffering from the disease, *anorexia nervosa*, or (*informal*) having an extremely thin body: *She's not just thin, she's anorexic.*

bony having little flesh, so that you are aware of the bones underneath: *His face was too bony to be really handsome.*

emaciated having a very thin body

as a result of starvation or disease: *the emaciated bodies of the victims of the famine.*

gaunt having a face or body that is thin and hollowed as a result usually of hardship or suffering: *You'd think he must have cancer, because he looks so gaunt.*

narrow small when measured from side to side or across its width: *a narrow gap.*

scrawny unattractively thin. *I'd like to wring her scrawny neck!*

slender attractively or gracefully thin: *long, slender fingers.*

skinny (used mainly to describe children or young people) having a thin body: *a skinny little kid.*

slim attractively thin: *The easiest way to get slimmer is to eat less.*

svelte having an attractively thin and graceful body: *You're looking very svelte as usual.*

think *verb*

to use your mind, for example, to produce ideas or to try to solve problems: *I have thought long and hard about this question and still haven't found a satisfactory answer.*

concentrate to focus your mind or your attention on something: *I'm trying to concentrate on my work, and she keeps distracting me.*

consider think carefully, for example, before making a decision: *Perhaps you like to take a couple of days to consider, before you finally make up your mind.*

contemplate to think about something, especially to visualize something and think about it: *The consequences of such a catastrophe are too awful to contemplate.*

deliberate to think about a matter, often to think about something and discuss it with someone else: *Members of the jury deliberated for several hours and then announced their decision.*

mull over to think about something, especially something that happened or was said at a previous time: *I've just been mulling over what you said yesterday and, actually, I think you're quite right.*

ponder think deeply about something, usually a serious matter: *pondering the mysteries of life.*

reflect to have a particular thought, or to consider: *She reflected that nobody had forced her to come; she had come of her own free will.*

ruminate think deeply for a long time:

She can spend weeks ruminating on some profound philosophical question.

take stock to think carefully about a situation so that you have a clear idea of what has happened or what you have done in the past: *It's time to take stock of what we have achieved so far, so that we can make realistic plans for the future.*

weigh up to compare different aspects of something and try to come to a judgment about it: *I'm trying to weigh up the advantages and disadvantages of working from home.*

See also **consider.**

threaten *verb*
frighten someone by saying or indicating that you will do something to harm them, unless they do as you wish, or to be a danger that could easily happen to someone or something: *He threatened to kill me if I moved or made a sound.*

bully to threaten or mistreat some one

who is weaker than you are persistently: *He says he's being bullied by one of the big boys at school.*

cow (usually used in the passive) make someone feel afraid and powerless: *Cowed by the teacher's icy stare, the boys slunk off back to their classrooms.*

intimidate to deliberately make someone feel afraid, usually so that they will do what you want: *He can threaten anything he likes, his threats won't intimidate me.*

lean on (*informal*) to use the power or influence you have over someone, often in a fairly discreet way, to make them do what you want: *The government obviously leant on the trade unions to make them agree to the plan.*

menace (usually used in the passive) to be a danger that could easily happen to someone or something: *The health of the population of Europe is being menaced by a new danger, Asian bird flu.*

pressurize to persuade someone or something to do something by using the power you have over them or telling them repeatedly what you want them to do: *I feel I'm being pressurized to sign up to the scheme, although it's not really in my best interests.*

throw *verb*
to make something travel through the air, especially by drawing back your arm, then thrusting it forward while releasing it from your hand: *Jenny caught the ball and threw it back to me.*

cast throw a fishing line or net into the water in order to catch fish, or (*literary*) to throw: *He glanced briefly at the latter before casting it aside like the rest.* Used in many metaphorical expressions, such as *cast an eye* and *cast a glance.*

catapult to throw or propel something or someone suddenly and with great speed and force: *The impact catapulted me out of my seat.*

fling to throw or propel something, someone, or yourself forcefully, dramatically, or carelessly: *She flung herself down on the bed and burst into tears.*

hurl to throw something with great force: *He was so frustrated that he picked up the typewriter and hurled it across the room.*

launch to make something leave the ground or leave your hand and begin a journey through the air: *She launched herself off the top diving board.*

lob to throw or hit something, usually a ball, so that it goes high up in the air before coming down again: *I was standing by the net, so he just lobbed the ball over my head.*

propel to use force to make something move in a particular direction, or to be the power source that makes a vehicle move: *She gave me a push in the back that propelled me through the open door and out onto the street.*

sling to throw something forcefully and often in a careless or casual way: *He came in, slung his coat on the floor, and flopped down on the sofa.*

toss to throw something without much

force, often in a casual way: *He screwed up the letter and tossed it into the wastepaper basket.*

tired *adjective* feeling the effects of effort or work and needing to rest or sleep: *I was so tired coming home from work that I fell asleep on the train.*

drained very tired, with no energy: *He felt very tired at the end of the all-day interviews.*

drowsy feeling ready to go to sleep:

After driving for several hours I began to feel rather drowsy and stopped at a roadside café.

exhausted very tired, having used up your strength completely: *They decided to run all the way home and were exhausted by the time they got there.*

jaded lacking energy and freshness and in need of a rest or change, especially after doing the same job for a long period of time: *The management team is looking distinctly jaded, and this is probably a good time to introduce some new talent.*

sleepy (used more often in everyday contexts and to describe children than *drowsy*) feeling ready to go to sleep: *We have two sleepy children here, who need to go to bed.*

weary tired, or (*literary*) causing you to feel tired or done while you feel tired: *We had many a weary mile to go before we reached home.*

worn out (*informal*) exhausted, especially after working for a long time: *I was completely worn out, and all I wanted to do was to fall into bed.*

zonked (*informal*) exhausted: *I must be unfit, because every time I play squash it leaves me completely zonked.*

top *noun*

1 the uppermost or highest part of something: *We climbed to the top of the tower.*

apex the upper angle of a triangle or a similar figure or shape: *A delta is a roughly triangular area of with its apex towards the mouth of the river.*

crest the uppermost edge or part of something, especially a wave, hill, or ridge: *We reached the crest of the ridge and could look down into the valley on the other side.*

crown the top part of the head or of a hat: *Baldness usually begins at the temples and on the crown of the head.*

peak the top part of the mountain, especially when it is pointed in shape: *a mountain with twin peaks.*

summit the top of a mountain: *We were only 500 metres from the summit when our oxygen cylinders failed.*

tip the very highest or furthest end of something, which is often pointed in shape: *a bud on the tip of the stem.*

2 (usually **the top**) the most important position, the most intense level, or the level at which the most important and successful people operate: *She has reached the top of her profession.*

climax the most intense moment in something, which usually follows a gradual build-up of intensity: *The brass blares out at the climax of the movement.*

culmination something that marks the successful end or climax of a process: *the culmination of the week's events.*

height the most intense point or period of something: *While the plague was at its height, more than 1000 people were dying every day.*

peak the topmost point, at which something is at its best or most intense, or someone is at their most successful: *She reached the peak of her fitness after completing all the exercises.*

pinnacle the peak of something: *the pinnacle of his career.*

summit the highest point of something, or a meeting between leaders of important nations: *To become head of her own department was the summit of her ambitions.*

See also **best.**

travel   *verb*
to go on a journey, to go from place to place, or to use a particular means of transport to go to a place: *I have to travel regularly to Paris and Rome on business.*

backpack to travel or hike carrying the things you need in a large pack on your back: *She spent part of her gap year backpacking in Thailand.*

commute to travel regularly between home and work: *We're trying to buy a house in town so that I don't have to commute so far every day.*

go to move by walking or in a vehicle, to make a journey or trip to a place, or to use a particular means of transport: *Wouldn't it be quicker to go by taxi?*

journey (*formal*) to travel: *We remained in Edinburgh while the rest of the party journeyed on towards Fort William.*

ride to travel while sitting on an animal, especially a horse, or a machine such as a bicycle, or to travel as a passenger in a bus, car, or taxi: *I learnt to ride a bike when I was six.*

roam to go around from place to

place, usually without a fixed plan or timetable: *They left us free to roam around the city and see some of the less well-known sights.*

take a trip to go or travel to a place, usually in order to stay there for a limited period of time: *Why not take a trip to London for the weekend?*

See also **go.**

trick *noun* an often cleverly planned action that is intended to deceive people or take them by surprise, either in order to cheat them or simply for fun or mischief: *He played a nasty trick on me, pretending to be asleep and then jumping up and scaring me.*

deceit the deliberate intention to deceive or mislead other people, usually thought of and condemned as being a bad quality in a person: *I didn't think you of all people would be capable of such deceit.*

deception the act of deceiving people, or an action that deceives someone, which may either be condemned as dishonest or admired for its cleverness: *The goalkeeper didn't spot the deception and went the wrong way.*

dodge (*informal*) an action that is intended to enable you to avoid doing something that you ought to do: *a new dodge to avoid paying tax on his profits.*

manoeuvre an action or movement that is intended to put you in a better position to do what you want: *a manoeuvre to outflank the enemy formation.*

ploy an action or manoeuvre that involves deception: *I think this is just a ploy to make us think they're not interested in taking over the company.*

ruse a cunning plan or idea, often 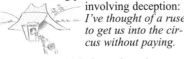 involving deception: *I've thought of a ruse to get us into the circus without paying.*

stratagem (*old-fashioned*) a clever and carefully planned action, often involving deception, that is intended to enable you to get the better of someone: *Odysseus, the most cunning of all the Grecian lords, devised a subtle stratagem to capture the town of Troy.*

subterfuge (*formal*) deception, or a deception, that usually involves secret or underhand methods: *When she couldn't achieve her aims by honest means, she would often resort to subterfuge.*

See also **cheat**.

trouble

1 *verb* to make someone feel worried and anxious or sad, often over a long period of time: *You look sad: what's troubling you?*

agitate to make someone worried and unable to rest or be still: *The loud music was agitating the residents of the nursing home.*

bother to make someone feel worried or upset: *Travelling by plane really bothers me.*

distress to make someone feel very sad: *The sight of the starving children on the news really distressed us.*

disturb to make someone feel worried: *There's no reason to be disturbed: this is just a fire drill.*

freak out (*informal*) to shock someone and put them in a panic: *It really freaked me out when all the lights suddenly went off.*

perturb (*formal*) to make someone worried or anxious: *He continued to believe that the plan would be a success and was not unduly perturbed by reports of early difficulties.*

upset to put someone into a sad or worried state: *I didn't mean to upset you by talking about your ex-boyfriend.*

worry to make someone feel anxious, thinking that something bad might happen: *It worries me that you work such long hours.*

2 *noun*
a state or situation characterized by violence and disorder: *They always call the police at the first sign of trouble.*

bother to make someone feel worried or upset: *The idea of travelling by plane really bothers me.*

commotion a situation where there

is a lot of noise and noisy or sometimes violent activity: *We heard a commotion in the flat downstairs and went to see what was happening.*

disorder a situation in which people behave violently and commit illegal acts: *The authorities will not tolerate disorder on the streets of our cities.*

disturbance an incident in which someone does something that alarms other people or causes trouble: *Someone reported a disturbance outside the pub, and police were sent to investigate.*

fuss noisy behaviour and complaints, often about a trivial matter: *She made a fuss because she thought the waiter was being rude to her.*

riot a situation in which a crowd of people behave very violently, usually attacking and destroying property and also attacking other people or the police and officials: *There were riots in which shops were looted and vehicles set on fire.*

unpleasantness (*euphemistic*) trouble, usually an argument or fight: *We don't want any unpleasantness, we're all friends here.*

unrest a situation in which there is disorder, usually because people are opposed to or angry with the government: *There is unrest in the southern region of the country and tourists are strongly advised not to travel there.*

See also **disorder; disturb; problem.**

true *adjective*
being in accordance with the facts, not a lie and not invented: *Is it true that you used to be a dancer?*

accurate conforming to fact, reality, or the actual state of affairs: *an accurate account of events.*

correct without error: *Is this the correct spelling of 'separate'?*

faithful in keeping with the facts, or with the essence of something such as a work of art: *a faithful adaptation for television of a classic novel.*

literal (usually used to describe the sense in which a word or phrase is being used) being the strictest or most basic: *Jim's hat wouldn't fit you; he has a big head, in the literal sense.*

veracious (*formal*) telling the truth, or

being in accordance with the facts: *a veracious witness.*

verifiable possible to be proved true or accurate: *an article containing verifiable information.*

See also **accurate; faithful; genuine.**

try *verb*
to take action in the hope of being able to do or achieve something, but without being sure of success: *He tried to put the fire out by pouring water onto the stove, but that only made things worse.*

attempt to try (used in more formal contexts than *try*): *I knew I would be unable to dissuade her, so I did not even attempt to.*

do your best to do everything that you can in order to achieve something: *I did my best to explain the situation to him, but I don't think he understood what I was saying.*

endeavour (*formal*) to try: *I shall endeavour to arrange matters to your satisfaction, sir.*

have a go/crack/stab (*informal*) to try: *He had a go at fixing the computer himself, but he had to give up and call in an expert.*

make an effort to devote more time and energy than usual to trying to do something: *He made a special effort to be on time for the meeting.*

seek (*formal*) to try to do or get something: *The publisher is seeking to recruit a new sales director.*

strive (*formal*) try hard to do something, often against opposition: *He was striving to make himself heard above the noise in the hall.*

struggle to put a lot of effort into trying to do something, but to have little success: *She was struggling to get the lid off a jar of pickles.*

turn *verb*

1 to move, or make something move, in a circle or part of a circle around a central point: *You turn the valve clockwise to let the water in.*

reel move unsteadily or drunkenly in a winding or circular way: *I punched him in the face and sent him reeling back.*

revolve to turn in a full circle, usu- ally at a speed that is or seems quite slow: *The little figure on top of the music box revolves as the music plays.*

rotate turn, or turn something, usually in a full circle, often fast: *The blades rotate to provide lift to the helicopter.*

spin to turn, or turn something, in a full circle or to face in the opposite direction fast: *The croupier span the roulette wheel.*

spiral move in a circle and upwards or downwards at the same time: *The plane spiralled downwards out of control.*

swivel to turn something around a fixed central point so that it faces in a different direction: *He swivelled his chair round to face them.*

twirl turn in a full circle fast and usually in a light-hearted way: *She twirled around, showing off her new skirt.*

twist to turn, or turn something, through part of a circle: *If you twist the top, it should come off quite easily.*

whirl to turn, or turn something, in a full circle very fast, often in a way that makes you feel giddy: *Couples whirled across the floor as the music got faster and faster.*

2 to change direction, for example to the right or left, or change the direction in which something is pointing: *Turn right at the next set of traffic lights.*

invert (*formal*) to move something so that the part that is usually at the top is at the bottom: *If you invert the letter M, it becomes W.*

reverse to move or change something so that the part that is usually at the front is at the rear or the thing that usually come first comes last: *We reversed the usual order and began at Z.*

shift to move or move something, often only a small amount, to be in a different position or facing in a different direction: *She shifted her chair a little to the right so that she could see the television better.*

swerve to change direction quickly or unexpectedly, especially to avoid something: *The car swerved to avoid a pedestrian.*

turn upside down to invert something: *The lid wasn't screwed on properly, so when he turned the jar upside down, all the beans fell out.*

veer to change direction, usually to a new direction at an acute angle from the previous one, or to change direction suddenly: *The wind veered round to the northwest.*

wind to change direction several times: *The path winds up the hill.*

ugly *adjective*
unpleasant to look at, through being shaped, arranged, or coloured in a way that people do not consider to be beautiful: *He has an ugly scar on his left cheek.*

deformed (used to describe a person or part of the body) that has not developed in the normal way and does not have the usual shape: *She was born with a deformed foot.*

grotesque ugly and very strange, and also sometimes intended to be funny: *At the site of the crash, the metal rails had been twisted into grotesque shapes.*

hideous very ugly, or frighteningly ugly: *a hideous monster.*

plain (usually used to describe a woman) having a face or appearance that either has no interesting or beautiful features or is definitely unattractive: *She was always such a plain little girl, so how did she grow up to look so stunning?*

repulsive extremely ugly or unpleas-

ant, so ugly as to drive people away: *Well, she's not very good-looking, but I wouldn't go so far as to say I find her repulsive.*

unattractive not having the qualities that appeal to people, especially in appearance: *I'm not wearing that outfit, as it makes me look so unattractive.*

unsightly very obviously spoiling the appearance of something: *George spilt coffee over the carpet, and it's left a very unsightly mark.*

understand *verb*
to be able to explain something or someone's character or actions, or to know what something means or what someone is trying to say: *I can't understand why I didn't think of it before.*

catch on (*informal*) to understand the meaning of what someone says or to understand what is happening: *I knew at once what she was hinting at, but it seemed to take everyone else a while to catch on.*

comprehend (*formal*) to understand: *I fail to comprehend how such a simple mistake could have happened.*

dawn on to become clear, understandable, or explainable to someone, especially suddenly: *It suddenly dawned on me that there was a much simpler solution to our problem.*

fathom (also *fathom out*) to under-

stand something after thinking about it carefully: *I can't fathom (out) what happened.*

follow to understand an explanation or a description: *The pictures will help you follow the story.*

get (*informal*) to understand the meaning of something, or understand a joke: *I don't get it. Why did he murder his aunt if she was going to leave all her money to his sister anyway?*

grasp to understand the meaning of something: *I'm not sure she fully grasped what I was saying.*

realize to become aware of or understand something that you were unaware of or did not understand before: *I finally realized that I had been approaching the problem in completely the wrong way.*

see understand or realize: *I see now why she was so reluctant to come to the party.*

unfriendly *adjective*

showing that you do not like someone or do not want to be with them: *He was most unfriendly and didn't even ask me to sit down.*

aloof not joining in with what people

are doing or not seeming to want to be with them or speak to them, sometimes because you feel superior to them: *While the others were chatting, she remained aloof.*

cold not feeling or showing any emotion, especially not showing any friendliness or affection towards people: *Even when he smiles, you can see he has very cold eyes.*

distant not seeming to want to communicate with other people very much or become involved with them: *He wasn't exactly unfriendly, but he was rather distant.*

hostile showing that you definitely do not like, approve of, or agree with someone or something and would rather act against them than be friends with them: *She greeted my remark with a hostile stare.*

inhospitable (used to describe people) not inviting people to your home or not making them feel welcome when they visit, or (said about places) not pleasant to be in: *The South Pole is one of the most inhospitable places on earth.*

unsociable not wanting to be with or talk to other people: *I don't want to seem unsociable, but I think I'd better go as I do have a train to catch.*

unwelcoming not making people feel happy and comfortable: *Plain white walls and hard wooden chairs create a very unwelcoming atmosphere.*

unpredictable *adjective*

that cannot be known in advance with any certainty, because very likely to change or do something unusual: *His moods are very unpredictable and seem to have nothing to do with whether things are going well or badly for him.*

changeable not likely to continue being the same as it is now: *The weather is very changeable at this time of year.*

fickle behaving in an unpredictable

way, because you are likely to change your mind about things unexpectedly: *He's too fickle to ever really know what he wants.*

unexpected that you did not know was going to happen: *Well, this is an unexpected pleasure!*

unforeseeable impossible to know about in advance: *You can't be blamed if the accident that happened was completely unforeseeable.*

unreliable that you cannot expect to do what he, she, or it is supposed to do: *The bus service is very unreliable in this part of town.*

unstable in a condition in which it is very likely to change, usually into a worse or more dangerous state: *mentally unstable.*

variable (often used in mathematics) changing, able to change, or likely to change, but not necessarily by a large amount: *a variable quantity.*

unusual *adjective*

not as you would normally expect: *It's unusual for him to be late.*

abnormal unusual, often in a way

that seems worrying or dangerous: *Surely that kind of behaviour is abnormal for a child of her age.*

extraordinary very unusual and usually very good: *I've had an extraordinary stroke of luck.*

funny rather unusual or strange: *I've got a funny feeling I've seen that man before.*

out of the ordinary unusual, especially unusual enough to be worth mentioning or commenting on: *Nothing out of the ordinary happened.*

remarkable unusual and usually impressive: *a remarkable achievement.*

surprising causing you to be surprised: *It's surprising how much you can get done in an hour if you really set your mind to it.*

uncommon not found very often, or happening rarely: *Red squirrels are very uncommon nowadays in most parts of England.*

unorthodox not what most people would have or use or would assume to be correct: *It's an unorthodox method of opening a can, but it seems to be quite effective.*

See also **eccentric; strange**.

urge *verb*
to advise someone very strongly to do something, or to use strong emotional pressure to persuade someone to do something: *I urge you to act now before it is too late.*

egg on to encourage someone to do something bad: *It's not like him to behave so badly, I expect the bigger boys egged him on.*

encourage to try to build up someone's confidence so that they feel able to do something: *She encouraged me to try again when I was feeling really depressed about my prospects.*

goad tease or taunt someone in order

to make them do something: *She goaded him into hitting the other fellow by calling him a coward.*

spur on to make someone more eager or determined to achieve something: *We were spurred on by the shouts of the crowd.*

will to wish very hard for something to happen or for someone to do something in the hope that the power of your wish will bring the result you want: *I was willing you to say yes.*

See also **persuade**.

useful *adjective*
helping you to able to do what you want to do: *I thought you might find this useful if you've got a lot of decorating to do.*

constructive giving you positive advice on what you ought to do or how you can improve: *constructive criticism.*

handy useful and easy to hold and use: *a handy little gadget.*

helpful useful: *helpful hints for newly married couples.*

practical that you can use to help you deal with real-life tasks and situations, not theoretical: *a practical guide to setting up your own business.*

profitable bringing you either financial profit or some other kind of benefit: *Surely there are more profitable ways of spending your time than reading comics.*

worthwhile worth the time, effort, etc., that you spend doing it: *You get a real sense of achievement when you finish the course, and that makes all the hard work and study worthwhile.*

useless *adjective*
not helping to achieve anything or bringing any benefit: *It's useless to complain.*

fruitless producing no result: *All attempts to trace the missing child proved fruitless.*

futile not serving any purpose or

having any chance of success: *Resistance is futile and will only lead to more bloodshed.*

ineffective not producing the desired result or effect: *Antibiotics are ineffective against diseases caused by viruses.*

in vain (*formal*) fruitless: *We tried several times to contact him, but all our efforts were in vain.*

pointless useless: *Going on would be pointless, since we know that all the mountain passes are blocked by snow.*

vain producing no result: *her vain attempts to make the unruly children behave.*

See also **inferior**.

valuable *adjective*
worth a lot of money, or very beneficial or important to someone: *She gave me some very valuable advice.*

costly that has serious bad effects, such as meaning that you have to spend a lot of money, or (*literary*) very valuable and splendid: *That mistake could prove costly in the long run.*

dear (used mainly to describe everyday items) expensive: *Strawberries are dear because they're out of season.*

expensive costing a lot of money to buy: *It's more expensive to eat in restaurants than to cook for yourself at home.*

invaluable extremely beneficial or important to someone: *Your assistance has been invaluable.*

precious having great value, either in terms of money or of its importance to a particular person: *Those memories are very precious to me.*

priceless so valuable that it is impossible to estimate its worth in money or its importance: *This manuscript is in Shakespeare's own handwriting, and it is quite literally priceless.*

treasured that a particular person loves and values greatly: *one of my most treasured possessions.*

very *adverb*
more than usually, to a greater extent or degree than normal: *It's very hot in here.*

awfully (*informal*) extremely: *I'm awfully sorry, I forgot.*

exceedingly (*formal*) (usually used with positive words) extremely: *I'd be exceedingly grateful for any advice you could offer me.*

excessively to a greater degree than is needed: *I think they're being excessively cautious, since the risks to them are fairly slight.*

extremely to a much greater extent or degree than normal: *He's extremely angry about it.*

highly (used only with certain adjectives) to a greater degree than normal: *a highly dangerous mission.*

quite completely: *'Are you quite sure that those were her exact words?' 'Quite sure.'*
Used mainly with emphatic adjectives to avoid confusion with the commoner sense of *quite* ('fairly').

really (often used emphasize your personal feeling that something is the case) very or genuinely: *I don't care what they think, I think he's a really nice guy.*

terribly (*informal*) extremely: *She's terribly upset.*

thoroughly in every respect: *I think you should feel thoroughly ashamed of yourselves.*

truly (often used emphasize your personal feeling that something is the case) very, genuinely, or sincerely: *For what we are about to receive, may the Lord make us truly grateful.*

vigour *noun*
a combination of strength and energy that enables you to do things in a brisk and powerful way *If you put a bit more vigour into it, you'd get the job done in half the time.*

animation liveliness, especially in a group activity: *It was only when the conversation turned to politics that people began talking with real animation.*

energy a usually physical force that is used in performing actions and doing work: *Some days I feel as if I haven't got enough energy even to get out of bed.*

liveliness an energetic and excited quality, often combined with a sense of enjoyment: *Anna organized some party games, which added greatly to the liveliness of the occasion.*

stamina the ability to continue doing something that requires strength and energy, for example running or working, for a long time: *Does she have the stamina to run a long-distance race?*

strength the ability to exert a lot of physical force, for example to move or lift things, or to resist weight, pressure, etc., without breaking or collapsing: *I haven't the strength to lift this on my own.*

vitality a combination of energy, eagerness to do things, and enjoyment of being alive and active: *She has so much vitality.*

zest a combination of vigour and enjoyment shown when you do something: *He's fully fit again now and beginning to make plans for the company's future with his usual zest.*

See also **active; healthy.**

violent *adjective*
using force to cause harm or damage, or
showing uncontrolled force or power: *a
violent storm.*

aggressive showing a wish to attack
someone: *Then he got really aggressive,
and I was frightened that he was going
to hit me.*

fierce suggesting that someone or
 something may
become angry or
violent and attack
you: *The lion let
out a fierce roar.*

powerful having or showing a great
deal of strength or ability to do things: *a
powerful blow.*

rough not gentle, careless or violent in
the way you handle things or people:
You're too rough, you'll hurt him.

savage very violent and very uncontrolled: *a savage attack.*

vicious deliberately intending or
intended to cause a lot of harm: *Don't
go near that dog, he looks vicious.*

wait *verb*
remain where you are or take no action
because you are expecting something to
happen: *I waited for half an hour at the
bus stop and then decided to walk home.*

bide your time to take no action,
especially because you think a
favourable opportunity to do some
something will soon arise: *I'm just bid-
ing my time until the share price falls a
little lower.*

hang around (*informal*) to stay in a
place doing very little, usually waiting
for someone or something: *I hung
around for hours outside the station, but
she didn't show up.*

hang on (*informal*) to wait, or to stop
what you are doing and wait: *Hang on,
I'll be with you in a minute.*

hold on (*informal*) wait, or to stop what
you are doing and wait: *Now just hold
on a minute, I didn't tell you could go.*

kick your heels (*informal*) to wait
unwillingly or frustratingly: *He left me
kicking my heels in the hotel lounge
while he went off to discuss business
with somebody.*

linger to remain in a place, often
 doing something in a
leisurely or relaxed
way: *We lingered by
the shore, just chatting
and enjoying the view.*

walk *verb*
to move, or to go somewhere, on your
legs at a fairly slow pace, as opposed to
running or riding in a vehicle: *The bus
service is so unreliable that it's often
quicker to walk to work.*

amble to walk in a leisurely way, especially for pleasure: *The couple ambled
slowly along the promenade.*

hike to walk a long distance, usually

for recreation: *We spent our holiday hiking in the Swiss Alps.*

march to walk in a disciplined and coordinated fashion, often in a group, or to walk in a determined and forceful way: *The soldiers marched across the parade ground.*

plod to walk with slow heavy steps: *She strode off in front, and the rest of us plodded along behind.*

saunter to walk in a casual, carefree manner: *A group of elegant young gentlemen were sauntering in the park.*

stride to walk with long energetic steps: *He strode into the room and started giving orders straight away.*

stroll to walk in a leisurely way, especially for pleasure: *We strolled along the Champs Elysées looking in shop windows.*

strut to walk in a proud or arrogant way: *From the way he struts around, you'd think he owned the whole estate.*

traipse to walk in a tired or reluctant way, often for a long distance: *I traipsed all the way to the post office, only to find it was shut.*

wander to walk about casually, not having a clear direction or purpose: *They spent the afternoon wandering around the shops.*

warm *adjective*
having a fairly high temperature: *Are you warm enough, or shall I switch the heating on?*

balmy (used to describe weather conditions) pleasantly warm and relaxing: *a balmy summer's evening.*

lukewarm (used to describe substances, especially fluids) not cold, but not at a high enough temperature to be described as *warm*: *The milk for the baby should be just lukewarm.*

mild (used to describe weather conditions) fairly warm: *It's actually quite mild for a winter's day.*

sunny when the sun is shining: *a sunny day.*

tepid (used to describe substances,

especially fluids, sometimes disapprovingly) lukewarm: *The soup was tepid, and the main course was stone cold when it arrived at the table.*

temperate having both cold and warm periods, but neither extreme heat or extreme cold: *a temperate climate.*

waste *verb*
to use or consume something such as money, time, or resources in a way that produces no benefit for anyone: *They wasted thousands of pounds on a luxury car that they don't really need.*

fritter away to use something up little

by little on useless objects or activities: *I didn't save all that money for you to fritter it away by gambling on fruit machines.*

misspend to spend time or sometimes money in an unprofitable way: *my misspent youth.*

squander to waste something, especially money: *The government is squandering taxpayers' money on more expensive equipment for the army.*

throw away not to make good use of something valuable that you have or that is offered to you: *He had the chance of really successful acting career and he just threw it away.*

watch *verb*

to look at something or someone or what someone is doing for a period of time, sometimes as a way of protecting or supervising them: *Now watch carefully while I show you how to do it.*

keep an eye on to watch someone or something, especially in order to protect or supervise them: *Do you mind keeping an eye on my suitcase while I go to the toilet?*

keep tabs on (*informal*) to keep an eye on: *Keep tabs on him – don't let him slip away into the crowd.*

keep under surveillance to watch something continuously, usually in order to detect or prevent crime: *The police suspected that the house was being used by drug smugglers and had kept it under surveillance for several weeks.*

keep watch to look out for possible danger, usually while someone else is doing something or you are guarding something: *You three can go to sleep, and I'll keep watch.*

look on to watch something happen without attempting to take part in it or get involved in it: *Three people were doing the actual work, and another three were just standing around looking on.*

monitor to watch something continuously or check it regularly in order to make sure that there are no problems with it: *This machine monitors the patient's heartbeat.*

observe (*formal*) to see or watch

someone or something, especially to watch something in order to learn from it: *Medical students are sometimes allowed to observe while the surgeons are carrying out operations.*

weak *adjective*

having little strength or energy or unable to resist much weight, pressure, etc.: *We think we've found the weak point in their defences.*

delicate thin, light, or fine and often beautiful or graceful, but easily damaged: *It's better to wash delicate fabrics by hand rather than in the washing machine.*

faint (used to describe a colour, sound, or quality) having little intensity and difficult to see or hear; (used to describe someone) feeling unsteady because they are hungry or very ill: *He heard a faint voice coming from behind the door.*

feeble (often used scornfully) showing a lack of strength or effectiveness: *her feeble attempts at humour.*

flimsy made of weak materials or not strongly constructed: *The strong wind soon blew down their flimsy shelter.*

fragile that can easily be broken: *This box is full of fragile ornaments.*

frail weak and in poor health, or flimsy: *He's getting very old and frail.*

puny (*formal*) (often used scornfully) having very little strength or power, and often small: *What can their puny forces do against our magnificent war machine?*

wealth *noun*

the money and other possessions that someone owns, especially a large amount of money and possessions, or the fact of having a large amount of money and possessions: *We wish you health, wealth, and happiness in your future life together.*

affluence a state in which someone has

plenty of money and is able to live relatively comfortably: *The affluence of most people in the West contrasts starkly with the poverty of the vast majority of people in Africa and Asia.*

fortune a very large amount of money: *He made a fortune from that invention.*

luxury a state in which you have a very easy and comfortable life and use the best and most expensive kinds of goods and services: *If you win the lottery, you'll be able to live in luxury for the rest of your life.*

means money that you have available or can use to live on: *Obviously, if you live beyond your means, you will end up in debt.*

prosperity a state in which things are going well for you and you have lots of money: *In the days of his prosperity he would think nothing of spending £500 on a night out.*

riches (*formal*) money and other valuable objects or products, or wealth: *The riches obtained from the rubber trade built these splendid mansions.*

treasure a collection of valuable objects such as jewels and coins, especially when hidden away or buried: *He dug up an old wooden chest full of treasure.*

See also **rich.**

wet *adjective*
covered in, or having absorbed, at lot of liquid, especially water, or (used to describe the weather) rainy: *I wore rubber boots so as not to get my feet wet.*

damp rather wet, especially to the touch, but not usually showing liquid on the surface: *Wipe the surface with a damp cloth.*

drenched (usually used to describe

people) very wet, usually because they have been in the rain: *I got drenched on the way home from work.*

humid (used to describe weather conditions) where there is quite a lot of moisture in the air: *It's terribly hot and humid in the jungle.*

moist (often used in an approving way) containing a certain amount of liquid inside itself, but less wet than something that is *damp*: *a nice moist sponge cake.*

rainy characterized by frequent rain: *a rainy day.*

showery characterized by frequent showers: *showery weather.*

soaked (usually used to describe people) very wet, usually because they have been in the rain: *You're soaked, come in and get dry.*

soaking wet very wet: *The clothes have just come out of the washing machine and are still soaking wet.*

sodden containing as much liquid as it can hold, so very wet and soft: *The pitch is absolutely sodden, you can't possibly play on it today.*

soggy having a very soft and yielding texture through containing large amounts of liquid: *The biscuits will go soggy if you don't keep them in an airtight tin.*

woman *noun*
an adult female human being: *There are only two women on the committee.*

bitch (*informal and very rude*) an unpleasant or spiteful woman: *The bitch took all my money and ran off with another man.*

chick (*informal*) (used mainly by men)

a young woman. especially an attractive one: *Who's that good-looking chick over there by the bar?*
Usually thought to be offensive.

female (used in an impersonal way) a woman or girl: *The number of households consisting of a single female has increased markedly in the past decade.*

girl a female child, or (*informal*) a woman: *a night out with the girls.* Sometimes felt to be patronizing.

lady a woman from the upper classes or who has very good manners, or a polite word for a woman: *Go and ask that lady if she'd mind if we opened the window.*

lass (*informal and old-fashioned*) a young woman: *She's a really nice lass, that daughter of yours.*

work

1 *noun* activity that involves physical or mental effort and is intended to produce a result: *There's still a lot of work to be done before the house is finished.*

drudgery boring and repetitive work that is also often physically tiring: *the drudgery of washing clothes and cleaning the house.*

effort the use of energy to produce a result, or an instance of using energy or a considerable amount of energy in order to achieve something: *With a bit more effort, he could do really well.*

exertion the use of physical energy to do something: *The slightest exertion makes her feel really tired.*

labour (*formal*) hard work, especially work that involves using your hands and body, or workers generally: *Machines have reduced the amount of labour involved in many household tasks.*

toil (*formal*) hard, usually physical, work that goes on for a long time: *It took hours of back-breaking toil to clear the ground so that it could be ploughed.*

2 *verb* to do work, especially in order to earn money: *I work in an office.*

be busy to be involved in doing something, especially work: *I'm afraid I can't talk to you now, as I'm too busy.*

be employed to work for someone who pays you money, or (*formal*) to be engaged in doing something: *For the last three years I have been employed in a bakery.*

earn your living to make the money you need to live on by working: *She earns her living as a secretary.*

labour (*formal*) to do hard work, especially works that uses you hands and body, or to use a lot of effort in doing something: *labouring on a building site.*

toil (*formal*) do hard, usually physical, work for a long time: *After toiling all day in the fields, he felt he deserved a rest.*

3 *verb* (said about a machine) to be carrying out a task, especially to be doing what it is designed to do effectively: *The computer's not working, because you forgot to switch it on.*

function (*formal*) to work: *In order to function effectively, the machine needs regular maintenance.*

go (*informal*) to operate: *I gave the lawnmower a kick to see if that would make it go.*

operate (said about a machine) to be using power and performing the task it was designed to do, or (said about a person) to control a machine: *The brakes are operated by pushing the foot pedal.*

run to operate, or to use a certain kind of energy in order to operate: *This engine runs on diesel.*

See also **job.**

worry *verb*

to have anxious thoughts about someone or something: *I always worry about the children if I don't know where they are.*

agonize to experience a lot of anxiety and distress in trying to do something such as reach a decision: *I agonized for a week over whether or not I should accept the offer.*

be concerned to feel anxious about something: *They should have been back three hours ago, and we're concerned about their safety.*

be on tenterhooks (*informal*) to feel very tense and anxious, usually while waiting for news of something: *We were on tenterhooks waiting to hear whether she'd passed the exam.*

fret to worry, and to show you are worried by being restless and complaining: *I told her not to fret, we'd soon have the damage repaired.*

have butterflies (in your stomach)

 (*informal*) to be very nervous about something you have to do: *I always have butterflies in my stomach before I have to speak in public.*

lose sleep (*informal*) to be unable to sleep through being worried: *I wouldn't lose any sleep over it, everything's sure to turn out all right.*

See also **anxiety; trouble 1**.

write *verb*

to put words on paper with a pen or pencil, or to compose a document, letter, novel, play, etc.: *I'm just writing a postcard to my sister.*

jot down to write something down quickly or in a brief form: *I jotted down a few points that I'd like you to raise at the meeting.*

make a note of to write something down briefly to help you remember it, or to pay special attention to something so that you remember it: *I made a note of his name and address, so that I can contact him again if necessary.*

note down write something as a brief record of what has happened or of information that you have been given: *I noted down the car's registration number so that I could pass it on to the police.*

pen (*formal*) to write something: *I sat down straight away and penned a letter to the editor of the local newspaper.*

put in writing to write something down, especially an agreement that you have made verbally with someone, in order to make it official: *I'm happy with the agreement we've just reached on the phone and I'd be grateful if you could put it in writing to me.*

scribble to write something hastily or

 carelessly, often in a way that is difficult to read, or to make meaningless marks on something with a pencil, pen, etc.: *I scribbled a note in my diary.*

sign to write your name in your own handwriting on a document, especially at the end of it, to show that it is from you or that you agree with its contents: *You forgot to sign the cheque.*

write down to put something on paper as a deliberate act, especially as a record of something or to help you remember it: *If you get a good idea, write it down straight away. Don't simply rely on your memory.*

Y

young *adjective* having lived only a

relatively short time: *You were too young then to understand what was going on.*

adolescent past childhood, but not yet fully adult: *the fantasies of adolescent boys.*
Usually used before a noun.

immature not having fully developed, especially not having the experience of life, the good sense, or the knowledge of how to behave that an adult has: *That sort of behaviour shows just how immature she is.*

juvenile (*formal*) young, or silly: *juvenile delinquents.*

little (*informal*) (used mainly when talking to or about children) very young: *Did you use to tell me stories when I was little?*

teenage aged between 13 and 20, or connected with people of that age: *teenage fashions.*
Usually used before a noun.

youthful having the appearance or the vitality of a young person: *I hope I still look as youthful as you do when I'm 40.*